Imported and Distribu___
in the United States
Tafnews Pres:
P. O. Box 29___
Los Altos, Calif. 94022

TRACK AND FIELD
The Great Ones

TRACK AND FIELD
The Great Ones

CORDNER NELSON

PELHAM BOOKS

First published in Great Britain by
PELHAM BOOKS LTD
52 Bedford Square
London, W.C.1
1970

7207 0352 2

Set and printed in Great Britain by
Tonbridge Printers Ltd, Peach Hall Works, Tonbridge, Kent
in Baskerville ten on twelve point on paper supplied by
P. F. Bingham Ltd, and bound by James Burn
at Esher, Surrey

TO
MARY

CONTENTS

FOREWORD 11

1 Nurmi 13

2 Owens 25

3 Warmerdam 36

4 Dillard 46

5 Zátopek 55

6 Mathias 70

7 O'Brien 81

8 Johnson 94

9 Davis 107

10 Oerter 116

11 Elliott 128

12 Brumel 139

13 Snell 148

SUPPLEMENT 160

INDEX 217

ILLUSTRATIONS

Paavo Nurmi	*facing* 32
Jessie Owens	33
Harrison Dillard	64
Emil Zátopek	65
Parry O'Brien	96
Bob Mathias	96
Rafer Johnson	97
Glen Davis	128
Al Oerter	129
Herb Elliott	160
Valery Brumel	161
Peter Snell	192
Roger Bannister	193
Ron Clarke	193

FOREWORD

If you want to start a lively conversation, try this formula :

1. Assemble some people who are enthusiastic followers of track and field athletics.

2. Ask them to name the ten greatest track and field athletes of all time.

If your group of people is large enough, there will be one who insists no athlete can be regarded as best in his event unless he now holds the world record.

Another will argue : 'A man who holds the world record now but is barely ahead of some other athletes, is not as great as an athlete of thirty or forty years ago who was far superior to everyone then known. This is true because most, or all, of the difference in performance between today's record holder and the one thirty years ago can be explained by better equipment and enlightened training methods.'

A third will state with absolute conviction that a world record is more important than an Olympic championship. A fourth will deny it.

A fifth will argue that an athlete's excellence in a second event doubles his greatness, and a third event triples it. A sixth will point out the great similarity between running 100 meters and 200 meters, or between 5,000 and 10,000. He will say :

'A man who dominates the javelin is greater than one who is barely superior in both the 100 and 220.'

A seventh track enthusiast will say a long career – many years of success – is necessary for true greatness. An eighth will argue that an overwhelming dominance in one year can prove greatness. For example, he might say, 'What if a man broke four world records in one year and then quit? Can you take away his greatness?'

A ninth might vote for the athlete who defeated all his opposition, while a tenth could argue that only the important competi-

11

tions count: 'A national championship carries a hundred times the weight of a casual club meet.'

If you ever settle those arguments, you have only scratched the surface. Now comes the problem of comparing two athletes, each of whom is on the winning side of two of the above questions and on the losing side of two others. The variety of possibilities is endless.

Our problem is truly complex.

I do not claim to have solved this problem in my selection of the greatest athletes. I discussed it with some good 'track nuts', notably Syd De Roner, Bill Peck, Dick Dodge, and Art Morgan. My conclusion was simple: the selection of the greatest athletes is not subject to scientific accuracy. It must be based, finally, on my own opinion.

I began with a list of about 116 athletes who have been both Olympic champions and world record holders. Then I added more than seventy truly great athletes who missed one or the other triumph for various reasons.

From this list of 192 athletes, I made the agonizing eliminations. I would be much happier with a book recounting the highlights of the careers of all the greatest athletes instead of a mere baker's dozen, but that is obviously impossible.

This book, then, is a compromise, like most endeavors in life, and I hope those who disagree with me can enjoy it for what it is and not condemn it because of what it could have been. When space is limited, a compromise is necessary between information and interest.

In addition to the thirteen athletes whose careers are recounted at length, the remaining 179 athletes are included in summaries of varied lengths. This supplement, comprising more than one fourth of the book, is arranged alphabetically in order to make an index unnecessary. Headings provide quick reference to each athlete's nation, event, and years of major competition.

1 NURMI

Around the Olympic stadium they ran, the two of them drawing steadily away from fourteen other 5,000 meter finalists. The taller man set the pace inside the white picket fence, but the little man was poised confidently near his shoulder, ready to strike.

On the last lap the little man bided his time, past the covered stands on the backstretch, around the last curve along the standing-room section beneath the white colonnade. Then the little man sprinted furiously and it was soon over. He established his superiority within a few yards and the other man was forced to let him go.

It was Antwerp, August 17, 1920, the last time for many years the taller man would lose an important race, for his name was Paavo Nurmi.

He wanted, more than anything else, more than almost any other man, to be a great runner. His desire began when he was nine, peering wistfully through a wooden fence at a boys' club track meet. Later, when he joined, he usually finished ahead of the other boys. At ten he ran 1,500 meters in 5 :43, and he ran 5 :03 at eleven.

When he was twelve, tragedy struck. His father died and the the family of six lived in one room while little Paavo worked as an errand boy, pushing a cart up hills. He was a vegetarian, not, as some historians say, because he believed in it, but because of necessity. Poverty helped make Paavo Nurmi a grave, unsmiling, silent man who knew no other way except hard mental and physical discipline.

In the 1912 Olympics, Hannes Kolehmainen won four races and became fifteen-year-old Paavo's idol. Inspired, Nurmi joined a club and began the training which carried him to fame.

'All my spare time was used in walking through the woods or in running.'

At seventeen, he won the 3,000 meter race in the junior nationals in 10 :06.5, but he attracted little attention otherwise. In 1917, at the age of 20, his 15 :47.4 was only the fifth fastest 5,000 meter time in Finland, and in 1918 he ran only 15 :50.7. As a mechanic in the army, he rose at 5 :00 a.m. to walk the icy roads, then ran in the afternoon.

In 1918, on the Russian front, legend has it that he ran 15 kilometers in 59 :24 with full equipment, including a knapsack containing 55 pounds of sand. He won a 20 kilometer race by over ten minutes. He received letters from Kolehmainen advising him to vary his training with speed work, but Nurmi did not absorb this advice immediately.

In 1920, he ran to a Finnish record of 8 :36.3 for 3,000 meters. On the sea voyage to Antwerp for the Olympics, he was miserably seasick and some blame this for his defeat, but Nurmi offered no alibi. Even then he was beginning to practice non-communication, even by smile or frown, which was to help weave a legend among the strands of fact.

One legend, based on fact, was Nurmi's invincibility. Some say he could run faster if he wanted to. Three days after his defeat at Antwerp, that legend began. A frustrated Nurmi his blue eyes hiding his disappointment over his 5,000 meter loss to Joseph Guillemot of France, trailed the little man to the home-stretch of the 10,000 meters.

Then the legend became reality, and all of Nurmi's desire and talent and hard training burst out into one massive show of strength. He rushed past Guillemot and won by eight yards in 31 :45.8.

Three days after the 10,000, the sandy-haired Nurmi ran his third Olympic race. He was behind in the last 200 meters of the 9,000 meter cross country race, but once again he thrilled the crowd with a strong finish. He won by four yards.

Nurmi returned to Finland as a minor hero, but he was dissatisfied. He continued his morning walk of at least an hour, with a few spurts of running. He continued his afternoon work-out of long, slow running from April through September. In his eagerness to improve, he added pace training.

He began to carry a stopwatch in his right hand, cocking his head to read it as he passed the posts along his training runs. His running style became a long, pleasing stride, heel touching first, his body and head erect and still, his elbows held high and wide.

It was his remarkable knowledge of pace which enabled him to set his first world record, in 1921. He ran 30 :40.2 for 10,000 meters at Stockholm. Testing himself at the short end of the scale, with no speed training, he lost the 800 meters in the Finnish Championships by one yard in 1 :58.4. He also ran a mile in 4 :13.9, third fastest ever run.

In 1922, he forced the track world to take notice. He traveled to England to win AAA championships in the 4-mile and steeplechase. He went back home and delighted the Finns with three world records on consecutive weekends – 3,000 meters (8 :28.6) on August 27, 2,000 meters (5 :26.3) on September 4, and 5,000 meters (14 :35.3) on September 12.

In 1923, a slender Swedish school teacher named Edvin Wide developed into a great runner and Swedes clamored for a race against Nurmi. Finns wanted Nurmi to ask for a distance of 10,000 meters to be safe, but Nurmi surprised them by asking for Wide's best distance – one mile. The classic race was seen by 18,000 spectators on August 23, at Stockholm's Olympic stadium, a long, low, gray-violet horseshoe with covered stands and two square watch towers at the north end.

According to legend, Nurmi had run a practice mile in 4 :11 at a pace of 63, 63, 63, and 62, under the world record of 4 :12.6, and he wanted to run such a pace here, but Wide had other plans.

The tow-headed Swede ran the first 440 yards on the 383-meter track in 58.6. Nurmi, stopwatch in hand, knew better than to follow such a suicide pace, but the excitement drew him down to 60.1.

With Wide ten yards ahead, Nurmi calmly continued his long straight-backed stride, making his own pace as if Wide did not exist. Wide led in 2 :01.9, still eight yards ahead of Nurmi's 2 :03.2.

The absurd pace began to take its toll. Wide slowed to 64.9 for the third quarter, and Nurmi moved ahead in 3 :06.7. Then the gallant Swede forged ahead. With the few Finns unheard in the din, Nurmi raced past Wide on the backstretch and pulled away. At 1,500 meters, on the last curve, Nurmi was eight yards ahead and he won the mile by 18 yards.

Jubilant Finns ran from the stands to congratulate him, and

15

then the announcer called out through a megaphone the electrifying results: Nurmi had run 1,500 meters in 3:53.0 and one mile in 4:10.4, both world records.

Legend has it, substantiated by those last 120 yards in a comfortable 17.4, that Nurmi could have run faster. Indeed, a year later, Nurmi's terse estimate of his own capability was 'Four minutes, four seconds, maybe.'

Whatever his capability, Nurmi helped build the legend most admirably the very next day. He set a world record for 3 miles (14:11.2) while defeating Wide by 90 yards in a 14:39.9 5,000. Then, on September 10 in Copenhagen, he lowered the 3,000 record to 8:27.8.

As world record holder at six distances from 1,500 to 10,000 meters, he was an outstanding favorite for any race he ran in the 1924 Olympics at Paris. He firmly believed he could win five races, but everything conspired to frustrate him.

First, the IAAF printed a schedule calling for the 5,000 meters to follow the 1,500 by half an hour. Outraged Finns protested and the schedule was widened to a hardly generous 55 minutes.

Second, he fell on an icy road on Easter Sunday and his knee was injured on a sharp stone. He could not walk for two weeks and then only with a stiff leg. When he attempted to run again he was shocked. He could not better 2:12 for 800 meters.

Third, Willie Ritola returned from the United States, where he had approached world record time at 4 miles and 10 miles. In the Olympic Trials in May, Ritola broke Nurmi's world record for 10,000 meters (30:35.4) and won a fast 5,000. A perturbed Nurmi could only win the 1,500 and 3,000 in slow times, and Ritola replaced Nurmi as Finland's current hero.

Grimly, Nurmi went to work, harder than ever. After his morning walk of 10 to 12 kilometers and some gym work, he rested an hour before going to the track. There he ran four or five furious sprints of 80 to 120 meters, then a fast 400 to 1,000 for time, followed by 3,000 to 4,000 meters with 'the last lap always very fast'. In the evening he ran 4,000 to 7,000 meters across country, punishing himself at the finish. He closed with four or five sprints.

'This daily training helped me to attain the condition I had at the 1924 Olympic Games.'

His condition became exciting in June. On the Helsinki track,

June 19, six days after his twenty-seventh birthday, he made a spectacular effort to prove he could run two races in one day.

He started the 1,500 meters with a deliberately reckless lap in 57.3. He passed 800 meters in 2 :01 and 1,200 in 3 :06. He finished comfortably with a new world record of 3 :52.6. Fifty-five minutes later, he started the 5,000 meters and he ran 14 :28.2, another world record.

Nothing like it had ever been done before, but still he was not permitted to run the Olympic 10,000. Finland did not want Nurmi and Ritola running each other into the ground in the first event. But if Nurmi would allow Ritola to win... No !

Nurmi, who had coached Ritola on pacing methods, now fumed in silence. He was king of the runners. Why should he take a back seat to Ritola?

Legend has it that on the first day of Olympic competition in Paris, Nurmi ran 10,000 meters in 29 :58 in solitary splendor on a training track while Ritola was winning the gold medal with a world record 30 :23.2. One Finnish expert, Lauri Pikkala, denies there was such a run, but he believes Nurmi was capable of 29 :30.

Two days later, Nurmi was untroubled in a heat of the 5,000 and the next day he won a mild 1,500 heat. The following day, July 10, he was determined to win the finals of both events.

The track in Stade de Colombes was 500 meters around and Nurmi aimed for 75 seconds for each of the first two laps, a bold pace of 60 seconds per 400 meters. Cocking his head toward the right to read his watch, he passed 400 meters in 58 seconds, 500 meters in 1 :13, and 1,000 meters in 2 :31, at least 15 yards faster than in his 4 :10.4 mile.

Coolly, he tossed the watch aside and looked back. The nearest runner was 40 yards behind. Satisfied, Nurmi coasted the last lap in 82 seconds to win by nine yards in 3 :53.6. Except for his need to save strength, he could have smashed the world record.

Excited thousands stood and cheered, but Nurmi ignored them. While some of his opponents collapsed, he stopped only to snatch up his sweat clothes. Then he jogged off to the dressing-room. He had expected victory; his concern was for the 5,000.

He rested on a mattress in the dressing-room and received a massage. Legend has it that he slept.

In less than an hour he was back on the track, running the 5,000 final. Ritola and Wide set out at a fantastic pace of 2 :46.4

for 1,000 meters and Nurmi trailed by 40 yards. The spectators knew Nurmi was attempting an unreasonable double and they were not really disappointed. Only Nurmi knew what he was doing. Calmly, glancing at his stopwatch, he gradually caught up.

They passed 2,000 meters in 5:43.6, and after another lap Nurmi took the lead. After 3,000 meters in 8:42.6, a suddenly discouraged Wide dropped far behind, but Ritola, who had set an Olympic record for the steeplechase the previous day, was determined to beat Nurmi.

Nurmi increased the pace by two seconds per lap, passing 4,000 meters in 11:38.8, but Ritola stayed on his heels. At the bell, Nurmi took one last look at his time and tossed the watch aside. The crowd stood, cheering.

Ritola fought alongside in the home stretch while Nurmi remained the gracefully erect stylist with long, bounding, hip-rolling strides, his arms carried high. Nurmi's blue eyes were coldly calculating as he looked over at Ritola, spurted ahead, and kept him a frustrating meter behind all the way to the tape.

This was the day Nurmi earned such nicknames as 'The Flying Finn' and 'The Phantom Finn'. As great as his double victory was – and it is not likely to be equalled – the strife between Ritola and Nurmi was not yet settled. Each had won two gold medals and Nurmi's close margin in the 5,000 left many fans unsure of his superiority over a longer distance. Two days later, a ruthless Nurmi set out to remove all doubt.

After a day of rest (nothing to do except run a heat of the 3,000 meter team race in 8:47.8 while running up and back to urge his team to a qualifying effort), they lined up for the start of the 9,000 meter cross country race under a blazing sun. It was the hottest day Paris had known in many years – 102 degrees.

Ritola set off at a vicious pace, obviously out to run away with it. Nurmi, knowing the pace was foolish, stuck with Ritola anyway. He had plans for Ritola.

After 3,000 meters, along the Seine, Wide let go and it was between Nurmi and Ritola on the cobbled streets. For four miles Nurmi stayed with this man who most seriously challenged his superiority. In that oppressive heat, behind such a fast pace, only 15 of the 39 starters finished, and many of them went to the hospital, but Nurmi prepared to go faster.

He felt as tired as Ritola looked, but he intended to crush him. Suddenly, Nurmi surged away. Quickly, he gained 100 yards. Ritola gave up and finished almost a minute and a half behind although still a minute ahead of the bronze medalist.

A great roar of cheering greeted Nurmi's entrance into the stadium. He ran to the finish magnificently serene, in sharp contrast to the staggering, collapsing runners who followed.

Nurmi had changed his shoes before Ritola entered the stadium and now a close friend, Hannes Kolehmainen, saw Nurmi do something he almost never did in public. He saw Nurmi inspect the bedraggled Ritola and smile.

Nurmi had run six times in five days, but one more day remained. Running against a much-subdued Ritola, Nurmi won the 3,000 meter team race by 50 yards in 8 :32.0. It was his fourth individual championship of the 1924 Olympics and he was further honored with two more gold medals as a member of Finland's winning teams in the 3,000 and cross country.

At this point in his career he was the proud owner of eight gold medals and one silver, plus six world records, and he was hailed as the athletic wonder of the world. Anyone except Nurmi might have been satisfied, but he knew he could have won the 10,000. He had lost his world record to Ritola, and he wanted it.

At Kuopio, Finland, on August 31, he shattered the unfortunate Ritola's 10,000 meter record with 30 :06.1. Nurmi also collected official records for 4 miles (19 :18.7), 5 miles (24 :13.1), and one-half hour (9,957 meters). Unhappily, his 29 :07.1 for 6 miles was not official.

A month later, at Viipuri, October 1, Nurmi added to his renown. He broke his 4-mile record with 19 :15.6 and went on to 5 miles in 24 :06.2. His collection of world records stood at the magnificent total of ten.

Nurmi had a good job as a paper-hanger, hired by the best families in Finland so they could point with pride to his work, but he gave it up to tour the United States in 1925. Americans stood in line and thousands were turned away without seeing the Olympic hero. Some American bankers appraised the good will Nurmi won for Finland as worth ten million dollars.

On January 6, at the Finnish-American Athletic Club Games in Madison Square Garden, Nurmi was first seen by the eager American public. They were shocked when he ran 2½ miles to warm up. They were enraptured when the balding, stolid man in white shorts and blue jersey set a pace of 59.0 and 2:02.5 trying to escape from Joie Ray in the mile.

They were excited when Ray passed Nurmi in the third quarter. But with 250 yards to go, Nurmi raced past Ray and won by three yards in indoor record time of 4:13.6, collecting the 1,500 meter record as well.

The crowd was surprised to see Nurmi on the track eating a large red apple shortly afterward. And they were amazed an hour and a half later when he defeated Ritola with an indoor record of 14:44.6 for 5,000 meters.

The spectators here, as everywhere, were most impressed because Nurmi never appeared to extend himself. And yet he broke seven indoor records in five races in his first 12 days.

He ran at least 68 races in the United States, setting records in many of them. Some, at odd distances, only bore the name 'Noteworthy Performances' in the record books, but they had the Nurmi quality. For example, his $1\frac{7}{8}$ miles in 8:29.0 was 20 yards farther than 3,000 meters, making his time superior to his outdoor record.

Enthusiastic crowds saw him circle the small tracks in record time for 2,000 meters (5:22.4), 3,000 meters (8:26.4), and 2 miles (8:58.2), all faster than the outdoor world records. He excited them with a mile record of 4:12.0 on Buffalo's flat floor on March 7. He disappointed them only twice. He failed to finish behind Ritola in a 5,000 when he suffered stomach cramps, and he lost a close 880 challenge to three-time AAU champion Allan Hellfrich.

Nurmi's tour was a great success athletically, but it was bad for him. His already withdrawn personality was further affected by ugly accusations of exorbitant expenses, later disproved. His health deteriorated. He suffered from shin splints and several other injuries. One historian wrote, 'It took Nurmi three years to regain his style.' Another, more gloomy, said Nurmi never fully recovered. In any case, Nurmi set no outdoor records in 1925.

But he once said, 'I love to run. It is my life. As long as I can run I shall do so.' And in 1926 he was good enough to lower his 3,000 meter record twice, to 8:25.4 and then to 8:20.4 at Stockholm, July 13. Four days later, at Viborg, Finland, he anchored a 6,000 meter relay team to a world record 16:11.4, breaking their own 16:26.2.

He was in Berlin on September 11 for the greatest 1,500 meter race ever run. Edvin Wide was there, better than ever, and Dr Otto Peltzer of Germany was to be feared. Peltzer was the world record holder for the 880 and so fast he had set a world record for 500 meters in June. Nurmi's only hope was to set a fast pace.

He passed 400 meters in 61 flat and 800 in 2 :02.2, but he was not the magnificent champion of two years ago. His pace slipped to 2 :34.4 at 1,000 meters, three seconds slower than his Olympic pace.

Wide and Peltzer passed him in the last stretch and Peltzer's finishing speed lowered Nurmi's world record to 3 :51.0. Wide, only three yards behind, was given 3 :51.8, while Nurmi approached his world record with 3 :52.8.

The next day, Nurmi knew he was not right and he endured another rare defeat. He lost the 2-mile race by 20 yards to Wide's world record 9 :01.4.

Further deterioration of Nurmi's supremacy came in 1927. He regained the world 2,000 meter record from Wide with 5 :24.6, but he lost it later when Eino Borg ran 5 :23.4. (Borg's time was not as impressive as Nurmi's indoor record 5 :22.4.)

Now Nurmi concentrated his ambition toward the Olympic Games. On July 29, 1928, he started off with 23 hopeful 10,000 meter runners on the 400 meter track in the Grand Stadium of Amsterdam. Around they went, past the covered stands on each stretch, separated from the cheering spectators by a 500-meter cycling track and a moat. At 5,000 meters in 15 :11, all had dropped back except Nurmi's two dangerous opponents, Ritola and Wide.

On the 18th lap, Wide began to fall behind and once again Nurmi was alone with Ritola. He kept the pace fast, but Ritola would not let go. On the last lap, Nurmi began a long kick. He built up a lead of four precious yards over Ritola. Around the curve he held it. Down the homestretch he held it, all the way to the tape. His time of 30 :18.8, good on the soft track, broke Ritola's Olympic record.

Two days later, Nurmi ran a comfortable heat in the 5,000, but on the next day he bore the indignities of the steeplechase. A novice hurdler, he fell heavily in the water jump. Wet and shaken, he climbed out and resumed running, and he managed to qualify for the final. Two days later they ran the 5,000 final.

Once again the three veterans ran together until the last two crucial laps. Then Wide dropped back. With 600 meters to go, Ritola began a long drive. At the bell, Nurmi was on Ritola's heels, 15 meters ahead of Wide. But on the last curve, with Ritola running hard for the tape, Nurmi could not keep up. He had to strain to hold off Wide by seven yards. He finished 12 yards behind Ritola and fell on the grass, exhausted.

The next day, Ritola dropped out of the steeplechase. Nurmi trailed early, but he moved up to a comfortable second place at the finish. Sports writers stated positively that Nurmi let his friend, Toivo Loukola, cross the line first, but once again this must be classified as interesting legend.

Nurmi, very disappointed, said later, 'If I had not been ill, my success at Amsterdam would have been as great as at Paris in 1924.'

Nurmi's dazzling collection now contained nine Olympic gold medals and three silver. As far back as 1925 he had declared his ultimate goal to be a victory in the 1932 Olympic marathon, and so now he was eager to run longer distances. On October 7, in Berlin, he ran one of his greatest races.

Circling the track at a steady pace, he probably bettered Shrubb's world record for 8 miles, but, unfortunately, no time was recorded. At 9 miles his pace was still fast and he was undoubtedly under Shrubb's record of 45:27.6. Lack of official timing deprived him of another world record. He ran past 15,000 meters (124 yards longer than 9¼ miles) in 46:49.6, 29 seconds under Jean Bouin's 15-year-old record.

Continuing his severe pace, Nurmi passed 10 miles in 50:15.0, 25 seconds under Shrubb's 24-year-old record. He increased his pace only slightly near the end, but he collected his third world record of the day by covering 11 miles 1,648 yards in one hour.

German observers were astonished because Nurmi showed no sign of distress, and yet his 10-mile and one hour records were to last 17 years.

In 1929, Nurmi was talked into another sea voyage to the United States for indoor racing, but he was in poor shape and after losing a slow mile to American indoor champion Ray Conger, he returned home, embittered. It appeared to be the end of the road for the 32-year-old Nurmi, but he still liked to run.

In 1930, he travelled to London, and on June 9, after a half-hour nap on a table, he added to his glory with the world 6-mile record in 29 :36.4, a time he had beaten in the 10,000 meters without official recognition. Afterward, in the shower, he commented, 'Not a good time; the track was bad.'

He won the Finnish 10,000 meter championship in 31 :04.6. Then, in Stockholm on September 3, his relentless pace carried him to another world record. His 20,000 meters in 1 :04 :38.4 knocked a minute and 51 seconds off the old record.

In 1931, great young Finnish runners were maturing while Nurmi's age and recurrent rheumatism were weakening his fierce claim to the number one position he had held for 12 years. On July 24 in Helsinki, he ran an exciting 2-mile race against Finland's three best: Lauri Lehtinen, Lasse Virtanen, and Volmari Iso-Hollo, who were to win a total of eight Olympic medals between them.

Nurmi, not one to give up easily, ran with his young rivals for lap after lap and they actually pulled away from Iso-Hollo. On the last lap, with the crowd cheering wildly, Nurmi was second behind Lehtinen, but Virtanen was on his heels. It looked bad for the old champion as they ran past 3,000 meters.

Suddenly, Nurmi electrified the crowd by passing Lehtinen. They pulled away from Virtanen. Then the old master gradually widened his margin over Lehtinen. All three finished under Wide's world record: Virtanen 9 :01.1, Lehtinen 9 :00.5 and Nurmi 8 :59.5.

After such a triumph, Nurmi's chances in the 1932 Olympics seemed good at his regular distances, but he was determined to run the marathon and, possibly, the 10,000. Then the IAAF shocked Finland by doing what no runner could do. They barred Nurmi for alleged violations of his expense accounts during the 1929 season.

'My heart bleeds to end a career by winning the marathon.' And the stoic Finn had tears in his eyes.

Never a quitter, Nurmi hoped he would be reinstated and so he continued to train. In a marathon race on June 26 in Viipuri, Finland, he led by a mile and a quarter over Armas Toivonen before he ran off course. His time for 35 yards short of 25 miles was 2 :22 :03.8. Six weeks later, Toivonen finished only 36 seconds behind the Olympic marathon winner at Los Angeles, but Nurmi's suspension was not lifted and his great international career was ended, with nine of his world records still in the books.

Since 1920 he had won seven Olympic races and set world records in the astonishing total of 16 individual events plus one relay, even though collecting records did not seem important to him. At least six times he lost the enjoyment of world records at intermediate distances because they were not timed officially. Seven other times he broke his own world record, and he bettered outdoor records in at least five indoor races. Thus, astounding as it may seem, he ran faster than an existing world record at least 35 times.

He lost three Olympic races, under extenuating circumstances, and only two other races of consequence – on consecutive days during a bad year. He was never beaten in a race longer than 5,000 meters. No runner before or since has been so successful over such a wide range of distances.

His imprint on the track world was greater than any man's, before or after. He, more than any man, raised track to the glory of a major sport in the eyes of international fans, and they honored him as one of the truly great athletes of all sports.

Even at the age of 36 he loved to run. In 1933 he was still an amateur in Finland and he entered the Finnish Championships at Turku. To get the maximum competition, he ran in the 1,500 meters against Lehtinen, who was now the Olympic champion and world record holder at 5,000 meters.

Calmly, Nurmi followed Lehtinen to the homestretch. Then he burst past with impressive power. The old man won by nine yards.

Nurmi's farewell comment was typically tart: 'I thought Lehtinen was better than that.'

Nineteen years later, when visiting spectators went into the stadium for the 1952 Olympic Games in Helsinki, they were stirred by a bronze statue of one of Finland's great heroes, Paavo Nurmi. Inside, the highlight of the opening ceremony was the appearance of the torch bearer, whose identity was kept secret until the gigantic electric scoreboard produced goose pimples, lumps in throats, and wild cheers from 80,000 people with the single word . . . NURMI.

2 OWENS

Right from the beginning, anyone who watched Jesse Owens run could see his unmistakable quality, both in his beautifully fluid grace and his sheer speed.

The first track coach who saw this graceful speed, in a game of tag, felt a surprise and pleasure like the first expert to recognize the Koh-i-noor diamond.

This obvious talent was properly motivated in 1928 when Charley Paddock, 'The World's Fastest Human,' stood on the stage in Cleveland, Ohio, and inspired the junior high school students.

'I met him later in the coach's office,' says Owens, 'and I was so impressed that I decided right then that I would become The World's Fastest Human by winning the 100 meters championship in the Olympic Games.'

Coach Charley Riley recalls, 'Jesse ran so fast I thought my stop watch was out of order.' As a high school junior at Cleveland East Tech in 1932, Jesse Owens hit the tape first in both sprints and won the broad jump in Ohio's state meet. His best jump was 24' 1¼", less than 1½ inches from the national high school record.

On June 11, he took his marks in a district Olympic qualifying meet in Cleveland. Local spectators were not surprised to see him win, but his time, even with wind, brought forth a surprised cheer. It was 10.3, equal to the world record.

Even though he failed to qualify in the regionals, track fans thought he was a remarkable prospect, but they had not seen anything yet. As a lithe, mature senior, Owens sailed through the air for a startling high school record of 24' 11¼". Only the best 15 men in history had jumped farther.

In the state meet, he won three events again, speeding gracefully along the track for a national high school record of 20.8 in his heat of the 220. On June 17 at Chicago's Stagg Field, he ran wild in the national interscholastic meet against the best available high school athletes. He broad jumped 24' 9½" and sped to amazing high school records of 9.4 and 20.7, compared with the world records of 9.4 and 20.6.

As the greatest high school star of all time, he returned to Chicago two weeks later for a hectic weekend in the national AAU meet. He ran behind Jimmy Johnson in the junior 100. He leaped to victory in the junior broad jump at 24' 2⅛". In heats and final of the senior 100 meters he ran against the great Ralph Metcalfe, the current Fastest Human. Metcalfe pulled away to win and Johnson also beat Owens. Then, easing his disappointment, Owens became a national champion with a broad jump of 24' 6¾".

Some twenty-eight colleges and universities sought Owens and he chose Ohio State. When he was born J. C. Owens on September 12, 1913, in Danville, Alabama, one of eight children of a cotton picker, his chances for a university education were limited. When he was six, he had to pick cotton to help out, and he was run over by a cotton drag. But his family moved to Cleveland ... and opportunity. He worked in a gasoline station as a freshman at Ohio State, became a good student, and developed his track technique.

Track coach Larry Snyder made some interesting discoveries : Owens' arm action was too short. Owens's broad jump run was 14 feet too short. Owens needed a hitch kick to maintain balance in the air. And surprisingly enough, Owens waited at the start of a race until he saw the others move.

'Jesse Owens listens,' Snyder said, 'and then he tries to put the suggestions into practice. He is so well coordinated that even a radical form change ... becomes part of his style after a very few practice sessions.'

Early in 1934 Owens opened a few eyes in New York with a world indoor record of 25' 3¼" in the AAU broad jump. He placed third in the 60 meters behind Metcalfe and Ben Johnson. Owens came back in exciting fashion to beat Johnson in the NYKC Games. He equalled the indoor record for 60 yards with 6.2.

Outdoors, he ran another 9.4 and defended his AAU broad jump championship with 25' ⅞", but in the 100 he again had to run against Metcalfe, the greatest sprinter in history. Owens had hopes all the way to the last 20 yards when Metcalfe's big figure powered past.

Thus, Owens entered his sophomore year as a renowned broad jumper, but he had yet to win a major sprint race. Working as the most popular page boy in the legislature, he competed in several indoor meets. He won the Millrose 60 in 6.3. He set a record of 6.6 for 60 meters in an AAU semi-final, but he lost to Johnson's incredible start in the final. He lost a dual meet 60 to Willis Ward in 6.2, but he avenged that defeat in the Big Ten Championship on a dirt track with the first 6.1 ever run.

The broad jump at the 1935 indoor AAU meet was fierce competition. Eulace Peacock broke Owens' indoor record with 25′ 3½″. Owens retaliated with remarkable jumps beyond 25 feet, including 25′ 9″ and 25′ 7½″. Later, in the NYKC Games, Owens lost to Peacock by 1¼ inches.

Owens worked hard in training. He began a session with comfortable striding. He ran a 50 to 75 yard dash five or six times from the starting gun. He toiled over three low hurdles, straining his natural 7-foot stride in order to clear the first hurdle. Three times a week he ran the first 300 yards with 50-second quarter-milers, then burst into an astounding 15 or 20 yard lead at 440 yards. He took a few carefree practice jumps three times a week.

Outdoors, he covered 100 yards in 8.4 with a running start. At the Drake Relays he ran 9.5 and broad jumped 26′ 1¾″, third best of all time. Only ⅜″ short of the world record, Owens took off seven inches behind the board. An enthusiastic coach Snyder said, 'Owens can jump 27 feet.'

Owens breezed to four victories in a quadrangular meet, including sprints of 9.4 and 20.7. The next meet was a day to go down in history.

Ten thousand people went to the Big Ten meet at Ferry Field in Ann Arbor, Michigan, on May 25, 1935, hoping to see a new broad jump record. But Owens was worried about his sore back, injured while rolling down stairs in a playful scuffle.

'I had to be helped to the automobile that took us to the field, and my teammates practically dressed me into my track outfit.'

It was the first really hot day of spring, with a wind under 3 m.p.h. At 3:15 p.m., when he was supposed to run the 100, he says, 'I could hardly go to my mark at the start . . . but when the starter said, "Get set," my pain left.'

The gun cracked and Owens was off fast. He pulled away steadily and beat Bob Gieve, one of the nation's best college sprinters. The time was 9.4, equalling the world record, but it was a yard or more faster than any modern 9.4.

The Michigan officials were more reluctant than any known timers to give fast times. They actually timed 'the center of gravity' instead of the first part of the torso to reach the line, as the rules specify. Secondly, the watches stopped surprisingly close to 9.3. Thus, Owens' time was certainly as worthy as a present-day 9.3 and probably 9.2.

Ten minutes later Owens half crouched at the head of the runway, ready for his first broad jump. In the sand near the world record distance, he had optimistically placed a piece of paper as a marker. Other athletes gathered to watch, and the avid spectators were so silent they could hear his footsteps as he sped toward the white board.

The steel spikes in his left shoe hit the board with a rousing sound heard high in the stands. Owens' left leg went forward once in a full stride as his body rose awesomely high. His feet thrust out ahead and cut into the sand, leaving the marker undisturbed.

After the suspenseful measurement, the announcer led Owens to the edge of the track and said, 'Ladies and gentlemen, I wish to introduce a world's champion.'

Owens' mark was 26' 8¼". It was the only jump he took that day, but it remained as the best in the world for 25 years.

At 3:45, far down at the end of the straightaway, Owens took his marks in the third lane, eager for a 220 record. At the gun he was off so fast he never saw his opponents. No longer worried about his back, he shot down the long straightaway, his lithe body erect, his legs flashing swiftly back and forth in beautiful strides.

As if two world records were not enough, his time here set the fans to shaking their heads in open-mouthed wonder. His 20.3 was a new world record for both 200 meters and 220 yards.

Fifteen minutes later, the now delirious crowd watched in tense silence as Owens ran as hard as he could, sweeping over the low hurdles on the now unkempt track. He was happy with his time, a world record 22.6, although two of the three official watches showed 22.4. Both the 200 meter and 220 yard records lasted 12 years.

Within one glorious hour, Owens had squeezed in a whole career of superlatives – six entries in the world record book.

'When the meet was over the pain returned to my back and I had to be practically carried to the dressing-room.'

After winning three firsts in the Central Collegiate meet and four in a dual meet against Southern California, Owens attempted the unprecedented feat of winning four events in the National Collegiates at Berkeley, California.

He jumped 26′ 1⅜″ in the trials on Friday. Then, running against a 9 m.p.h. wind on June 22, the 5′ 10″, 160-pound 'Ebony Antelope' thrilled the crowd with his graceful speed. He defeated Peacock by a surprising two yards in a 9.8 100. He beat George Anderson by two feet in a 21.5 220. He rested while the 2-mile was run, and then he beat the great Glenn Hardin by three yards in a 23.4 low hurdles race.

No other man has ever won more than half as many events in one NCAA meet.

After the meet, coach Snyder told Owens, 'So far as we are concerned, the keyed-up, highly competitive track season is over.' He advised Owens to make no particular effort 'to keep in strict training.'

A relaxed Owens beat Peacock again in the Far Western AAU. In the national AAU, before 15,000 people at Lincoln, Nebraska, he faced Peacock, Metcalfe, and George Anderson, who had been timed in an unbelievable 9.2 by seven timers in May. Peacock beat Owens in a heat in 10.2, fastest on record, but it was disallowed because of wind.

In the final, Owens ran well for half the distance, but an inspired Peacock pulled away and Metcalfe passed Owens. Peacock won in 10.2 with a wind of 7.76 m.p.h., 3¼ m.p.h. too fast for a record.

In the broad jump, Owens came through in a courageous defense of his championship with a good 26′ 2¼″, but Peacock leaped ¾ of an inch farther.

Owens needed his best to win in that company, and Peacock edged him out twice more in 100's in the next week. Thus, three of Owens' four failures since high school came at the end of a hard season after his coach told him to ease off.

He went back home for a well-earned rest. He resumed his $3 a day job in the Ohio State House, and he was married. One reporter described him as a 'mannered, suave college student'.

Owens was ineligible for indoor collegiate competition in 1936. He lost to Peacock by one foot in the Cleveland 50 yard dash. Outdoors, in practice, he ran 300 yards in 29.5, a remarkable time when compared with the official world record of 30 seconds flat.

He won four events in three dual meets and he was well on his way to repeating his four Big Ten championships when disaster struck. He fell in the low hurdles, and at the halfway point he was far behind Bob Osgood of Michigan, a 23.5 man. Owens began to run as he never ran before.

Coach Snyder raved about it: 'Jesse gained the 19 plus one yard to win by a yard. I think it was the fastest 100 yards ever run by any human being and he cleared five hurdles while doing it.' Owens' time was 23.5.

He defended his three Central Collegiate titles. His great performances for the season included another 9.4 100, a 9.3 with wind, the second fastest ever 220 in 20.5, and an American record 21.1 220 around a turn.

The important NCAA meet was at Stagg Field, Chicago, June 19 and 20. In a heat of the 100 meters, Owens ran a puzzling 11.2. The distance turned out to be 110 meters, and so Owens had the finest time ever recorded for 110 meters or 120 yards.

In the final, Owens flashed past 100 yards in another 9.4 and won in 10.2, a world record good enough to last 20 years.

Owens defended his broad jump title at 25' 10⅞", glided around a curve to win a 21.3 200 meters (and 21.4 220), and completed his second brilliant quadruple victory with a 23.1 in the 220 low hurdles.

Next came the AAU meet at Princeton, N.J., on a hot July 4. Owens regained his broad jump title with only two jumps, reaching 26' 3", but his most significant event was the 100 meters where he had yet to win an AAU championship.

He was behind Sam Stoller at 50 meters, but he led Metcalfe by a safe three yards. He ran away from Stoller, while the powerful

Metcalfe could gain only four feet on him. Owens had his first victory over Metcalfe, in 10.4.

The suspense-filled Final Trials for the Olympic team, held on the following weekend in the humid, 100 degree heat of Randall's Island, New York, was the most important meet yet for Owens. He broad jumped 25' 10¾" to win. The way he was running this season, he was favored in the 100 and he beat Metcalfe by five feet in 10.4. He was now on the team in two events, but the 200 promised trouble.

Coming off the curve into the homestretch, Metcalfe was leading, but Mack Robinson was catching him. Owens was challenged for the third spot on the team by Bobby Packard. For a moment Owens was in danger, but he turned on his smooth power and swept past spectacularly to win by two feet in 21 flat, an American record around a curve.

Next came a sea voyage to Germany with a dangerous loss of conditioning. Owens seemed vigorous in Berlin, but then came Hitler's 'Aryan superiority' and some unexpected German triumphs on the field. It was a nervous Jesse Owens who took his marks for the 100 meters heat on August 2.

The expectant morning crowd of 80,000 was far larger than any track crowd Owens had seen. No runner in Owens' heat could threaten him, but he ran fast anyway, winning by an extravagant eight yards. His Olympic record equalling time of 10.3 was not allowed because of wind.

He had left the village on the bus early that morning, and he had to wait nervously for the 12th heat. Now he was afraid he would miss the bus back for lunch. After this first day, coach Snyder arranged for a cot in the peaceful quiet of the dressing-room, and Owens carried a cold lunch.

Owens 'ran scared' again in the quarter-finals that afternoon before 110,000 spectators including Adolf Hitler, rocking with frenetic excitement in a box jutting out from the second deck. Owens ran 10.2 again with wind.

On August 3, Owens was more composed, and he breezed home confidently in 10.4 against Frank Wykoff and Lennart Strandberg in the semi-final. But in the final he was anxious to win, and, as coach Snyder says, 'He was always best when the blue chips were down.'

The big German starter in his white coat raised his pistol and said, 'Get set,' in German. Owens came to the set position. Then the anxious wait. Two seconds seemed like ten. The gun fired. Owens shot out of his holes with a good start. With one of the fastest accelerations ever seen, Owens drove to a startling 10-foot lead over Metcalfe in the first 25 yards.

Then the powerful Metcalfe began to reach full speed, and he cut down the distance between them alarmingly. Owens ran smoothly through the tape, four feet ahead of Metcalfe and he was an Olympic champion, exactly as he had planned eight years before. Only he was not quite through yet.

With the theory of Aryan supremacy crumbling before his very eyes, Hitler was seen to make a hasty exit before Owens mounted the victory stand for his gold medal. Der Führer presented no more medals.

August 4 was a busy day for Owens, with four appearances. In the morning he sped around the curve and qualified safely for the 200 meter quarter-finals in Olympic record time of 21.1, but the broad jump qualifying was exciting.

He jogged unsuspectingly to the broad jump runway and awaited his turn. Still in his sweat clothes he ran down the runway to check his step. To his horror, an official waved a red flag, signalling a foul jump. Owens' protest was to no avail. He had one foul against him and he still did not have his step.

Hopefully, he sped down the runway, but his left foot hit two inches beyond the board and again the ominous red flag waved. Now he was within one jump of being eliminated from his best event and all he needed was a jump of 23' 5½".

Worried now, Owens walked away from the pit. Someone put a hand on his shoulder and said hello. He turned to see a smiling Luz Long of Germany, his chief rival for the broad jump championship. Long, a blond Aryan in plain view of about 70,000 Germans, offered advice to his black rival. Gratefully, Owens drew a line a foot behind the line and moved his takeoff back accordingly.

Faced with disaster, he raced down the runway, holding his stride in so he would not foul. He overdid it and took off two feet behind the board. It was not a good jump, for him, and he watched anxiously while the officials measured a mark perilously close to the qualifying standard. His jump measured 23' 5 9/16". One eighth of an inch less would have meant shocking failure.

PAAVO NURMI   Stopwatch in hand, pale skin gleaming in the May sun, 34-year-old Nurmi wins the 4-mile at the British Games of 1931 on the soft track at Stamford Bridge

Top left: JESSIE OWENS Owens (*left*) poses with his friend and arch rival Ralph Metcalfe, world's greatest sprinter through 1935. *Top right:* High in the air, Owens completes his hitch kick before 110,000 spectators in Berlin's Olympic Stadium. *Below:* In a rain-blurred Olympic 200 metres final, a relaxed Owens reaches the tape for his last great triumph

In the afternoon, a strong wind came up, and all the jumps in the final were wind-aided. Almost casually, Owens sandwiched in a quarter-final of the 200 meters in 21.1, aided by a wind of 8.27 m.p.h.

Owens' first jump was 25′ 4¾″. It was a relief to be in the lead, but Luz Long came back on his second trial to tie. Owens, who had expected this to be his easiest event, had to draw upon his competitive courage. On his second jump, his heels cut the sand at 25′ 9¾″. Long's third jump fell an inch short, but it was a threat. Owens jumped 25′ 5¼″ and then fouled his fourth trial.

Long's fifth jump was 25′ 9¾″, an exact tie, and the German crowd roared. Now Owens felt the pressure, but to him that meant a better effort. He sprinted down the runway, leaped high into the air, and whipped his legs in a graceful running motion to keep from falling to his left. His jump was 26′ ½″.

Long fouled his last jump and Owens was the champion, but he increased his Olympic record to 26′ 5¼″ on his last attempt. Long was the first to congratulate Owens and they walked arm-in-arm.

Owens bubbled with joy. When photographers asked for a jump for the cameras he agreed readily. Fully warmed up, he streaked down the runway and gave it all he had. The jump was not measured, but Brutus Hamilton is sure it was over 27 feet and he told Owens so.

'I wouldn't be surprised,' Owens agreed. 'I felt good, hit the board just right, and thought for a moment I wasn't coming down.'

That was his last broad jump. Hamilton says, 'I'm certain in my own mind that Jesse could have leaped at least a foot farther had he taken a few weeks to concentrate upon his event in his prime. . . . He didn't care much for the event and never practiced.'

August 5 was 200 meters day. Owens coasted prettily through his semi-final in 21.3, saving himself for what he knew would be a difficult race. His team-mate, Mack Robinson, had finished only two feet behind Owens in the Final Trials and today Robinson won the first semi-final in an alarming 21.1.

The wind let down a little for the final and a light drizzle began to fall. Owens kept a wary eye on Robinson ahead of him to the right, and he ran the curve to catch him. Into the stretch he led Robinson satisfactorily by two yards, but he was tired from four days of competition. He forced himself down the homestretch as the rain fell harder, and he gained another yard.

He hit the tape three yards ahead in 20.7, a time superior to his straightaway record of 20.3.

Row upon row, the spectators rose to their feet before Adolf Hitler and paid tribute to this Negro youth whose talent and competitive courage were unsurpassed. Owens stood in the rain for a moment of wonder. He had come a long way from Alabama.

He was bothered constantly by autograph hunters and photographers – at the stadium, at the dormitory, at meals. On August 8, after two days of 'rest', Owens ran the important leadoff leg in a heat of the 400 meter relay, followed by Metcalfe, Foy Draper, and Wykoff. They ran 40 flat to equal the world record.

Next day, in the final, Owens showed his marvelous pickup. He blasted out in front and beat his nearest opponent by about six yards. His team-mates increased the lead to 11 yards and they set a new world record of 39.8.

On the victory stand, with a laurel wreath on his head, a diploma in one hand, a tiny potted oak tree in the other, and his fourth gold medal around his neck, Owens felt wonderful. 'That's a grand feeling, standing up there. I never felt like that before.'

He was the toast of the athletic world. Invitations poured into compete all over Europe, and the AAU, in need of money to pay for the Olympic trip, signed contracts for his services without his knowledge.

He had to run a 100 meters race the very next day at Cologne. He was more than two yards ahead of Metcalfe with 20 meters to go but he eased up to let his friend win. When Metcalfe's time was announced as 10.3, it was obvious Owens had given away a world record. Tired, he also lost the broad jump for the first time that year, to Wilhelm Leichum.

Owens ran several times, including 10.3 at Bochum, August 12, and then his last competition was in a relay in White City, London, on August 15. The AAU had rented him out for more races in Sweden, but he was tired. Telegrams had been coming in streams, offering money, and Owens was advised to take what he could and set himself up for life. He returned to New York on the Queen Mary instead of going to Sweden, and he was suspended by the AAU even though he had never signed an entry blank for a Swedish meet.

'I've lost six pounds,' he explained, 'being circused and pushed all over Europe. I'm burned out and tired of being treated like a head of cattle. I'm turning professional because I'm busted and know the difficulties encountered by any member of my race in getting financial security ... because if I have money I can help my race like Booker T. Washington ... because I owe it to my wife ... and because after I have made some money I hope to go into politics and do something for my people.'

He still had a year of college eligibility and wonderful potential, but the most sensational career in track history came to an abrupt end. Ironically, none of the 'fabulous' offers were acceptable.

Owens had stopped the watches at 9.4 five times; only Frank Wykoff had ever done it twice. No other man had cleared the uncommon distance of 26 feet more than once; Owens did it seven times. He never lost in outdoor college competition; in only two years he won more events than any other collegian. His indoor and outdoor world records in the broad jump and his Olympic record each lasted an astounding 25 years, longer than any other records in modern history.

He set official world records in seven events, plus two unofficial records and three indoor records. He never lost at 220 yards or 200 meters.

Sportswriters and fans, individually and in polls, have proclaimed Jesse Owens the greatest track and field athlete of all time. Certainly, he accomplished more in two years than any other athlete ... or in one week ... or in one hour ...

3 WARMERDAM

Greatness comes in many forms. It can appear in a single moment or accumulate over a long career, but all great athletes have one thing in common ... an unquestioned superiority over their opponents.

In the entire history of track and field, no athlete's superiority has been so unquestioned as Warmerdam's.

To Cornelius Warmerdam, bright, tow-headed third son of an American immigrant from Holland (and thus affectionately known as 'Dutch'), the concept of himself as a superior athlete was distressingly slow in coming. Modesty is not an outstanding characteristic of the very great, but Dutch Warmerdam was different. He was unassuming to an unusually pleasant degree.

In his early years as a vaulter, he had something to be modest about. A fine student who skipped the third grade, he received his diploma from high school in Hanford, California, before he was seventeen. Handicapped by his tender age, his vaulting progress had reached only 12' 3" from his eight feet at age 12 and nine feet at age 13. His greatest triumph was a tie for third in the 1932 California state high school meet.

College coaches did not clamor for his services. 'The opportunity of going on to school was limited in those days. Junior colleges did not exist and money was scarce.' Dutch farmers work like beavers, and Warmerdam had worked hard from the age of ten on his father's 40 acres of peaches and apricots. Now he worked on the ranch for a year and a half instead of attending college.

He liked to pole vault, however, and he had built his first uprights at the age of ten. Now his runway and pit were on their fruit drying field.

One summer day in 1933, a curious salesman, tipped off by the high school track coach, stopped his car on the road and watched with amazement as a lean, fair-haired youth sprinted on the other side of a spinach patch carrying a long pole. He saw the boy vault over a crossbar more than twice his own height. Soon after, the excited salesman was talking to Fresno State track coach Flint Hanner.

'I just saw a kid jumping well over 13 feet . . . in a spinach patch.'

Hanner said, 'That's not much of a broad jump.'

Soon after being corrected on that point, Hanner hastened to the ranch. Warmerdam was happy to begin Fresno State in the spring of 1934, when he vaulted a promising 13' 6".

In 1935, still not quite twenty years old, Warmerdam squirmed over the bar at 14' 1⅞" in a dual meet, less than five inches from the world record. In the West Coast Relays at Fresno, he tied for first at 13' 6½" with five men, including Earle Meadows and Bill Sefton.

Warmerdam's progress was now satisfactory, though hardly world-shaking. Unfortunately for his track career, his personal philosophy prevented him from faster development as a vaulter. He valued other things in life besides pole vaulting. He never trained in the summer, as all successful athletes must do now. In the fall, he trained only when he wanted to prepare for indoor meets, and those did not begin until 1939. In college, he enjoyed bastketball during the winter months, and he was good enough to be a high scorer and captain of the team.

In 1936, he raised his personal record only one inch, hampered by a bad ankle. 'I missed several meets because it hurt to jump.' His only triumph was a tie for first in the Drake Relays at 13' 8". At the end of June, he competed in the Far Western semi-final trials for the Olympic team. Only two men at the Los Angeles Coliseum meet were to qualify for the Final Trial in New York.

Suffering from his sore ankle Warmerdam struggled over 13' 6". After one miss at 14 feet, he had to stop. The next day his ankle was swollen to twice its size. 'I could hardly walk.'

Instead of competing in New York, he picked cotton in the hot San Joaquin Valley. His father told his unhappy son, 'Don't quit; keep at it.' He had a tooth pulled and the ankle gave him no more trouble. 'It appears that the abcessed tooth had caused the irritation in the ankle joint.'

Weight training was not used by athletes then, and Warmerdam's only strength training came from wielding heavy pruning shears three months a year. He helped develop his speed and an even step by training over the low hurdles.

'It's practically all speed. If you can't get up speed on the runway, you can't get your weight up the full 80 degrees.'

In 1937, his last season as a collegian, Warmerdam was free from injury and he vaulted well. In the dual meet with Southern California, he flew over the bar at 14 feet to tie for second with Sefton behind Olympic champion Meadows. At the Pacific Association AAU meet, he was pleased to swing over 14′ 4″ even though he lost on fewer misses to Jack Mauger. He also lost ground on the world record, for Sefton and Meadows had raised it to an awesome 14′ 11″.

At the famed Princeton Invitational, he won at 14 feet over Mauger. In his first national AAU meet, at Milwaukee, Wisconsin, on July 3, Warmerdam became embroiled in a long and exciting competition against the co-holders of the world record, plus former record holder George Varoff.

Warmerdam and Varoff missed once at 14 feet. None of the four missed again until the bar reached 14′ 7⅝″. All four missed on their first attempts. In the second round, Sefton and Warmerdam sailed over. Meadows and Varoff cleared on their third jumps to make it the greatest 4-way vaulting ever seen. Warmerdam thus defeated Meadows and Varoff, but he lost to Sefton because of his single miss at 14 feet.

The Pan-American Games were held in Dallas, Texas. On July 17, Warmerdam won his first major championship by clearing 14′ 3″ and defeating Varoff and Meadows. Then Warmerdam enjoyed his first trip to Europe and he cleared 14′ 3″ in Stockholm.

In 1938, he graduated from Fresno State. In the spring he won the Compton Invitational at 14′ 6″. He cleared 14′ 6″ again, in the Princeton Invitational, but Meadows beat him with the same height after Warmerdam had loaned him his spare pole.

Warmerdam soared over 14′ 5½″ to defeat Varoff for his first victory in the national AAU. He beat Varoff again in Berlin during USA's first international dual meet. He set a British All-Comers record of 14′ 3″ at Glasgow, vaulting from a runway on a soccer field into a pile of sand.

He was now good enough to be sought after for indoor meets.

On February 11, 1939, in Boston, he propelled himself over the bar at 14′ 6⅜″ for a world indoor record. He added the indoor AAU championship to his small collection of honors, but he lost his outdoor title in Lincoln, Nebraska. At 14′ 4″, he knocked the bar off and lost to Varoff. He still had much to be modest about.

In 1940, he was teaching history and geometry in a mountain high school. Pole vaulting, in his philosophy, was something he did for fun, and training was more difficult now. As his weight went near 180 pounds he added more tape to his old bamboo pole, 'picked out of the Stanford University discard rack.'

He did not compete in the indoor meets, and Meadows took over as indoor champion. Warmerdam's first meet, in the cool spring air of the Long Beach Relays, resulted in a ridiculous 12′ 6″. 'I was in fairly good shape but I was eliminated before really getting warmed up.'

Dutch Warmerdam had a quiet maturity which put pole vault-ing in its proper place, but he also had some pride. He took sprint starts, worked on the parallel bars, and vaulted tenaciously until dark. His weight was down to 170 pounds.

Now a member of the San Francisco Olympic Club team, he won at 14′ 4″ at Stanford on April 6. On April 13, he drove to an insignificant meet with California and Washington State in Berkeley. 'I knew I was in good shape.'

Down on the runway at Edwards Field, he lifted over 14 feet easily, on his first attempt. He felt good clearing 14′ 2″. The bar was raised to 14′ 5″ and he missed. On his second attempt he cleared easily. Exhilarated now, he had the bar raised to a personal record height of 14′ 8½″. Why not? He had nothing to lose.

When he shot over the crossbar on his first vault, he was a little puzzled. It seemed too easy. Quietly excited, he asked the officials to raise the bar to 15 feet. He had wondered what it would be like to attempt a world record.

He soon found out, for he missed. But he was far from dis-couraged. 'I knew I could make it after the first miss because it was a close miss and fairly easy for me.'

The few spectators watched silently as he stood 140 feet from the pit, holding the heavy bamboo pole in front of him. They saw the lean, broad-shouldered man start his purposeful run, lop-sided because of the pole on his right side. His left elbow pumped in lieu of an arm swing as he gathered speed. He approached the pit at a dangerous pace and lowered the tip of his pole until it jarred to a halt in the box. Simultaneously, his arms went high, transferring forward speed into upward energy with a sudden shock.

For a moment his body was alongside the pole. Then he lifted his feet, turned on his side, and pushed his body upward, feet first. It was a hard, struggling effort, but his body flew off the pole, and he was above the bar, wonderfully free. He pulled his hands up barely in time. Then he concentrated on landing safely in the low pile of shavings.

It was the world's first 15-foot vault.

The cheers were loud, joyful, and not a little surprised. Even Warmerdam, known as a calm, quiet individual, expressed his pleasure. In one marvelous second over that crossbar came his transition from good vaulter to world record holder.

The AAU meet was held in Fresno and Warmerdam knew that pit well. They started vaulting at 6:30 p.m. on the warm evening of June 29, at a height of 12' 6".

Warmerdam cleared each height with calm confidence, on his first attempt. Meadows and Bud Deacon went no higher than 13' 6", leaving Ken Dills, a 14' 8" vaulter, as Warmerdam's only threat. Dills cleared 14' and 14' 4". On his first trial, Warmerdam sailed skillfully over 14' 8", and Dills failed. Warmerdam was the national champion, breaking the 4-way meet record, and now he wanted another world record.

The people in the two long stands on either side of the track watched keenly as Warmerdam raced unevenly down the runway. There was the smooth pole plant, taking some of the shock out of his sudden halt, and then he was up, arching over the bar. He landed in the shavings with the satisfaction of another world record – 15' 1⅛".

'It was big for me because it was in Fresno and my folks were there to see me.'

He took no European trip in 1940. He was married in August and he did not compete indoors in 1941, but he ran with a dedication and he kept up his strength. His training now required almost no vaulting.

On April 12, in a dual meet with Stanford, he was ready. Starting at 12' 6" again, he cleared each of six heights through

14′ 8″ on his first attempt. Then, with the bar at 15′ 2⅝″, he missed. He missed again. A third time he charged at the bar with determination, and this time he went over the record height.

Without doubt, he was vaulting better than ever, but two weeks later, in Los Angeles, he lost at 14′ 6″. 'Officials asked me to jump at 15 feet anyway. I did, and cleared on my first attempt. This was not an official jump.'

Two days after that, in Visalia, California, he cleared 15 feet. On May 24, in the Coliseum Relays, he cleared 15 feet. He was now consistently better than the best of all the other vaulters in history.

At the invitational in Compton's little stadium on the night of June 6, he zoomed over 15 feet for the fifth time in 1941. Few, if any, track and field athletes had turned in so many performances better than all other men, but it seemed as if he had reached his ceiling.

Still, he was hopeful as he attacked 15′ 4¼″, more than an inch and a half above his world record. Seven thousand alert specators in the old wooden stands watched the lean 6-footer in his red shorts and his white shirt with its red winged 0. Warmerdam seemed perfectly calm as he peered down the runway, then launched into his loping run.

He missed.

In pole vaulting, a miss is not a tragedy; you keep on trying. Warmerdam, who had kept trying for 11 years, tried once again, and this time he sailed over. The crowd's roar shattered the silence. He put on his red sweat suit and tried to be patient during the long process of measurement, with an official holding a tape high up on a ladder.

The crowd cheered when the announcer confirmed the new record, but Warmerdam felt too good to stop. The bar was raised another inch and a half, but he knocked it off, of course. The crowd could not reasonably hope for another world record the same night, but they enjoyed watching. On his second miss they applauded his effort and prepared to go home.

After a short rest, he tried again, racing hopefully down the runway, shooting toward the dark sky. A sudden surprised roar burst upon him as he fell triumphantly to the pile of shavings. He had cleared 15′ 5¾″. The crowd was delirious. Two world records in one meet!

The rest of the season was disappointing by comparison. He won twice more at the now disdained height of 15 feet. Then, at the AAU, after winning at 15 feet, he had 'Three very good attempts at 15′ 7″.'

In the fall, he taught at Piedmont High School, near Berkeley. On December 28, in New Orleans, he won at the Sugar Bowl with 15 feet and he was ready for an even greater season. His presence was desired in the Millrose Games and he wrote out a telegram to the meet director :

'There is no use crossing the continent to vault 14 feet. But if you will extend the runway from 125 feet to 137 feet, I can almost guarantee you a fifteen-foot jump.'

The eager director granted his request, but on his flight to the February 7th meet, Warmerdam had to change airplanes in Chicago. To his dismay, his pole was lost. Vaulting with Milt Padway's pole, two feet shorter than his own, he cleared 14′ 8⅝″ to regain the indoor record Meadows had taken from him in 1941.

'Then, with the bar at 15′ ⅜″, he sped down the board runway, unsure of his borrowed pole, and sailed over. It was the first 15-foot vault indoors, and 16,000 fans went wild. Hats sailed into the arena. Promoter Fred Schmertz says, 'I think it was the greatest ovation ever given to a single individual.'

Warmerdam stayed in the east for the Boston AA meet. Using his own pole, he cleared the first five heights, through 14′ 8¾″, without a miss. He wanted a new indoor record height of 15′ 2″, and he made it on his second attempt.

After the cheering and measurement, the bar was set at 15′ 7¼″, an inch and a half higher than he had ever vaulted outdoors. The crowd in the double-decked Boston Garden watched intently while he held his pole in the box, adjusting the standards. He missed, but he was confident tonight.

He went back to the far end of the runway. When he started his second run he could hear nothing except his spikes pounding into the wooden runway like a suspenseful drum roll.

He watched with satisfaction as his left foot hit his check mark at 120 feet and again at 70 feet. He slid the end of his pole into the slot and swung up smoothly. 'A vaulter must have a body as hard as a prize fighter's to absorb the shock.'

He rode the straight pole patiently for a moment, then twisted and shot his feet toward the roof. His left leg bent under his right in a scissors motion and he struggled to a face-down position as he went over the bar sideways. His 167 pounds landed on his hands and knees in a dangerous pile of shavings only as high as the runway. 'Once, in an indoor meet, my knee went through and hit concrete.'

The spectators left their seats in a frenzy of admiration. Two hundred youngsters pursued him. Everybody wanted to shake his hand and congratulate him. Even a quiet Dutchman had to smile with pleasure, but he wanted to vault some more.

The bar was raised to 15' 10". He missed the first attempt, but he felt good. He missed the second, but he knew the height was possible. On his third trial, his remarkable shoot lifted his body cleanly over the bar, but he did not bring his left elbow up in time and it knocked the crossbar off. After the meet, the crowd pursued him out of the building and he almost missed his plane.

With almost routine skill, he left the crossbar on at 15 feet to 15' 2" in four more meets. Then, at the district AAU meet in Berkeley on May 2, he went over 15' $\frac{3}{4}$" without a miss and he asked for an outdoor record height of 15' 6". He missed twice. Then, as on his two previous world records, his third jump brought triumph.

The bar was measured carefully at 15' 6$\frac{7}{8}$", and he had the satisfaction of his fifth world record.

He bettered 15' 1" in Memphis, Tennessee, and Fresno. On May 23 he went to the town of Modesto, 90 miles north of Fresno, where eager local people promoted a new meet called the Northern California Relays. The spectators in the low wooden stands were pleased when he vaulted 15' 3" without a miss. Few big meets had such a fine meet record.

Delayed an hour because one 14-foot standard fell from its improvised perch on a wooden crate and had to be taken to a shop and welded, the vault lasted long after the meet ended, but Warmerdam wanted to try 15' 8".

On his third attempt, his faithful bamboo pole, heavily taped, rode high ahead of him, then dipped and thudded into the deep slot. His left hand shifted up to his right, an extraordinary 13' 11" from the end of the pole. He was jerked violently upward, then swung smoothly. He twisted over and thrust himself skyward.

'No athlete has much left after sprinting 50 yards at top speed, yet I still have to figure on the body shock that comes when the pole strikes the ground. The pole vibrates, jars your whole system. It can tear loose the grip of your right hand. It can do something to destroy the physical coordination so necessary to finish the job after momentum ends at the crossbar.'

He arched sideways over the bar and dropped free.

The small crowd roared. An excited official knocked down the crossbar. Measured again, it was only 15' 7¾", but it was a world record by ⅛ of an inch. Another roar of pleasure and admiration, but Warmerdam seemed almost embarrassed.

Next came a trip to Pocatello, Idaho, for the Intermountain AAU and a victory at 15' 1⅛". 'This vault was very difficult, running into a wind.'

On June 20, he was in New York for the national AAU. He won at 15' 2½" and stood alone on the victory stand in his bare feet to receive his medal from Mayor Fiorello La Guardia.

For his unprecedented achievements and his good character, he won the Sullivan Award for 1942.

In 1943, he returned in triumph to the Millrose Games and won at 15' 1½". He repeated his indoor AAU victory, leaving the crossbar undisturbed at 15' 3⅞", and he cleared 15' 1¾" in San Francisco.

On March 20, 1943, as a brand new ensign in the U.S. Navy, he flew to the Chicago Relays for the finest vaulting of his career. He knocked the bar off only once through 15' 3⅝" and it was raised to 15' 8½".

He stood for a moment at the head of the runway, concentrating his desire. Behind him, across the banked board track, the crowd in the triple-decked stands grew quiet with anticipation. When he launched into his loping sprint, his footsteps were the loudest sounds in Chicago Stadium.

He knew he could vault this high, but he had never succeeded a 15' 4" or higher on his first attempt. He swung into his vault at full speed, swung up, twisted, and pulled, then pushed his whole body toward the lights. Elated with his zooming push, he flattened out on top only a little sideways.

He was over! It was the highest vault ever made, and it came on his first attempt. Exhilarated, he had the bar moved to 16' ½".

Three times he raced down the runway and flung himself

hopefully toward the bright ceiling, and three times he missed but two of his jumps were the best ever seen. Of those two, he says, 'I thought I might have cleared 15′ 11″.'

One writer, years later, called this, 'Perhaps the greatest performance seen on any track at any time.'

Outdoors, Warmerdam vaulted well, soaring over 15 feet nine more times, but he never matched his impressive Chicago vaulting. He won the AAU title again at 15′ and later thrust himself over laudable heights of 15′ 4″ and 15′ 3″.

In 1944, his duties as a naval lieutenant and his location at Monmouth College in Illinois frustrated further improvement. He cleared only 14′ 5″ in the Chicago Relays. His only 15-footer came in his farewell appearance when he won his sixth AAU championship in New York. He would have been everyone's favorite for Olympic champion in 1944, as well as in 1940.

Warmerdam's outdoor world record lasted 15 years and his indoor record stood for sixteen years. No other man cleared 15 feet until 1951, but Warmerdam had driven his body over that height an astounding total of 43 times, plus twice in exhibitions.

Bob Richards, the second man to vault 15 feet, said, 'Warmerdam was part sprinter, part shock-absorber, part acrobat, and part strong man. He wasn't human.'

No athlete ever had so many marks so far ahead of the next best man of all time, in any event.

Nat Cartmell, 1904 Olympic double silver medalist in the sprints, summed it up when he said, 'Warmerdam is the only all-time, indisputable, supreme champion the athletic world has ever known.'

4 DILLARD

In August of 1936, a skinny black boy of thirteen sat on the curb of Cleveland's Central Avenue watching a parade for a hero. He saw Jesse Owens sitting high on the back seat of an open car, smiling and waving to the crowd. He felt the wonder and awe of Owens' Berlin triumphs. Four gold medals!

'I certainly was hit by the spark that afternoon,' says Harrison Dillard.

His junior high school team-mates laughed at this scrawny, undernourished child of poverty, and they called him 'Bones', and the coach said he was not strong enough to sprint. One man took an interest in the frail boy – his idol, Jesse Owens.

Owens gave him his famous shoes from Berlin, and helped form young Dillard's love of hurdling.

'I've always felt,' Dillard once said, 'that sprinters, including me, are a dime a dozen. That's just running. But when you combine running with the gymnastic ability required in the hurdles, you have a high art in track and field athletics.'

In the spring of 1941, Dillard had begun to develop his art. Proudly, he wore Jesse Owens' shoes and he won both hurdles in the Ohio state high school meet.

Dillard enrolled at Baldwin-Wallace College because of his deep friendship with Coach Eddie Finnigan, and he worked toward filling Jesse Owens' shoes. His only significant competition in 1942 came at the AAU championships on Randall's Island, New York. Dillard did well to place third in the junior high hurdles. He lost the junior low hurdles by only three inches. In the senior intermediate hurdles, the only time he ever attempted that event, he placed fifth in 53.7.

In the spring of 1943, he began to fill those shoes. Although his best time over the high hurdles was 14.8, he won at the famous Penn Relays. In the Ohio Athletic Conference meet, he led little Baldwin-Wallace to a surprising championship by winning both sprints, both hurdles, and the sprint relay. His promising season came to an abrupt end when, at the age of 19, he was drafted into the army.

Army service during a world war is not the ideal training climate, especially when you are under fire in Italy, and Dillard's career could have suffered immeasurably. But when you are trying to fill Jesse Owens' shoes you simply carry on. When the war ended in Europe in that joyous spring of 1945, Dillard began training and he ran in seven service meets. He ran 10.6 for 100 meters, 14.6 for the high hurdles, and he was voted the outstanding competitor of the climactic meet in Frankfort.

In the spring of 1946 there was no longer any doubt about Dillard's future greatness. At the Kansas Relays he flashed over the hurdles in 14.2. In the Ohio Conference, June 1, he won in 9.7, 14.6, and 22.8. In the Ohio College meet, June 8, he ran 9.6 and 14.2. Then he stirred a somnolent track world by equalling the world record of 22.5 for the low hurdles.

He lost only twice in 1946, once while injured at the Penn Relays and once to dangerous George Walker in the Central Collegiate highs.

He went hopefully to the NCAA Championships at Minneapolis and he hit the tape first in both hurdles. His 14.1 was a personal best and his 23 flat was a world record around a curve. Once again he gave Owens credit for changing him to a left-footed hurdler, an advantage in curve hurdling.

In San Antonio, Texas, he won the AAU highs in 14.2 when a charging Walker hit the ninth hurdle. Dillard completed his notable sweep of four national championships with 23.3 for the 200 meter hurdles around a turn.

He was even better in 1947. In Madison Square Garden, he won both hurdles championships in the indoor AAU and completed an undefeated indoor season. Outdoors, he equalled his previous best of 14.1 three times and ran 14 flat five times. Undefeated in the highs, he tied the world low hurdle record again at 22.5. Then he lost his only race of the year to Bill Porter's fine 22.7 in the Coliseum Relays. It was only his third loss in 137 races.

The NCAA meet was at Salt Lake City. Dillard defeated Porter by two yards in 14.1, but he was concerned about the fast low hurdlers he must face. He left nothing to chance. He started as fast as possible and kept going. He never saw his opponents and he beat Porter by over two yards. His 22.3 was a new world record for 220 yards and it equalled Fred Wolcott's 200 meter record. Considering the 6-mile headwind and 50-degree temperature, it may be the best ever run.

The next weekend he was in Lincoln, Nebraska, for the AAU championships. He won both hurdles again, in 14 flat and 23.3, an unprecedented sweep of eight outdoor national gold medals in two years.

'Bones' ranked No. 1 in the world for both hurdles for the second year, but he also began to be recognized as a sprinter. Although his best 100 was 9.6, he ran four commendable 10.4's for 100 meters in Europe. At Stockholm on August 5, he ran 10.3, only one tick of the watch off the world record. He ranked ninth in the world in the 100 and he was good enough for fourth in the 200, where he ran 21.2 twice around a curve.

In 1948, Dillard was phenomenal. He began indoors with a perfect record of ten high hurdle victories and four low hurdles. His 7.2 while defending his AAU title was a record, but he surpassed it with 7.1 at the Chicago Relays.

Outdoors, he ranked No. 1 for the third consecutive year in the lows, his last year of serious competition over the 2′ 6″ hurdles. His excellent record included 22.4 and 22.5, plus a wind-aided 22.3.

On April 17, in the Kansas Relays at Lawrence, Dillard took his marks in the highs alongside Clyde Scott of Arkansas, a hurdler good enough to win the Olympic silver medal four months later. Dillard's new winning streak was up to 53, and he wanted to win this one.

At the gun, his golden uniform flashed to the front sensationally. He charged each hurdle wildly, taking off eight feet in front. As he whizzed over the 3′ 6″ barrier, he brought his right leg forward incredibly fast. His right foot was within 15 inches of the track when his left foot came down a long five feet beyond the hurdle. This was the style criticized by coaches but later used by short, fast men to become great hurdlers.

Now it drove his 5′ 10″, 150-pound body down the Kansas track faster than any hurdler in history. He sat on the sixth hurdle and rode it down but he kept going. He finished an astounding ten yards ahead of Scott in 13.6, a new world record both for

120 yards and 110 meters. One official watch showed 13.5.

He reached the AAU meet in Milwaukee with an incomparable win streak of 82. He wanted to make the Olympic team in two events, but the AAU was still organized under the archaic system which required heats and finals all in one day, and Dillard had to take his marks four times in 67 minutes. His third race was the 100 final and he lost to Barney Ewell. By then he was too tired for the high hurdles final and he lost to Porter's 14.1 by five feet.

In spite of that sobering lesson, he went to the blocks in both events in the Final Trials at Evanston, Illinois, the following week. In both heats he won promisingly, but in the 100 final, hampered by a bad start, he was beaten by Ewell and Mel Patton in a record tying 10.2. But he was on the Olympic team.

The next day, he was at the start of the high hurdles. He was the outstanding favorite to be the Olympic champion and all he needed here was a relaxed third place.

The gun cracked and he left his blocks with his great pickup. He reached the first hurdle ahead of the others, as usual, but he hit it. He almost never hit hurdles, but at this important time he hit the hurdle. To his dismay, he lost stride. Falling behind, he drove desperately to make up the lost ground, but he was not at the right place on the track and he hit another hurdle, and another. Disastrously far behind now, the greatest hurdler of all time came to a helpless stop, his hands against the seventh hurdle.

With his Olympic dream shattered, the shock must have hurt, but the horrified spectators would never know it. Actually smiling, Dillard jogged to the finish and threw both arms around Porter. People were there to sympathize with him, but he kept a tight little smile on his face and said, 'I can run some, too.'

And so he resigned himself to being a sprinter in the Olympic Games in London. Courageously, he prepared to meet those great sprinters on their own terms. Coach Finnigan said simply, 'They'll never meet a guy with a greater desire to win.'

On July 30, Dillard was on the track at Wembley for the first round. He raced resolutely through his heat in 10.4, fastest of the 12 heats. In the afternoon, he ran 10.4 again, matched only by Patton, the favorite. The next day, Dillard won his semi-finals in 10.5.

In the final that same afternoon, before 83,000 spectators,

Dillard fidgeted in the outside lane. He was supposed to finish fourth. At the gun, Dillard sprinted off his blocks and into the pickup admired by experts as one of the fastest ever. While the ill-fated Patton was stumbling far behind, Dillard shot into the lead.

Patton was gaining, but he was too far back to threaten. Lloyd LaBeach was gaining, but not fast enough. Dillard sprinted smoothly toward the tape, his hopes rising, but Ewell was gaining rapidly at the end. Ewell hit the tape, stopped, jumped for joy, clasped his hands in a boxer's handshake, and grinned.

Dillard waited quietly, keeping his thoughts to himself, and his hopes. The silver medal was more than he was expected to win, but a man can't help hoping. Later, he said, 'I never went through anything like that wait.'

Then came the official announcement: First, Dillard, United States. Time 10.3, equalling the Olympic record. Into a wind of five miles per hour, this was a great performance.

'Aw nuts,' Ewell said, 'I thought I had it.'

Dillard patted him sympathetically on the back. Later he said, almost wistfully, 'I won something, anyway.'

Coach Finnigan vaulted the rail on to the field and ran to Dillard. They embraced and Dillard lifted him off the ground. Tears streamed down Finnigan's cheeks. Overcome, he went to his hotel room and wrote a note to Jack Clowser, Dillard's Boswell:

'This was the day we waited for so long. To think it came not in the hurdles but in the event we all thought Dillard couldn't win. Fate is strange and wonderful. I'm going out to find a church somewhere. My heart is bursting.'

Now Dillard was a select sprinter. On the third leg of the 400 meter relay team, he flew around the curve, passing everybody to give the U.S. a commanding lead. In post Olympic meets he triumphed over Ewell three times, in 10.4, 9.6, and 9.5. In Paris he ran 20.8 for 200 meters around a curve, time bettered by only five men in history. He scurried over the high hurdles four times in 13.9. For the year 1948, he was ranked best in the world in the 100 and low hurdles, No. 2 in the highs, and No. 4 in the 200.

A smiling, likeable man, Dillard worked in the promotion department of the Cleveland baseball team. He had not filled Jesse Owens' shoes completely but his name was honored in the world record books for the 120 yard and 110 meter high hurdles, the 220 yard and 200 meter low hurdles, the low hurdles around a curve, and indoor bests in both high and low hurdles. In the hazardous sprints and hurdles, his competitive record stood at 201 races won and only six lost. He could have retired gracefully, content with a collection of medals and clippings surpassed by few athletes.

But the spark inside him, ignited by Jesse Owens, had grown to a raging flame, and he still ached over his failure in the hurdles. Even though he admitted, 'I've lost some of my zest for competition,' he would compromise. He would run indoors and hope to keep in shape for a comeback in 1952.

On the indoor boards in 1949, he won his first five high hurdle races. He seldom hit a hurdle. He had one stretch over 200 hurdles where he knocked down only two. But he ran into trouble in the NYKC Games and finished third, his only failure in ten races. In the Chicago Relays, he beat Craig Dixon by two feet to tie his own indoor record of 7.1 for 60 yards.

He ran very little outdoors in the United States in 1949, but he took two tours. In Georgetown, British Guiana, he ran an excellent 13.8, 10.4, and 9.4, the best time in the world that year. Later in April, in Trinidad, he ran a 9.4 100 with wind. In the fall, not at his best, he ran a 10.4 for third place in the meet against the Scandinavian countries. He also lost in the AAU high hurdles, running 13.9 to Dixon's 13.8. Thus, his World Ranking, in a poor year, was No. 2 for the hurdles and No.7 for the 100.

In 1950, he ran only indoors (with the exception of a 14.4 in Glasgow, which left him unranked). He tied the board track record of 6.1 for the 60 yard dash at Philadelphia, but he lost the hurdles to Jim Gerhdes. That was his only failure in three indoor seasons, through 1952. Now called, 'Old Bones', he raced over the hurdles to victory in all three AAU championships.

He resumed his quest for an outdoor championship with 14.4 on May 3, 1952, in Berea, Ohio. He flew out to Los Angeles for the Coliseum Relays and ran a first-rate 14.1 for third place after leading for half the race.

Three weeks later, at Compton, he was given third although he ran 14 flat and actually finished second. Having finished behind Billy Anderson, Dixon, and Jack Davis, and with world record holder Dick Attlesey making a strong comeback, Dillard was lightly regarded, but he phoned Jack Clowser :

'Don't worry, I'll be ready. I can feel the improvement with my new double-arm style. It makes up for the trifle in flat speed I may have lost.'

He ran a 14.2 in the Ohio AAU, and then he went out to Long Beach, California, to seek the AAU title on a cold, windy night.

Dillard waited patiently on his marks, head down, while four false starts by Dixon and Davis upset the others. At the gun, Dillard was off fast. Any doubts as to his merit were dispelled in a few seconds. His speed was startling over the first hurdle. At the fifth hurdle he led by four yards. He lost almost half of that to Davis' formidable finish, but he won in 13.7.

A week later, a few miles away in the imposing bowl of the Los Angeles Coliseum, the U.S. team chose itself in the heat of competition. Cold weather and the threat of rain held attendance to 22,000 on Saturday, but the high hurdle field was stronger than it could possibly be in the Olympics.

The tension was so great that the hurdlers went to their marks six times without a start. Dillard appeared cool and calm, knowing his start was faster than any hurdler who ever lived, for he had never been beaten to the first hurdle.

Tense and jumpy, they took their marks for the seventh time. This time, when the gun fired, there was no recall Dillard charged the first hurdle and cleared it safely with a lead of a full yard. He built up a comfortable lead. Then he sat on the seventh hurdle, and it was like four years ago. He was in danger of missing the team, and this year he had no 100 meters to save him.

He was unable to recover his proper stride. Fear ran through him as he hit the eigth hurdle. They were gaining on him now. A man of less poise might have charged desperately, trying to regain speed, but he knew the important thing was to clear the barrier in stride. He adjusted his step and cleared the last two safely. He hit the tape ahead of Davis in 14 flat, and he now had his chance – the one he had lost in 1948.

Now it was the Olympic championship he wanted . . . the gold medal. He was favored to win, but he knew better than most the hazards of hurdling. In Helsinki, he went to his marks for the final a determined man, for this was the race 'on which I had set my heart.'

After a false start by Davis, Dillard was more keyed up than he had ever been. He tried to ignore the crowd in the flag-rimmed stadium. On his marks, he looked down at the red brick track. He came to the set position, head down. Suddenly, his nerves failed him and he started to move. He rocked forward. Desperately, he caught himself and pulled back as the gun sounded. His start was poor, for him, but his great pickup carried him to a one-yard lead at the third hurdle.

This was not enough, for Davis was terrifying at full speed. Dillard sped forward, driven by the aching desire from his 1948 failure, his legs a whirl of blurred speed over the obstacles. Three lanes over, to his left, he glimpsed the dreaded figure of Davis gaining on him, but he could not run any faster.

He concentrated on the one thing which could win for him. If he could avoid hitting a hurdle and maintain full speed . . . All his poise and experience and careful training came into play. It was his competitive skill against Davis', with Davis the stronger runner.

At the ninth hurdle, Davis pulled almost even. Still Dillard could do nothing except his best. Coolly, he flashed over the next to last barrier. Davis, under the same pressure as Dillard, hit the hurdle hard, crashing it down and landing flat-footed.

Over the last hurdle, Dillard flew with bird-like grace. He sprinted for the tape and thrust his head forward in a victorious lunge. He won by more than a foot as both men ran 13.7.

Dillard shed his calm dignity and whooped for joy. 'Good things come to those who wait.'

Few men ever won gold medals in two different Olympiads. Nobody ever did it in two diverse events. After he ran the second leg on U.S.A.'s victorious relay team, he mounted the victory stand in front of the covered main stands and received his fourth gold medal. In world records and gold medals he had done a good job in filling Jesse Owens' shoes.

For all practical purposes, that was the end of Dillard's career as an outdoor runner, although he beat Davis by two yards in 13.9 in the White City meet against the British Empire and ran a commendable 10.4 in Vienna even though slowed by a muscle strain in the last 20 meters. He did not run outdoors again for four years, and he never reached satisfactory condition in his abortive attempt in 1956.

Indoors, however, he ran with distinction. He lost only two indoor races over the next three years. One was to Davis in 1954, but he beat Davis in 1955 for his eighth triumph in indoor AAU high hurdles. He was also ranked No. 1 indoors as a sprinter in 1953. Three times his superior start and pickup won sprint-hurdles doubles.

In 1956, at the age of 32, Dillard slipped to No. 3 in indoor hurdling, placing third in the AAU behind Lee Calhoun and Davis. In his first outdoor competition since 1952, he ran 14 flat with wind, but unusually bad weather and pressure of his job prevented full training.

Explaining sadly, 'I'm a little out of shape,' he placed only eighth in the AAU and seventh in the Final Trials. 'Old Bones' great career was over.

He won four Olympic gold medals. He won an unmatched two consecutive doubles in both the NCAA and AAU, plus one other AAU title. He won nine indoor AAU championships. His name appeared in the record book in all the high and low hurdles available. He approached world records in the sprints and defeated some all-time great sprinters. His won-lost record was almost incredible for such hazardous events. In 1947–48 he built up the longest winning streak of any runner in history.

He was second in the voting for the Sullivan Award in both 1947 and 1948, and he won it for 1955. As somebody said, 'It couldn't happen to a nicer guy.'

Coach Larry Snyder once appraised Dillard's potential as a sprinter, had he not run the hurdles, by saying, 'He might have been the best of them all.'

Jesse Owens showed great perception when he chose Harrison Dillard to fill his shoes.

5 ZÁTOPEK

The crowd of 60,000 at Wembley could scarcely believe their eyes. They were watching the 10,000 meter run of the 1948 Olympic Games, but this Czech, Zátopek, was the worst looking runner they had ever seen.

He was an awkward, scrawny little man, 5' 8½" tall, wearing a faded red shirt of Czechoslovakia, and he seemed to be in pain. Corn silk hair bobbed on his wobbling head. Periodically, his face twisted into an agonized grimace. His tongue flopped out of his mouth. His shoulders hunched grotesquely. He puffed and blew alarmingly. Every few strides his right hand stretched down toward his knee as if to scratch. His heels seemed reluctant to lift behind him, as if they were weighted. He looked, in short, as if he might be having a fit. At the very least, he seemed about to drop out.

Never has a runner been so deceiving.

The crowd had heard little of this awkward runner, even though only last month he had run 10,000 meters in an excellent 29:27 – 1.6 seconds slower than Viljo Heino's world record. A combination of indifferent athletic reporting plus iron curtain secrecy had conspired to deny Emil Zátopek his due publicity.

His position far back in the pack of runners and his apparent exhaustion did nothing to enlighten the crowd. After each lap, he looked alertly at a certain point in the crowd, and each time a rabid Czech held up a white sock. But now, after eight laps, a red vest was held up. The undesired signal meant the pace had slowed below 71 seconds per lap. Instantly Zátopek responded. He moved awkwardly up to fifth place, and now the crowd cheered the ugly duckling, more because he was the under-dog than because they fancied his chances against the great Heino. For even though he had edged Heino last year at 5,000 meters, this was twice the distance, where Heino excelled and Zátopek had run only two races.

Little did they know.

A few Czechs in the stands were chanting, 'Zátopek,' and the crowd's excitement grew louder. When he galloped past the light blue vest of Heino to take the lead at 4,000 meters, the applause was great.

Heino passed him, and the crowd responded with excited shouts. The red signal showed and he burst past Heino with a startling spurt. He pulled away to a lead of 30 meters and the crowd joined in the chant of 'Zá-to-pek, Zá-to-pek.'

He began to lap runners, but his pace was slower than his planned 29:35. The red vest kept waving, and he became confused.

He shouted anxiously to an official, 'Where is Heino?'

Came the reply, 'Heino is out.'

Zátopek struggled on in the stiffling heat. More confusion resulted from a mistake by the lap indicator, but Zátopek calmly ran the correct distance and ended with a blazing finish. His time was 29:59.6, a new Olympic record, 47 seconds ahead of Alain Mimoun. High in the stands, his joyful countrymen sang their national anthem. No less joyful was Zátopek, whose personality exudes friendly enthusiasm and the joy of living.

The next day the crowd cheered the new hero as he ran 30 seconds faster than necessary in his qualifying heat of the 5,000 meters. Two days later, the exciting final was held on a track drenched by a downpour. Zátopek led the pack into the tormenting wind and rain. His pace was a reliable 68–69 for eight laps and the others were content to follow.

At 3,500 meters, Gaston Reiff of Belgium rushed past. Zátopek, paying for his excesses of the previous days, was too tired to follow and Willi Slykhuis of Holland moved past. The two favorites ran away from Zátopek and he was soon a hopeless 65 yards behind Reiff, with Slykhuis between them.

Zátopek's legs felt heavy and he kept slipping in the slush. He tried to go faster, but the laps went by and he was far behind. On the backstretch of the last lap, still a distressing 30 yards behind Reiff, he felt his courage return.

He began to sprint, awkwardly but fast. He rushed past Slykhuis and the crowd was up and roaring. As Reiff turned wearily into the homestretch, Zátopek was twenty yards behind, charging like a runaway locomotive.

The astonished crowd screamed his name and Reiff heard. Amazed, he turned his head and saw the madman charging down on him. He gave everything he had and barely moved faster, but it was enough. He hit the tape with Zátopek two yards behind.

Zátopek's wild finish seemed to impress observers even more than his overwhelming victory in the 10,000. Now, everybody wanted to know about him. What made him so good?

It began in 1941 when he was 18. He had moved to Zlín when he was 16. Full of ambition, he worked in a shoe factory and attended technical school at night. The shoe company sponsored a race in the streets and young Zátopek was forced to run even though he tried to get out of it and said, 'I'm no good at running.'

That, of course, was not quite the truth, for he had proved himself better than his contemporaries in a few runs for fun, and he finished second out of a hundred boys in this race. During the next year, he ran a few more boys' races, still with no enthusiasm. But when he was singled out for training in 1942 he was happy.

His first formal race was at 3,000 meters. He finished only three seconds back of his trainer in 9:12 and the newspaper reported, 'A good performance by Zátopek.' He read it over and over again.

Now, training became the most important part of his life. Where others searched for races they could win, he searched 'for stiff competition he would surely lose, and his times grew promisingly faster. In 1943, he began to work at rudimentary interval training, striving to increase his speed.

'You must be fast enough. You must have endurance. So you run fast for speed and repeat it many times for endurance.'

He trained hard and began to break national records each year. When the Russian army drove the Germans from Zlín, Zátopek, enthusiastic as ever, became a soldier and after the war he began officer's training at the Military Academy.

His first race outside Czechoslovakia was in the 1946 European Championships at Oslo. He was enthralled. When he first saw the great Heino he approached him with deference and timidly touched those world-record legs. At the start of the 5,000, his knees trembled.

He ran with Europe's best until Slykhuis pulled away. Then Sydney Wooderson shot away from Slykhuis with dazzling speed.

Over 100 meters behind, Zátopek was narrowly beaten by Evert Nyberg and Heino, but his good 14 :25.8 was another national record.

All winter he trained with stupendous energy. He found a quarter-mile path in the woods near the military camp and he labored through rain, mud, snow, and ice ... in military boots. Sometimes he had to carry a flashlight to see his way. He said simply, 'There's a great advantage in training under unfavorable conditions.'

He was so fit that his first 5,000 meter race of 1947, against Nyberg in Prague, resulted in 14 :08.2, second only to the peerless Hägg's 13 :58.2.

Immediately, he had to fly to Finland, where Heino waited for him in Helsinki. Zátopek had lost his freshness and he was nervous, but he tried to run away from Heino. After 3,000 meters it became a fierce battle, with the lead changing on every lap. In the homestretch they fought side by side until Zátopek struggled one yard ahead at the tape in 14 :15.2.

Suddenly, everybody wanted him to run. He graduated as an army lieutenant, and his entire month's leave was spent in fiery competition. He was undefeated at 5,000 meters in 1947 and he was No. 1 in World Ranking. At 3,000 meters he ranked No. 3, because of a defeat by Reiff. Zàtopek's 8 :08.8 was second only to Hägg's record.

One reason he was not a favorite for the Olympic 10,000 meters was because his first attempt did not come until May of 1948, at Budapest. He had prepared strenuously. He ran as many as 60 runs of 400 meters in one day, with only a 200 meter jog in between. And yet the race was difficult. He ran a good 30 :28.4, a national record by two full minutes.

Next came 3,000 meters in 8 :07.8, and then his 29 :27 at Prague on June 17. Five days later, he ran Slykhuis off the track in a 14 :10 5,000. He was in great shape, and yet the track world was not prepared for his triumph in London.

After the Olympics, Zátopek was worn out and his hip hurt, but it was impossible to avoid racing, even though he was badly off form. He lost his second race of the season, to Reiff's 14 :19 at Prague.

On October 24, he was married. His wife, Dana, had placed seventh in the women's Olympic javelin at London, and she shared Emil's superabundance of high spirits and energy. Denied permission by her parents to participate in a handball championship that morning, she went cycling with Emil and they crashed while kissing. Late for their wedding, they made up for it by dancing until dawn, after the other guests had all dropped out.

The combination of marriage, a new job, and his Olympic success would put an end to most careers, but Zátopek only tried harder. His third race of 1949 was 14:10.8 for 5,000 meters, and he knew he was better than ever.

On June 12, he ran in the Army Championship at Ostreva.

'I was in Zlín all day Friday. On Saturday around 11 o'clock I got an express train for the race at Ostreva. I had to stand all the way and had only beer and biscuits to eat. It was a five hour trip. I was dead tired when I arrived and boarded a street car to go to the stadium. I went to sleep and a soldier awoke me just in time to get off at the stadium.'

Naturally, he planned no special effort in the 10,000, but he felt unusually strong. In the seventh kilometer the announcer said Zátopek had a chance for the world record and the crowd began to cheer him on. With a hard finish, he crossed the line in 29:28.2. He was a world record holder!

He ran 14:14.4 and 29:49.6, then he had to stay out of competition for a month with a leg injury. He beat Heino in 29:58.4. On September 1, Heino regained the world record with 29:27.2.

Czechs begged Zátopek to reclaim his record, but he answered, 'Perhaps in the spring,' for his training had suffered from the excess of races and travels. He ran three more 10,000 meter races with one good time of 29:38.2.

Then a world record attempt was organized for Ostreva on October 22 and he had three weeks to prepare. For fourteen days he ran ruthlessly – five times 200 meters at full speed, 30 times 400 meters at racing speed, and five more 200's, with only fast 200-meter jogs for recovery. Then a leg injury slowed him, but he trained carefully, with two days of rest.

A cold wind quieted before the race, but dark clouds threatened. Zátopek wore blue shorts and a white shirt with his army sports club initials, ATK. At 7,000 meters, in 20:35.5, he was well ahead of a record pace when a crisis struck and he slowed. At his new pace he would fail. The crowd pleaded with him.

He fought his weariness with all his willpower. On the last

lap he ran as hard as he could. In the homestretch he suddenly waved to the crowd and smiled. His time was 29 :21.2.

The world record was his again. Dana's words describe his feelings : 'He glowed like a meteor and couldn't fall asleep all night for excitement.'

He had finished 1949 undefeated except for one 1,500 meter lark. His next goal was 10,000 meters under 29 :15. He had given runners a new philosophy which was building a chasm between those who are great and those who play only for fun.

'If one can stick to the training throughout the many long years, then will power is no longer a problem. It's raining? That doesn't matter. I am tired? That's beside the point. It's simply that I just have to.'

With snow on the ground, Zátopek wore an extra jersey, sweat pants, a knit cap, and heavy boots to protect his ankles. One exercise he invented was bounding exuberantly through the snow with exaggerated knee lifts.

In 1950 he won many easy races in times which would please almost any other runner. In June he increased his training load to its highest intensity. For two weeks he ran at least 40 times 400 meters each day.

On August 2, in Helsinki, he lowered his personal record for 5,000 meters to 14 :06.2. He was ready. Two days later, he ran 10,000 meters on the famous track at Turku.

He found himself running exceptionally well. He increased his pace. Heino was there as a spectator, cheering him on. The entire Finnish crowd cheered him. He ran faster and faster, finishing with a wild sprint. His time took a stunning 18 seconds off his world record – 29 :02.6.

After two more good 5,000's, he went to the hospital with food poisoning from a goose. His stomach was pumped, and the doctor ordered him to withdraw from the European Championships, but the doctor did not know his patient.

Zátopek went to Brussels anyway, and a crowd of 60,000 saw him run the 10,000 on a puddled track in a foolhardy 29 :12.0. He won by more than a minute even though he had to race Reiff in three days.

In the 5,000, he clung grimly to Reiff's desperate pace, then raced past him at the bell. There was a great silence from the Belgian crowd. Reiff almost collapsed and finished 23 seconds behind. Later, he commented, 'I was beaten by Zátopek's strength, by his courage, and by his amazing energy.'

Zátopek's time was 14 :03.0, his fastest ever.

Four days later he ran 29 :54.6 and the next day, a fine 14 :05.2. Thus, in one great month, the doctor's patient had run the two outstanding 10,000's of all time, plus the second, third, and fourth best 5,000's. Once again he finished the year unvanquished.

That winter he decided to train indoors. His bold experiment in weight training included hours of labored riding the bicycle with 4.4 pound weights on each foot, deep knee bends, and knee raising against the stubborn resistance of a wall exerciser. A near-disastrous ski accident put one leg in a cast for a month, and his desire to run was frustrated until April.

For him, most of 1951 was a bad year. He lost a race at 3,000 meters. He won all his 5,000 meter races, but his times were not sensational and he lost his No. 1 ranking to Reiff. His record remained untarnished in the 10,000 meters, with a best of 29 :29.8, but his real honors came at longer distances.

At Prague, on September 15, he set out to break the national record for one hour. He ran his first 10,000 meters in 31 :06. Then, 'I knew that I would have no problem in lasting out and so I ran as fast as I could.'

His second 10,000 was a good 30 :10. In one hour he covered 19,558 meters (12 miles 268 yards). That, plus his 20,000 meter time of 1 :01 :16, ruined Heino's world records.

Heino's comment was, 'Believe me, Zátopek could run twenty kilometers in one hour.'

People talked about such a fantastic possibility. Other than Heino and Zátopek, only four men had ever run under 30 minutes for one 10,000. Zátopek was relied upon to do it twice, back to back. Zátopek, himself, was doubtful, but he knew he could do much better than his own record, and so, on September 29 at the excellent track among the trees at Houstka Spa near Stará Boleslav, he tried.

It was a warm, windless day, and he felt fine. He led the other 16 runners from the start, passing the first 5,000 in 14 :56. At 10,000 meters he felt confident in 29 :53.4. The spectators were agog. He passed 15,000 meters in 44 :54.6, a surprising world record.

Suddenly, he felt a painful stich in his side. He knew it came from eating before the race, but he had needed the strength and now he fought against the pain. He passed 10 miles in 48:12, another world record.

The stitch went away after a few minutes, but he had to fight his fatigue. He waited in suspense for the gunshot which would signal 59 minutes. He approached the post marking only 400 meters to go for his 20,000 meters. If only he could run a few yards past that post before the shot, he could finish under one hour.

Still no shot. Puzzled, he entered the curve. Then the shot rang out. He tried hard, all the way around to the finish, in 59:51.8. He had done it! Still the timer had not fired the final gun He had to continue. He ran another 52 meters before the hour ended – his fourth world record in one stunning race.

He sighed. 'Today I really had more than enough.'

He ran three more 5,000's in October. Then he rested and enjoyed ice skating with Dana and running in deep snow. He had to his credit four of the five fastest 5,000's ever run, and six of the seven best 10,000's. It was time to prepare for the Olympics.

In April of 1952, he caught a chill but he ran anyway. He became ill and was confined to bed. After a few days he could stand it no longer. He sneaked away from the doctors and nurses, and he ran.

With the Olympics only two months away, he ran 5,000 meters in a horrifying 14:46.4. In Kiev on June 11, he was badly beaten by two Russians, but his time, 60 yards back, was down to 14:22.0. Two days later, after Aleksandr Anufriev had built up a lead of 120 meters in the 10,000, he gave all he had to win in 29:26.0.

He became depressed, but he won his national championships in 14:17.6 and 30:28.4. After three weeks of preparation, he felt confident of his ability to win the 10,000, but no more.

In the beautiful stadium at Helsinki, 32 intense runners lined up for the start of the 10,000 meters on the first day of competition. Zátopek, in his bright red vest, was in the second row, and he started calmly, letting the others struggle for the lead.

He was a wise veteran now, cool and collected. He ran to his own pace, placidly watching the times on the gigantic electric scoreboard, easily visible from the backstretch. His first lap was in 68.9, in tenth place. He tried to stay in the first lane, for a wiry moss had been built into the red brick and clay track for buoyancy.

At six laps, in 7:02.4, a rousing drive put him in the lead, and he began his effort to shake loose from the others. He increased his pace cold-bloodedly on each curve and his lap times swung between 68 and 72. At 5,000 meters, in 14:43.4, only two brave runners hung on.

After 13 laps, young Gordon Pirie could stand it no longer, and then there was only Mimoun. Since 1948, the courageous little Algerian in the blue of France had lost only to Zátopek. Now he hung on grimly as 70,000 keen fans howled appreciation and advice.

Zátopek increased the pressure for six laps. Then, slowly, the dark little runner faded behind him. Zátopek continued a safe 71-second pace. On the last lap, with the crowd cheering louder than in 1948, he increased to 64 seconds. He won his second gold medal by 90 yards in 29:17.0, his third best time.

He was in high spirits for the third heat of the 5,000 meters two days later. At the start he said, 'Shall I ever get into the final?' but during the heat he was a friendly extrovert. He encouraged Curt Stone of the United States in English: 'Come along, Stone, if you want to qualify.' He spoke in Russian to Anufriev, 'Sasha, come on, we must get a move on.' Desiring to remain on the pole, he gently took hold of one runner's shorts and moved him aside. On the last lap, when only five were left in contention, he lulled them to an easy pace with five fingers held up in front of their faces.

Two days later, the final was serious business. Still, he was smiling and at ease in the dressing room and on the starting line, greeting his opponents in his warmest English, French, and German. Then the gun sounded and a capacity crowd stirred to one of the greatest races in history.

Zátopek was willing to help set the pace, but Herbert Schade of Germany, a threat because of his 14:06.6 in June and his Olympic record 14:15.4 in his heat, wanted to lead. At 4,000 meters it was the bespectacled Schade in 11:24.8, followed by Zátopek and Reiff.

To many onlookers, Reiff was still the favorite, with his smooth stride and great speed, but suddenly he stepped off the track and quit with 500 meters left. Four runners entered the last lap together.

As the bell clamored, Zátopek heaved himself into the lead.

Fighting hard on the backstretch, he was startled to see a red-headed runner appear alongside. It was Chris Chataway, Britain's 22-year-old wonder, sprinting into the lead. To his dismay, Zátopek saw Schade and Mimoun go past. Zátopek, six yards behind, looked a tired and beaten runner, and he was full of despair.

At the same time he was calculating where he would attack. He could not allow himself to be fourth. Into the last curve he suddenly threw everything he had into a straining, heaving, awkward sprint. The crowd roared, almost hysterically excited.

Running in the third lane, he went past Schade. Mimoun swung out to pass Chataway and bumped Zátopek, but Zátopek was once again the runaway locomotive, charging past all of them.

He was not aware of the hapless Chataway's fall behind him. His only thought was to give everything he had. He thundered down the homestretch, pulling away from Mimoun on sheer strength and will power.

He won in 14:06.6. His last furious 200 meters was in 28.3, his last 400 was 58.1. Everybody was surprised by such a glorious finish. Probably, he could not have done it unless it was necessary.

The crowd remained standing in quiet awe. They had witnessed an amazing demonstration of courage.

Exhausted, Zátopek returned to the Olympic village and so he did not see Dana win the women's javelin. When he heard the good news, he said, 'This gold one pleases me more than all the other ones so far.'

Zatopek's double victory in his regular events was no surprise, even though some experts had favored Schade and Reiff. But the marathon was a baffling matter. He had never endured even half that distance. He was uncertain of his training. The whole thing was a gamble, and nobody knew it better than Zátopek.

He had two precious days of rest. He spent some time learning patience at the slow marathon pace. Then, at 3:30 p.m., he took his marks with 67 other runners before an expectant crowd of 80,000. He felt unsure of himself; his three gold medals meant nothing here. This was the strongest field of marathon runners ever assembled.

He started near the head of the pack for three laps around the red track. Then, with a wave to his friends, he left the stadium, keeping a wary eye on Jim Peters ahead of him. Peters,

Left: HARRISON DILLARD At the peak of his form in April, 1948, Dillard demonstrates his style in a training session. *Below:* London, June 6, 1949: Dillard anchors a United States medley relay team at the British Games

who had the fastest time ever run, feared Zátopek and tried to run away with a long, stretching stride and an awkward head roll.

At 10,000 meters, in the village of Molmi, Zátopek was running comfortably with Gustaf Jansson of Sweden, 17 seconds behind Peters. The next 5,000 meters included some hills, but Zátopek still felt fresh. This was still a familiar distance. Jansson finally spoke to him in Swedish, challenging him to catch Peters. At 15,000 meters in 47 :58, they caught the white-clad Englishman, and they ran together amicably for 3,000 meters.

Zátopek asked Peters if the pace was fast enough. Peters, almost out on his feet, said it was too slow.

Incredulous, Zátopek said, 'You say "too slow". Are you sure the pace is too slow?'

'Yes,' Peters answered.

Zátopek shook his head and increased the pace.

'Come with us,' he encouraged Peters. 'It's much easier when there are three together.'

Zátopek and Jansson rounded the turning post side by side, with Peters falling behind. Now they ran into a breeze and running became harder.

At 25,000 meters on the now-familiar road, Zátopek led Jansson by five seconds after the Swede stopped for fruit juice. Zátopek fought down his desire to drink, for liquids did not agree with him when he ran.

Now was his chance. He ran over two hills at a good pace. Then, hopefully, he looked back. He was relieved to see Jansson far behind.

Now it was a question of being able to finish at this pace. Many an unhappy track runner has run well for 20 miles only to fall apart with miles still to go. Zátopek feared this invisible barrier, and he ran carefully.

His feet were beginning to blister, and his legs had lost their spring, but he gritted his teeth and kept running. He knew how to fight.

At 30,000 meters, his 1 :38 :42 was 12 seconds faster than the world record. His legs ached and he seemed to have a chest full of needles. He relaxed his arms and opened his mouth wider to get more air.

At 35,000 meters, in 1 :56 :50, he was over a minute ahead of

Jansson. The crowd shouted encouragement, but the clamor only made his head ache.

He ran steadily, fighting the pain, through the outskirts of Helsinki. At 40,000 meters, in 2 :15 :10, he led by a satisfactory $2\frac{1}{4}$ minutes. Now he knew he could do it. Only eight more minutes to go.

The Zátopek who entered the stadium through the marathon gate to a blare of trumpets seemed frail and timid compared to the man who had charged down the homestretch of the 5,000 meters. His face was ashen, his red vest was soaked and hanging outside his shorts. His legs barely lifted high enough.

The crowd, however, did not notice. All they saw was the most glorious triumph in the history of sport. Wildly, they came to their feet. Whatever their language, they chanted with all the rest, 'Zá-to-pek, Zá-to-pek, Zá-to-pek.'

He pushed himself wearily around the track. He lifted his arms above the tape. He smiled. He had won a triple victory impossible to evaluate. It was certainly the greatest in Olympic history. The crowd loved him.

He sat down. Cautiously, he removed his shoes to examine his bloody feet. He heard his time – 2 :23 :03.2 – fastest ever run on an out-and-back course. People congratulated him. Not the least of his rewards was a real kiss from the women's javelin champion.

He greeted the other finishers with slices of orange – Reinaldo Gorno, $2\frac{1}{2}$ minutes behind, then Jansson. He munched an apple, smiling and talking. After the victory ceremony he jogged a lap of honor and his ovation has never been surpassed.

After the Olympics he could have taken a welcome rest, but he was reaching top form and he wanted to make use of it. He ran 5,000 meters in 14 :06.4 early in October. Then he returned to the forest stadium at Houstka for another record attempt on October 26.

After a hard rain, the track was in good condition. Zátopek ran around and around, monotonously strong. In one hour he had covered 18,970 meters. At 15 miles in 1 :16 :26.4, he triumphed over the world record by more than a minute. At 25,000 meters, his 1 :19 :11.8 took another minute off Mikko Hietanen's record. Zátopek seemed fresh. He finished, smiling and waving. His time for 30,000 meters was 1 :35 :23.8 an impressive minute and a half under the record. Now the Czechs pointed with pride to every official world record from 10,000 meters on up.

Czechslovakia awarded him the Order of the Republic, its highest honor, never before given to an athlete. But an illness threatened to end his career in 1953. He had his tonsils removed and spent several days in the hospital. His 5,000 meter times were mediocre, for him, and he lost one race at 3,000 meters.

On August 5 he was in Bucharest for the biggest race of the year. Anufriev had run 13 :58.8, Kovacs had bettered Zátopek's best time with 14 :01.2, and a new threat was named Vladimir Kuts. Zátopek was 30 meters behind with two laps to go, but a savage 800 meters sent him past Kuts on the last turn and he won in 14 :03.

He became ill again and he missed six weeks of competition. On October 17 in Prague, he appeared hopelessly beaten, 30 meters behind Kovacs with a lap to go. Once again he won by fighting harder than even he thought possible. He ran the last lap in 57.8 to win in 14 :09.0.

On November 11, in good shape again, he ran 10,000 meters in the three-lined Houstka stadium where his tenacious pace had broken six world records. This time he passed 6 miles in a world record 28 :08.4. He fought hard during the last lap and ran 10,000 meters in 29 :01.6, a full second under his own world record.

He ended the year with a pleasant trip to Brazil for the famous New Year's Eve race. An estimated 800,000 people cheered him along as he won in record time.

In 1954, the world began to catch up with Zátopek. Younger, talented runners used his example to train more intensely. He began the year free from handicaps and ran 14 :04.0 on May 14.

On May 30, in Cólombes Stadium in Paris, he roused a small crowd of 6,000 with something special. In a 5,000 meter race, he was 4.4 seconds behind Hägg's world record pace at 4,000 meters, but his last raging 1,000 in 2 :43.8 brought him across the line in 13 :57.2. He had broken the honored 12-year-old record by one second. He now held the wondrous total of ten world records – everything longer than three miles.

With only one day of rest, he amazed the track world again. Running almost alone in Brussels, he was a man inspried. He pushed himself as if his life depended upon it, and he broke his records for 6 miles (27 :59.2) and 10,000 meters (28 :54.2).

A month later, July 3, he ran into trouble against Kovacs before 80,000 partisan fans in Budapest's Népstadion. Zátopek was slightly ill and feverish, while Kovacs ran faster than any other man except Zátopek. At 6 miles Zátopek managed to lead, but Kovacs went ten meters past him on the last curve. All of Zátopek's fighting courage could gain only four meters in the stretch and Kovacs won in 29 :09. The Hungarians were overjoyed, for this was Zátopek's only failure in any race over 5,000 meters.

Zátopek went to Bern for the European Championships knowing he was no longer invincible. An eager crowd packed the small Neufeld Stadium, expecting an exciting 10,000 meters, but Zátopek took no chances with tactics. He ran with determination from the start and he beat Kovacs by a satisfying half lap in 28 :58.0 on a wet track. Zátopek now claimed seven of the eight best 10,000's ever run.

He had given too much in the 10,000, however, and he allowed Kuts to go far ahead in the 5,000. Kuts won by a shocking 100 meters in a new world record time of 13 :56.6. Zátopek was out-kicked by Chataway, and he finished a dispirited third in 14 :10.2.

He tried to regain his 5,000 meter record at Stockholm on September 3. He came heartbreakingly close with 13 :57.0.

In Prague, on October 23, Zátopek's demise was near completion. In the dual meet with the Soviets, he was helpless as Kuts went far ahead. Kuts kept going and set a world record of 13 :51.2. Zátopek suffered his worst defeat, half a lap behind.

In 1955, he trained harder than ever, running as many as 90 times 400 meters in a day in a vain effort at improvement. Although he ran 10,000 meters under 30 minutes on seven occasions, in two of them he placed a sad third – against Hungary and against Pirie and Ken Norris in London. He ranked only fourth in the world after seven consecutive years as first, six of them un-defeated. He also lost six 5,000 meter races.

His hard training paid off in one great achievement, on October 29 at Celakovice. Albert Ivanov, a Russian friend, had bettered Zátopek's 25,000 meter record by two minutes on September 27, and Zátopek wanted it back. He passed 10,000 meters in 30 :24.2. He passed the 15-mile mark in 1 :14 :01.0, almost $2\frac{1}{2}$ minutes under his own world record. He continued his steady pace and broke Ivanov's record by almost half a minute, in 1 :16 :36.4.

In 1956, he was definitely poorer, set back both by age and a hernia operation, and yet he ran 29 :33.4 in October, approached within 27 seconds of his 25,000 meter record on October 21, and placed sixth in the Olympic marathon at Melbourne. His enthusiastic followers claim he would have won except for his disastrous hernia operation, causing a three-month layoff in the summer.

For most runners, sixth in the Olympic marathon would be a crowning achievement, but to the balding Colonel Zátopek it was the end. Grinning, he said :

'I realized I was licked at the halfway point. I started confident that I could make a good race of it, but I suddenly realized about all that was left was to go out like a champion. That was when I decided it was no use breaking my neck with any more speed and risk collapse. . . . This was my last race.'

Actually, he ran with spirit in 1957, and won half of his ten 10,000 meter races. His times for the last five ranged between 29 :47 and 29 :25.8, excellent for a man of thirty-five. He lost a 5,000 meter race while running 14 :06.4.

Emil Zátopek's problem was that he became a legend before he lost his zest for racing. Nobody can remain the greatest forever, not even with the greatest of courage.

6 MATHIAS

'Boy,' said Bob Mathias in May of 1948, 'the more I hear of the decathlon, the less I like it.'

Coach Virgil Jackson, however, was determined to prove the worth of his prize 17-year-old. He wanted Mathias to begin training for the decathlon and enter a meet only four weeks away.

'By 1952,' Jackson argued, 'you will have had the benefit of college coaching, and if you keep at it I'll bet you can make the Olympic team then.'

In retrospect, that is quite funny, but it was enough to persuade the boy. On June 10, he was on the field at Pasadena, California, competing against some of the best in the United States in the Southern Pacific AAU decathlon.

He ran 100 meters in 11.3 and broad jumped 21' 4½", not what he had hoped. In the 16-pound shot put, he lost more than the expected ten feet from his high school best, reaching only 43' 1". He high jumped only 5' 10", a disappointment after his second place in the high school high jump at the West Coast Relays. He lifted no eyebrows with his 52.1 for 400 meters.

None of his marks were noteworthy, even for the tender age of 17½, and he was beaten several times by his more mature opponents. Such is the peculiar nature of the decathlon, however, that it pointed out one virtue in young Mathias : he had no weakness. He was in first place.

People who saw him take a cat nap while he waited between events thought he was lazy. They did not know about his anemia at the age of 11, curtailing his beloved sports. They did not know the hours his mother had spent teaching him how to relax.

On the second day, Mathias ran the hurdles in 15.7, no surprise to his opponents, for they knew he was state high school champion in both hurdles. He threw the discus 140' ⅛", more than ten feet short of his excellent personal record.

Now people began to believe he had no weakness. They

70

did not know he had first attempted the pole vault and javelin only four weeks before. In the pole vault he missed his first two attempts at nine feet although he had cleared ten feet in practice.

He worked feverishly on his step on another runway, and on his third trial he cleared easily. He went on to clear 11′ 9″, much higher than he had hoped. The dazed observers were discovering one more quality about Bob Mathias: he was something of a genius at rising to the occasion.

In the javelin, the best he could do on his first two throws was 155 feet, good for a beginner. On his last throw, he sent the spear flying out 175′ 4⅝″, surprising everybody.

For an athlete over six feet tall and weighing more than 185 pounds, the 1,500 meters is a difficult and unpleasant event, but he ran it in 4:59.2.

He had accomplished more than anybody hoped. He won with 7,094 points. As a result of this sensational beginning, he was in Bloomfield, New Jersey, two weeks later for the AAU championships, hoping to be among the first three and represent the USA in the Olympic Games.

Surprising the easterners, Mathias improved on four of his Pasadena marks the first day with 11.2, 21′ 6⅝″, 6 feet even, and 51 flat. But he was a disheartening 354 points behind three-time champion Irving Mondschein.

One of the few who was confident was the 17½-year-old boy himself. Starting the second day he drove over the high hurdles in 15.1 to put fear into Mondschein. He sailed the discus 139′ 7″, a disappointment to him, but he gained 124 points. Then a thunderstorm halted competition for an hour and a half.

With the field turned to mud, pole vaulting became dangerous. Al Lawrence, a 13-footer, cleared only 11′ 6¼″ and the surprising boy tied him. After a mediocre javelin throw of 157′ 3″ from the muddy runway and a personal record 4:55.2 in the 1,500, Mathias was the national champion.

His 7,224 was the second best score in the world since 1940. And he was on the Olympic team!

He traveled to England by ship as the youngest track and field member of any U.S. Olympic team in history. He knew he needed more training and he worked hard, staying close to the yellow and blue RAF barracks at Uxbridge. His hard work hurt his elbow and his knee. These injuries and the international competition threatened his chances, but he still hoped for a medal.

At seven o'clock on the morning of August 5, Mathias wakened, calmly drank orange juice and ate a steak, and rode the bus ten miles to Wembley, where 70,000 spectators braved the rain. Not allowed to warm up properly, he ran his 100 meters at 10:30 a.m. in 11.2, equalling his best time.

His first broad jump was over 23 feet. Unfortunately, he fell back, and an hour later, when his second turn came, he could jump only 21' 8¼". He was far down in the field of 35, and he had to start gaining.

He put everything he had into his first shot put and the ball sailed over 45 feet. Smiling with satisfaction, he stepped out toward his put. To his dismay, a red flag waved, indicating a foul, and then, for the first time, he heard of the bizarre Olympic rule requiring him to step out of the back half of the circle. He had to settle for 42' 9¼".

He had to wait in the rain, wrapped in his blanket, for the high jump. He missed at 5' 9", an easy height for him in high school. When he missed for a second time he began to worry. If he cleared no height all his chances for a medal were gone.

He remembered a happy day when he was ten. He had tried to jump four feet high with no previous experience and, somehow, his formless dive had carried him over the bar. Now he determined to try the same dive. With everything riding on his gamble, he swung around almost directly in front of the bar. He ran hard and used all his strength. His form amazed everyone, but he cleared the bar.

Up in the stands, coach Brutus Hamilton whacked coach Dink Templeton on the back and cried, 'The kid's going to win it.'

Templeton agreed wholeheartedly and called Mathias a 'competitive genius'.

Mathias went over the bar at 6' 1¼", his best height. He gained on almost everybody, including the stunned Mondschein, a 6' 7" jumper. Ten weary hours after he started competing, Mathias ran 400 meters in 51.7. He was in third place, 49 points behind cocky Lt Carlos Kistenmacher of Argentina.

Kistenmacher boasted to his young opponent: 'Whatever you do in each event, I'll do better.'

Mathias was not worried enough to miss his nap on the bus

back to the Olympic Village. He ate and went to sleep. At seven the next morning, he was disappointed to find it was raining harder than ever and his legs were stiff and sore.

At 10:30 a.m., he ran the worst hurdles race ever. He hit the first hurdle and lost balance and momentum. His 15.7 was a tribute to his ability to come back.

Kistenmacher slipped badly to 16.3 and Mathias passed him, but Simmons, a fine hurdler, ran 15.2 to take the lead. Mathias was a good third behind Ignace Heinrich of France.

Aroused, Mathias threw the discus 145 feet, but Mondschein's discus slid along the wet grass and knocked over Mathias' marker. Half an hour later, frustrated officials placed a marker about a foot and a half short of his throw. Even so, his 144′ 4″ was so good it put him in the lead by 48 points.

It was noon and Mathias wanted to leave the field. He was hungry and he wanted to get out of the rain. An official warned him he might be called to vault at any moment, and so Mathias returned to the meager comfort of his blanket. The competitors were divided into two groups, and Mathias was in the second group. By the time the hungry boy was allowed to vault, six hours had passed.

The other entrants were slipping on the pole and sliding on the runway, but Mathias coolly passed until the bar reached ten feet. He cleared it easily.

Miserably wet and muddy, Mathias continued vaulting. It was dark now and there was unsatisfactory illumination from the flickering Olympic torch and a pitiful string of 50-watt bulbs along the stands. Vaulting was dangerous.

Meanwhile, the more fortunate group finished the competition. Heinrich was the winner, unless Mathias could triumph over the rain, the poor light, and fatigue from the late hour.

Courageously, Mathias kept vaulting. He cleared 11′ 5¾″, near his best height. He missed twice at 11′ 9″. Then he decided to stop. He could win . . . if nothing went wrong.

Harried officials used flashlights so the javelin throwers could measure their steps. A flashlight illuminated the foul line. Mathias ran down the wretched runway and threw, but he crossed the line. Another foul would put him in grave danger. On his second throw, he concentrated on avoiding a foul. He put his whole arm into a desperate throw and the javelin disappeared into the night. His elbow hurt, but the javelin stabbed into the mud at 165′ 1″. He was only 189 points behind Heinrich.

Now, if only he could finish the 1,500 meters, he could win. The track was soaked, and he had cramps in one foot and in his empty stomach, but he was not about to give up. He put on a sprint toward the finish line, lighted by flashlights. His time was 5:11, and those 354 dearly bought points boosted his total to 7,139.

He was the Olympic champion...at the age of 17 years, 8 months, and 3 weeks. Wearily, he plodded barefoot to the stands and hugged his mother while his father and two brothers grinned.

At that moment, tired and hungry after 12 hours in the stadium, he did not consider that all decathlons are not conducted under such distressing conditions. He said, 'No more decathlon, Dad ...ever again.'

Reaction to Mathias' cinderella victory was stupendous. President Truman sent him a telegram and, later, greeted him in person. The people of little Tulare, California, erupted in a joyous victory celebration which shut down the town and clogged Highway 99 for three hours. Coach Virgil Jackson 'found myself alone, in a city park, sitting on a park bench for 20 minutes and crying like a baby.'

Mathias was besieged for autographs and interviews. A crowd of 5,000 people met him at the Visalia airport, nine miles from Tulare, and thirty state highway patrolmen handled traffic. At a testimonial dinner the next night, he was praised by Governor Earl Warren and decathlon world record holder Glenn Morris. Mathias was honored the next night in Fresno, and later on 'Bob Mathias Day' at Sacramento's State Fair and in Los Angeles.

He was voted the Sullivan Award for 1948, for his good character as well as his dramatic victory. And still later, the Tulare court reporter stated, 'Bob Mathias' victory in the Olympic Games and his all-around fine sportsmanship in school here have done more to combat juvenile delinquency in Tulare than any other happening.'

Mathias played football that fall at Kiski prep school in Pennsylvania, then started track in the indoor season. In the National Interscholastics at Madison Square Garden, he showed his class by winning the prep high hurdles and placing second in both broad jump and high jump. During the easy spring season he concentrated on the AAU decathlon to be held June 28 and 29. Eager citizens had secured the meet for Tulare.

Mathias' home town numbered 12,000 total population, and each evening 7,000 enthusiastic spectators watched the decathlon. Mathias was second at the end of five events, but he crushed Mondschein the second night and won with 7,556 points, a total bettered by only four men before him. He said, 'It seemed to come a lot easier this time.'

In Oslo, Norway, he won a decathlon with 7,346 points, and then he enrolled at Stanford. In the spring he was all over the track and field. He lowered his best high hurdle time to 14.5, raised his vault to a good 12' 10", and lengthened his shot and discus marks impressively to 49' 6" and 157' $5\frac{1}{4}$", each one a record for Stanford freshmen.

In the important meet against the California frosh, not content to win those four events, he also won the low hurdles and placed second in the high jump and fourth in the javelin. In a low-pressure practice decathlon he scored 7,602 points.

He sought the national AAU decathlon title again in zealous Tulare on June 27 and 28, and he faced the toughest opponent of his career. Bill Albans, an Olympic hop-step-jumper, was fresh from scoring an amazing 22 points in the NCAA meet.

Mathias was happy with his 100 meters in 10.9, but Albans ran 10.6. Mathias rose to the occasion with a personal broad jump record of 23' $3\frac{3}{8}$", but Albans leaped 24' $6\frac{7}{8}$". Mathias put the shot 47' $6\frac{1}{4}$", his best in a decathlon. Albans could do only 39' $\frac{3}{8}$" and Mathias passed him, but Albans high jumped 6' $2\frac{3}{4}$", two inches higher than Mathias, to regain the lead. Mathias ran 400 meters in 51 flat, equal to his best ever, but Albans ran 49.5.

At the end of the first night, Mathias had scored 4,230 points, a total bettered by only three men before this meet. But Albans was 101 points ahead with the highest first-day total in history.

Starting the second night, Mathias ran the hurdles in a good 14.7, but Albans ran 14.1, the fastest time ever recorded in a decathlon. After 6 events, Mathias was 210 points behind and the 6,500 spectators were worried.

Mathias, however, had only begun to fight. He threw the discus a good 146' 5". He set a personal record with a vault of 13' $\frac{3}{4}$".

He threw the javelin for a personal record of 182′ 4½″. A bewildered Albans said, 'He isn't human.'

Mathias, with the event won, set out after Morris' world record of 7,900 points. The temperature had reached a nearly unbelievable 114 degrees, making distance running most difficult, but he pushed himself around the track in 5 :05.1.

His score was a superb 8,042 points. He was now, at the age of 19, world record holder in the event demanding the most experience.

For the third summer, the teenager toured Europe. On August 6, exactly two years after his Olympic triumph, he won the Swiss Championship with 7,312 points on a wet track.

In the spring of 1951, a muscle spasm in his back limited his action. In the low hurdles, he ran 23.5 and placed fourth in the conference meet. In the shot, he was a highly regarded prospect at 51′ 2½″. He placed sixth in the NCAA and seventh in the AAU. How won the conference discus, placed second in the NCAA and fourth in the AAU, for a remarkable seventh in World Ranking. In the dual meet against the Big Ten conference at Eugene, Oregon, on June 19, he threw the discus 173′ 4″ and set another excellent personal record with 24′ 5″ in the broad jump.

Stanford coach Jack Weiershauser tried to explain Mathias' success without full training in any single event : 'He just does it, that's all. Especially when we need it. It's all in his mind.'

In the fall of 1951, Mathias played football and helped greatly in Stanford's surprise appearance in the Rose Bowl. Then he did some skiing and led his fraternity to the intramural basketball championship. Critics said he was not developing his great track potential. He did no weight training and not enough technique training.

In the 1952 collegiate season, he cut his high hurdle time satisfactorily to 14.3. In the NCAA, he ran 14.2 for a laudable second place behing Jack Davis. He also placed sixth in the discus and seventh in the shot. He competed in all three events in the Final Trials, but his mind was on the decathlon at Tulare, three days later. It meant more than the AAU championship this time. It also served as the Final Trials for the Olympic team.

On the night of July 1, before 6,000 hometown fans, Mathias was invincible. He ran the 100 meters in 10.8, his best time.

He broad jumped 23′ 5¼″, his best decathlon broad jump. He put the shot 49′ 10⅞″, also his best decathlon mark. In the high jump he never touched the bar. After clearing his best ever height of 6′ 2¾″ he stopped to conserve energy.

In the 400 meters, he raced hard against young Milt Campbell and finished in 50.8, his best time. His first-half score was higher than Albans' best-on-record.

He hit three hurdles to begin the second night and the crowd felt disappointed in his 14.6, but it was his fastest time in any decathlon. He threw the discus 157′ 11⅝″, his best in a decathlon. After seven consecutive decathlon bests he vaulted only 12′ 3¾″, but he came back with a personal record of 193′ 10⅜″ in the javelin, He ran 1,500 meters in 4:55.3, almost his best. He was the only man ever to win four AAU decathlons.

This magnificent world record, under the newly adopted tables, totaled 7,829 points. Under this new system, his battered record of two years ago was only 7,444.

At 21, Mathias stood 6′ 3″ and weighed 195 pounds. He was an outstanding favorite to win the Olympic decathlon when they assembled in the beautiful stadium at Helsinki, but he had butterflies in his stomach. He was experienced enough now to know the hazards of decathlon competition. More than ability was needed. A man had to survive. Any injury or even bad luck could eliminate him from contention. No man had ever won the Olympic decathlon twice.

The bad luck struck him at the very beginning. On his marks for the 100, he heard a click and started running. A camera had set him off, but it cost him a false start. One more and he would lose all of the points from the 100, enough to beat him. He hung back until certain he heard the gun, but even with that bad start he ran 10.9.

On his third broad jump, trying to improve on his 22′ 10¾″, injury struck him. He felt a pain in his left thigh. Worried, he went to the Olympic Village and ate a large steak for lunch.

Somebody asked Brutus Hamilton, now head U.S. coach, if Mathias could continue.

'Yes, of course,' Hamilton said. 'Bob not only is the greatest athlete in the world but he's also the greatest competitor. You watch him now. When the pressure is on, he's at his best.'

A little later, a pressured Mathias stepped into the shot put ring. On his first put, he sent the ball out 50′ 2⅜″, his best ever in a decathlon. He overwhelmed his competition by at least five feet and took the lead.

In the high jump he cleared 6′ 2⅘″, his best ever. Then he studied his decathlon scoring tables. Satisfied, he stopped jumping to rest his sore leg.

It was cold and windy on the field. He took his mattress under the stands and calmly went to sleep. Refreshed, he returned to the field wearing a heavy overcoat under his blanket.

At 8:00 p.m. he ran his 400 meters. He sizzled around the wet track with a 22.5 200 meters, then hung on for 50.2, again his best ever.

Thus, backing up Brutus Hamilton's confidence in him, he had recorded three consecutive decathlon bests. His score was only 27 points behind his recent world record.

After a good night's sleep, he had a rubdown and heat for his injured leg. The trainer put on an elastic bandage. Still, when he tried to lift his leg over a hurdle, the pain was intense. He hit the first hurdle and never regained his timing. He had hoped for 14.2, but his time was 14.7. He was now only 179 points ahead of Campbell, still vulnerable.

During a light rain, he threw the discus 153′ 10″, an excellent decathlon mark but a disappointment to him. Then he omitted lunch at the Village in favor of another rubdown.

The pole vault lasted five dreary hours, through rain, sunshine, and a cold wind. He cleared 13′ 1½″, his best decathlon height. Coolly, he examined the scoring tables. His leg hurt more with each vault, and so he withdrew, satisfied to be 26 points ahead of his world record pace.

After another rubdown, he was ready for the javelin. He needed around 195 feet to stay ahead of his record pace, but he had never thrown that far. His first throw fell hopelessly short. His second was also short.

Up in the stands, coach Weiershauser urged some American youths into a rooting section, and they chanted, 'Oh, Bob. Hey you. Don't forget to follow through.'

Mathias smiled, and shouted to his coach, 'I got you.' His last throw brought a different cheer when it landed at 194′ 3⅛″.

At 10:00 p.m. he paced himself cautiously around the red brick track in the 1,500 meters. His taped leg ached with every stride, but when he was sure of himself he increased the pace and ran his fastest 1,500 meters – 4 :50.8.

For the third time in his unparalleled career, he improved the world record. His 7,887 was equal to 8,450 on the old tables – 550 points better than the second best man of all time. He won his second gold medal by 912 points, largest victory margin in history.

Coach Hamilton was one of the first to shake his hand.

Mathias said, 'I'm glad I didn't let you down, Mr. Hamilton.'

Hamilton, himself a former Olympic decathlon silver medalist, had a film of emotion in his eyes.

'Bob, you'll never let anyone down.'

After the interviews, the remaining 15,000 spectators wanted a victory lap and Mathias jogged around to loud cheers. At the same moment, in a little town so far away it was barely afternoon, the citizens of Tulare paraded and danced in the street.

In a post Olympic meet in Zurich, Mathias was credited with 13.8 for the high hurdles, a time bettered by only eight men before him. 'I felt very good, had an excellent start, and was helped by ideal weather conditions and a very fast track.'

In the 1953 conference meet at Stanford, 8,500 fans were on hand to say farewell to Bob Mathias as a track man. He was cutting his season short to be married, and he had the Marine Corps ahead of him. His last event was a stirring low hurdle race against Jack Davis, one of the world's great hurdlers. Mathias pressed Davis all the way, barely losing in 23.2

Further honors as an amateur ended when he signed a contract to play himself in a film, 'The Bob Mathias Story'. He retired undefeated in the decathlon even though his remarkable potential was never fully developed.

Postscript : in 1956, three years after his last collegiate competition, he competed briefly in the maroon and gold of the Marine Corps. His quite remarkable feats proved better than anything else that his natural ability and competitive genius counted for more of his success than did his training.

After that long layoff, he threw the discus 162′ 5½″, better than most of his throws in his final year at Stanford. In the Marine Corps Championships he won the hurdles in surprising times of 14.4 and 23.4.

In the Interservice decathlon at the Coliseum, he was amazing. He ran 100 meters in 11 flat broad jumped 22′ 8¾″, and put the shot 50′ 4¼″. He was near a world record pace. He fell off a bit in the high jump, to 5′ 11¾″. Not in the best of shape, he ran a good 51.9 for 400 meters.

The next day, he ran 14.9, threw 160′ 2¼″, and vaulted 11′ 11½″. He took only one javelin throw but it sailed 204′ 1¼″, his best ever. The winner at 7,193 points, he was happy to withdraw from the 1,500 meters.

Obviously an Olympic contender except for his professional status, he said somewhat wistfully, 'I'm a little sorry I turned pro.'

O'BRIEN

Success in athletics, as in many other fields, comes from a combination of natural ability plus hard work, intelligently directed. All great athletes had unusual natural talent, and a few of them tried as hard as humanly possible, but most of them received their coaching from others.

One notable exception, whose creative thinking taught the world's coaches how to coach, was Parry O'Brien.

One night in 1951 at Fresno, California, O'Brien shoved a 16-pound iron ball 53′ 6⅞″ for second place. This was almost two feet shorter than his best mark and even shorter than his national freshman record 53′ 10½″ of the previous year. He had improved impressively over his 57′ 9½″ with the 12-pound shot in 1949, but he was disappointed.

When the event was over, he stayed at the shot put circle. For two hours, while the meet went on under the lights, he practiced intensely with the help of 1948 Olympic champion Wilbur Thompson. He almost missed his airplane, but he arrived home in Santa Monica at 1 :30 a.m.

At 3 :00 a.m. his father was startled from a sound sleep by heavy thuds. Sleepily, he investigated and saw his son in the asphalt alley, putting the shot from a chalked circle under the street light. After each put, Parry had to search among the weeds of the vacant lot with a flashlight to find the iron ball.

'I think I've discovered something,' he told his sleepy father. 'I couldn't wait until morning.' And he continued his intense concentration until 4 :00 a.m.

His father's affectionate summation was : 'He has more determination than four mules.'

O'Brien hoped he had improved, but in the NCAA meet at Seattle he put only 53′ 10″ and he lost by one frustrating inch to Darrow Hooper, who was the high school record holder two years before.

The defeat hurt O'Brien. He had fouled on puts near 55 feet, and it was his first loss to a collegian. Then, in a mid-week meet at Eugene, Oregon, against the Big Ten conference, he put only 53′ 9½″. Disgusted, he worked out for 2½ hours after the meet.

A week after his NCAA failure, he was in Berkeley for his first national AAU meet, and he had 'psyched himself up' into a heated determination to beat Hooper.

'I try to whip myself into a frenzy. When I'm ready for a toss I'm in a different world.'

He was also competing against world record holder Jim Fuchs, victorious in 88 consecutive meets. Fuchs was not at his best because of a sore back, but he put 55′ 2″.

Without warning, the track world was forced to recognize O'Brien as an unusually reliable competitor, able to focus his hours of strong self-discipline and intense concentration onto the best put of his life at the right moment. For he came through with 55′ 9¼″ to win his first great victory.

Next came a significant trip to Europe with too many meets too close together. 'I was looking for a way to throw that was easier but with which I could get the same results.'

He reached 55′ 5″ at Paris on July 8. Then he began his daring experiment. At the start of a put, he began turning his right foot farther and farther toward the back of the circle, like Fuchs, but he also shocked coaches by turning his whole body so that his back was toward the direction of his throw.

'I was severly criticized by German coaches and other experts who said it wasn't natural for the body to go that way, and it was too unorthodox to succeed. But I was thoroughly convinced that with the orthodox method I was, and always would be, no better than a 56-foot shot putter. I was certain that I could not achieve the kind of marks I had in mind – 59 and 60 feet – with this orthodox technique.'

In the fall of 1951, he gave up football in favor of track. 'I wanted to be able to take the credit or the blame for what I did myself. I always wanted to be a soloist.'

He began training for the 1952 season and he made another important decision. He would go all-out with his new form. He drew a chalk circle under the street light behind his fraternity house and he put the shot into a parking lot. He worked day and night.

His coach, Jesse Mortensen, did not try to restrain O'Brien's experiments. In fact, he pointed out two advantages of O'Brien's discovery : (1) more power from the right leg, and (2) a push of a foot longer, giving O'Brien valuable time to work up speed and force.

'For quite a while I had to be my own coach, work out my own technique, correct my own faults. That's why I wanted to be off somewhere doing it alone where I could get greater concentration.'

About two evenings a week that spring, O'Brien went secretly to the nearby Coliseum. Shamelessly, he tossed his shot over the chain-link fence and climbed over. Down on the field, lighted and inspired by the Olympic torch, he practiced diligently for an hour and a half to two hours.

His work paid off. He beat Hooper by $\frac{5}{8}$ of an inch in a triangular meet. He won at Fresno with 55' 9$\frac{3}{4}$", his best yet. The next week, in the Coliseum Relays, he progressed admirably to 56' 6$\frac{3}{4}$" but he lost to Fuchs by half a foot. At Compton, O'Brien challenged with 57' 3$\frac{3}{4}$", but Fuchs put 58' 5$\frac{1}{2}$", only five inches from his own world record.

For two weeks O'Brien kept a picture of Hooper on his desk, concentrating on the moment he would avenge his NCAA defeat of last year. The shot put consists of many arduous hours of training for each split-second explosion in competition, but that explosion is what counts.

O'Brien went to the NCAA meet at Berkeley and exploded with 57' $\frac{5}{8}$". He won the shot easily. In the discus, which he threw for fun but with his own peculiar concentration, his unexpected 170' 4$\frac{1}{2}$" was second only to soon-to-be Olympic champion Sim Iness.

In the AAU meet at Long Beach, California, O'Brien controlled his explosion perfectly in the cool night air to reach his best distance of 57' 4$\frac{3}{4}$". It beat Fuchs by five inches and set a new meet record. Now only two men had ever put farther than O'Brien.

As one of the established favorites, O'Brien ran into the fiercest competition yet recorded, in the Final Olympic Trials in the Coliseum. Hooper came through with a great 57' 1$\frac{3}{8}$" on his first put. O'Brien's first put thudded into the turf at 56′ 3⅞″ and he was a vulnerable third, behind Bernie Mayer.

Mayer arched the shot 56′ 7¾″ and O'Brien reached 56′ 9⅜″, but Mayer and Fuchs were still threats. O'Brien had to improve. On his fourth effort, he put all his concentration into it and reached 57′ ½″.

As the Olympic shot put began, clouds as black as ink crowded toward the stadium in Helsinki. O'Brien studied the clouds and 'put everything I had into my first try. I could see it might rain.'

He took his strange position in the ring, facing backward, shot nestled against his neck. He puckered his lips and bent double, left arm high. He shoved across the ring, building up to his explosion. Turning with all his strength and desire, he straightened his right arm behind the shot. He released his pent-up air with a loud 'Pow.' The shot went 57′ 1⅜″, his sixth consecutive meet over 57 feet.

The rain came, hindering his opponents. For a long time it looked as if O'Brien's tactics had won easily, but Hooper was not finished. A crippled Fuchs could manage only 55′ 11¾″, within an inch of Hooper, but Hooper had one chance left.

O'Brien watched tensely as Hooper pushed out his last gallant effort. A roar went up from the crowd. Many were sure Hooper had won. The suspense was almost unbearable. Then the figures went up on the field board.

O'Brien's mark was 17.41 meters. The figure 17 appeared under Hooper's number, quickly followed by 39. O'Brien had won the Olympic championship by ¾ of an inch. He showed little emotion, for his thoughts were on the future. He wanted to reach 60 feet in 1953. 'I feel sure I can do it.'

After a tour of Europe in which he lost only once, in the discus, he returned home and devoted himself to weight training, pioneered by Otis Chandler but never fully exploited. In February, O'Brien flew to New York, curiously examined the leather-covered indoor shot for the first time, and put it 55′ 10¾″ to win the AAU title over Fuchs and Mayer.

His intensive practice lasted three hours a day, with as many as 150 throws. 'I don't quit until my hands are bleeding.' As a result, in April, he increased his personal record impressively, to 57′ 10½″, 58′ 1⅞″, and 58′ 8¼″.

On May 7 he was in Fresno for the West Coast Relays, build-slowly to a climax. He wore two sweat suits against the chill wind for his first put of 57' 5½". He stripped them off and put 58' 4¾". He put them on and moved to keep warm while he waited.

He worked on himself carefully. He took a swig of honey from a plastic bottle. 'The fastest energy there is.' He worked himself into a frenzy at the proper moment. 'The shotputter has to know when to blast and when to rest, when to take it easy, and when to give it all he's got.' For his third put he was fully clad and barely reached 55 feet.

He shed the two sweat suits and stepped into the ring for his fourth put. He was ready. He placed his right toe at the rear of the circle. His 6' 2½", 225-pound body bent low. At that critical moment the national anthem began. Spectators and athletes alike came to attention, but O'Brien's concentration was on his effort.

He dipped his body. He shoved his body a foot and a half across the ring, landing in the same position. Then he uncoiled explosively, with the fluid movement of a medium tank. The shot made a silver arc under the lights.

Suddenly, the usually stoic O'Brien was dancing up and down with joy. Abruptly, he heard the national anthem, and he stood at attention, impatient for the measurement.

It was 59' ¾", a new world record.

Four weeks later in the Compton Invitational, he raised it to 59' 2⅜". A shocked Hooper, beaten by more than three feet, said, 'O'Brien's weight training gives him unbeatable power.'

In the NCAA, O'Brien won at 58' 7¼". In the NCAA discus, after upsetting the Olympic champion at the Coliseum Relays and Compton, O'Brien threw a personal record 173' 8", but he lost to Iness' world record 190' ⅞".

O'Brien pushed the iron ball to a meet record of 57' 11¼" in the AAU, and placed fourth in the discus. In an extended tour of Europe, he finished the year victorious in the shot put in more than 45 meets He ranked sixth in the world with the discus.

From his high school marks it seems O'Brien did not have outstanding natural ability, but he did have unusual speed for a big man. He once ran 100 meters in 10.8. In Europe, he ran the first leg in six relays and was never beaten.

He was now the greatest shot putter in history, but he was

only beginning. With his collegiate competition ended, he competed in fewer meets in 1954, but his quality improved.

He began in the indoor AAU meet at Madison Square Garden. His 59' 4" was the best in history, indoors or out. His first outdoor meet was the Drake Relays in Des Moines, Iowa, on April 24. He dented the turf at 59' 9¾", another world record. His second meet was a special competition in which he bettered all previous records for combined right and left hand – 102' 1¾".

His third meet was an added event during a dual meet in the Coliseum. News came that Stan Lampert had put 59' 5⅛", second best ever. 'I could just see all my records going down the tubes.'

Fired up, he fouled his first toss. His second went 60' 5¼", the first 60-footer in history, two days after the first 4-minute mile.

His third put sailed 60' ½". Then he put 59' 10¼", foul, 59' 10¼" again, and 58' 10¾". Thus, his answer to Lampert's threat consisted of the four longest puts in history.

On May 15, at Fresno, he upset the great Fortune Gordien in the discus with a mighty 184' 1½". That night, he completed the best double ever with a 59-foot put.

At the Coliseum Relays on May 21, he started with five good puts, all over 58' 6". His sixth went 60' 5¾", adding another half inch to his world record.

At the Southern Pacific AAU meet in the Coliseum on June 11, he surpassed any shot putting he had done previously. In a period of five minutes he took four puts : 60' 5½", 60' 6", 60' ½", and 60' 10".

Only five weeks before, the 60-foot shot put had been rated as an ultimate performance comparable to the 4-minute mile.

O'Brien closed out a short but spectacular season with a new AAU meet record of 58' 11¾" in St. Louis, plus a second place in the discus. He ranked third in the world in the discus. No other modern athlete has ever ranked so high in two field events.

He became an Air Force lieutenant and 1955 was a year of poorer performances. He raised the world indoor record to 59' 5½" in the AAU. In Mexico City, he won the shot at the Pan American Games and placed second in the discus. In the AAU meet at Boulder, Colorado, he became the first man in thirty years to triumph in both the shot and discus. He was an undefeated first in the shot, but his best marks were 59' 4½" and 175' 7", and he slipped to sixth in the discus world placings.

O'Brien was still not satisfied with his efforts. He explored every conceivable possibility for improvement, digging 'deep into what you might call an inner reserve of strength.' He investigated the possibilities of physics and aerodynamics, of religions and Yoga, and of self-hypnosis.

Olympic year found him better than ever. He trained at the University of Pennsylvania the week before the indoor AAU at Madison Square Garden. He brought himself to such a pitch that he fouled his first two puts and had to be careful to qualify at 58' 6". His fourth put was 59' 4", still short of his indoor record, and he fouled his fifth.

On his last attempt, the leather-covered ball crunched into the boards farther away than any other throw ever recorded anywhere – 61' 5¼" – and the fans sprang to their feet, roaring with surprise. Most amazing of all, the shot was found to be five ounces heavy.

In early outdoor meets, he threw the discus 184' 10" and put the shot 60' 8½". On May 5, in Salt Lake City for the Intermountain AAU, he raised his world record to 61' 1" and threw the discus 179' 7" for the world's best double.

On the night of June 2, in Stockton, California, O'Brien won the Pacific AAU at 60' ½", then reached a best-ever 61' 8¾" on an unofficial 7th put. He also threw the discus 180' 4½". After raising his outdoor world record to 61' 4" in the Service Championships and doubling in the discus, he seemed to be good enough to make the Olympic team in two events.

Then came disaster. A ganglia cyst in his right wrist cut him down to 58' 11½" in the AAU and he lost to Ken Bantum. The longest winning streak in athletic history came to an end at 117.

He also slipped in the discus and placed fourth. After a week of concentrating on the shot to the neglect of the discus, he finished only fifth in the discus in the Final Trials, but he was successful in the shot at 60' 10".

He had the cyst removed, gained to 235 pounds with intensive weight training, and after seven weeks he returned to competition in great shape. He added a quarter of an inch to his world record with 61' 4½" at Pasadena on August 18. On September 3, in Eugene, he went wild.

His first put was a mighty 62′ 3″, the tenth time he had broken the world record. His second put was 62 feet even. His third left the fans dazed. It was 62′ 6⅜″, another world record. As if the three longest puts of all time were not enough, he threw the discus 181′ 7¾″, second to Al Oerter by four inches, giving him another best-ever double.

His great condition was proved at Santa Ana, California, on October 27 when sloping ground invalidated a world record 62′ 8½″ and a series of six throws all longer than 60′ 11″. But that was nothing compared with his next meet.

It was November 1, in the Los Angeles Coliseum, and the U.S. Olympic team was in its final meet before leaving for Australia. An eager O'Brien put 62′ ½″ on his trial and 62′ 2½″ on his second. His third measured 62′ 8″, the twelfth time he had bettered a world record. His fourth went 62′ 5¾″.

When his fifth throw left his finger tips he knew it was a good one. He thrust both arms into the air and jumped slightly off the ground – his equivalent of the mad leaps of other triumphant athletes. The throw measured 63′ 2″, almost three feet farther than the next best shot putter in history.

His sixth put was 62′ 1″, completing the greatest series of marks anyone had ever accomplished in track and field.

He appeared to be the surest favorite of the 1956 Olympic Games, but in the huge, round Melbourne Cricket Grounds anything could happen. He was up against the only other 60-footers in history – Bill Nieder and Ken Bantum.

'You wouldn't think I'd be nervous, but man, I really was.'

He stepped into the unfamiliar concrete circle for his first put. He moved well across the ring, but the shot slipped off his fingers and went only 58′ 9½″. 'The shots were new and there was nothing to grip on.'

He had to wait a long time between throws, and twice more the shot slipped off his hand. His best mark was only 60′ 11⅛″, but five of his puts were better than the best of his competition and he was still Olympic champion.

For the fifth year in a row he ranked as the world's best shot putter and he was fifth in the world among 1956 discus throwers. At the end of 1956 he had made the twenty-one best winning puts in history, plus almost as many other puts longer than Nieder's best of 60′ 3¾″. He could have retired then as one of the greatest athletes of all time, but competition was in his blood.

In 1957, after he put 62' 2" in an exhibition in Manila on January 11 and won his fifth indoor AAU championship at 58' 8", he neglected the shot in an effort to reach the top in the discus. Even so, he lost only once in eight meets, to Nieder's great 62' 2". He ranked second behind Nieder in the world ratings.

In the discus, his efforts were rewarded with the coveted first in World Ranking. He was undefeated, with a best mark of 183' 3".

His true love was the shot put, however, and in 1958 he hardly threw the discus. Indoors, he won the AAU shot at 60' 1¼" then traveled to Frankfort, Germany, and set an indoor record of 61' 8½". He regained his first ranking with an undefeated season, including a 63' 1" put in the California Relays.

In 1959, O'Brien was honored as first in the shot for the seventh year, although a young giant named Dallas Long beat him twice and broke his world record with 63' 7". O'Brien had fine exhibition puts of 63' 6" and 63' 8", but his best official mark was 63' 4". He won against Long at Compton (62' 7"), in the AAU (62' 2¼"), and in the Pan American Games (62' 5½"). Track fans shook their heads in wonder. He had lost only four times in 7½ years.

In the discus, O'Brien ranked seventh in the world with a best of 185' 1½". He sailed the platter far enough for second in the AAU and third in the Pan American Games.

O'Brien made a real effort for his third Olympics, ignoring the discus. He won the indoor AAU again, at 61' 8". He put 63' 5" and 63' 1¼" in early meets. He won at the California Relays and Compton. He won an AAU victory at 62' 6¼". He made his third Olympic team with 62' 3¾" for second place in the Final Trials. He had good puts of 63' 2" and 63' 3¼" in two more meets before the Olympics.

Down on the green turf of Rome's Stadio Olimpico, Parry O'Brien stalked about, waiting his turn. No man in track and field had ever tried harder to win than he had, and almost nobody was so successful, but now he had reached his limit. Now, at the age of 28, he had ceased improving and others were better.

The Europeans had cracked badly under the stress of Olympic

competition, but he worried about Nieder and Long. Nieder, with a brace on his right knee, had raised the world record to 65′ 7″ in April and again, to 65′ 10″ on August 12. Long, 6′ 4″ and 260 pounds, had put 64′ 6½″ in March, before he was 20, and he had a much greater potential. All O'Brien could do was his best.

He led off with 61′ 7″, possibly good enough for the bronze medal now that Britain's Arthur Rowe had failed to qualify. Nieder put only 61′ 3″ and Long's first effort was a poor 55′ 1⅜″.

O'Brien stepped into the ring for his second trial. He knew exactly what to do. He had more throws over 62 feet than everybody else in history combined. If he could get off a good one, the others might fold. He bent low, shoved off, and pushed the shot 62′ 8¼″.

Nieder followed with 61′ 7″. Long, with shoulders like a block of granite, moved to second with 61′ 11¼″. Now O'Brien could do nothing for himself. He stalked grimly back and forth, flexing his muscles and manipulating a white towel. He neither spoke nor smiled.

They all failed to improve on their third round and in the fourth. The suspense was almost frightening. O'Brien's game fight thrilled onlookers as he led against overwhelming odds.

Then Nieder did everything right and the shot sailed 64′ 6¾″ and O'Brien's dream was over. He stayed ahead of Long and won a silver medal, but on the victory stand his eyes were on Nieder's gold. He announced his retirement and he was hailed for his great competitive ability.

He could not stand retirement, though, and in February of 1961 he won his ninth consecutive indoor AAU title, at 61′ 3″, then upgraded the indoor record to 63′ 1½″. Outdoors, he lost only to Long, put 62′ 3″, and placed second in the AAU. He was ranked third in the shot put world ratings, and he threw the discus 188′ ½″, plus two over 189′ on sloping ground.

In 1962 he concentrated on the discus and ranked tenth in the world in both events. His best shot put was only 61′ 4½″, but he threw the discus 193′ 2″.

In answer to a pertinent question, he said, 'Quit? What for? I'm as good as ever. . . . You may see me in Tokyo.'

In 1963 he improved to fourth in World Ranking, the same as in 1951, but this year his best was 62′ 8″, almost seven feet farther than in 1951. He was second in the AAU and in the meet against Russia.

In the seldom seen two-handed shot put he raised the unofficial record to 106' 10¼", reaching 45' 9½" left-handed.

After an absence of two years, he competed in the 1964 indoor AAU. His 62' 10" was good, but he lost to Gary Gubner's 63' 2½". Outdoors, he raised his personal record, astonishingly, to 63' 10", but he lost the Southern Pacific AAU to Long's world record 66' 3½". In the AAU, O'Brien placed third, but his best distance was the same as John McGrath's fourth place and only two inches ahead of Dave Davis.

Like Zátopek, O'Brien was honored as a living legend while still competing far beyond his time. His opponents respected his achievements and they used his methods, but none of that counted for him in the heat of competition. They were passing him by.

The Final Trials, to choose the U.S. Olympic team, were held in the Coliseum in mid-September. Long was considered certain to make the team. Randy Matson, off his 64' 11", seemed sure. O'Brien was everybody's favorite for third although he was threatened by 63-footer Davis, by McGrath, and by Gubner, off form from his 64' 11" of 1963.

Matson led at 63' 10" with Long second. Davis's second put went 62' 8", placing him third. O'Brien could do only 61' 5". With only four men qualifying for another three puts, Gubner stepped into the ring for his last chance and put one out near O'Brien's mark.

The crowd, pulling for O'Brien as they never had when he was king, waited in suspense until the measurement showed Gubner half an inch behind.

Now as nervous as he had ever been, the 32-year-old O'Brien took his place on the concrete for his fourth put. His desire to beat Davis's 62' 8" burned inside him. He went through the familiar movements. Carefully, using all the wisdom he had accumulated in 17 years of effort, he directed his body toward one perfectly-timed instant of explosion.

The round ball made an arc and landed heavily. The measurement – 63' 2" – delighted the crowd, but O'Brien worried about Davis. He paced about beyond the 70-foot line until Davis's last chance was gone. Then, and only then, did he shed his reserve and flex his biceps for the crowd. They gave him the loudest cheer of the meet.

He was on his fourth Olympic team. At Tokyo, he had no hopes for an upset victory. All he could do here was hope for a medal. He shoved the weight a full 63 feet, his longest Olympic put, but he placed only fourth. Time marches on.

He retired again, but not from the discus. 'Traditionally, the careers of discus throwers last longer. Some of the greatest have hit their peak in their late 30's or early 40's. A throw of 200 feet will win a lot of meets in this country and abroad, and I have a career best of 193′ 7″.'

He sent the platter spinning out over 190 feet several times in 1965 and he improved his record to an excellent 196′ 10″.

In 1966, he retired from the discus. Nobody should have been surprised when he made a comeback in the shot at the age of thirty-four. Nor should they have been surprised at his performances. But they were.

Now successful in the banking business, he had the time and opportunity to train in the new UCLA gymnasium, and new weight equipment also helped. He began indoors with 62′ 9½″. Then, at Seattle, he threw 63′ 9″, only an inch short of his best ever.

In Canada for the Achilles Invitational at Vancouver, February 19, O'Brien trailed a new star, Neil Steinhauer, on his last put. The amazing O'Brien came through with 64 feet, his best ever.

'I used to compete against the lines, but now I can throw against somebody and it's stimulating. I'm in it for what I can get out of myself. I don't need the trinkets ... just the satisfaction of knowing I've produced my maximum.'

Outdoors, he increased his personal record to 64′ 2¾″ at the Coliseum Relays. Then, on May 28, in Honolulu, he arched the heavy ball 64′ 7½″. This greatest put of his life contained an element of sadness, for it was his farewell to striving.

In addition to his contributions of a new technique, proof of the value of weight training, and new ideas in mental preparation, O'Brien had now showed the world something new in the field of longevity.

'It's gratifying to know I have contributed something to the sport that has done so much for me ... travel, friends, education.'

In 1967, he placed third in the indoor AAU with 61′ 9″, but he did almost nothing outdoors. His bests were 60′ 2″ and 175′ 2″. Old soldiers never die .. They just fade away.

During his unparalleled career, O'Brien placed high in World Ranking more often than any other man. He scored more points in U.S. national meets than any other athlete. In addition to his two firsts, a second, and a fourth in four Olympics, he won two firsts, a second, and a third in Pan American Games. He triumphed in more than twenty major relay meets. He won five medals in NCAA meets and thirty in AAU meets – eighteen of them gold.

In no other athlete has so much quality come in such quantity.

8 JOHNSON

About the time the little town of Tulare, California, was going wild in celebration of 17-year-old Bob Mathias's Olympic victory in the decathlon, a 12-year-old boy in Kingsburg, twenty-five miles south, was painfully trapped in a peach cannery conveyer belt. The front half of his left foot was 'hanging by the tissue near the toes.' He needed twenty-three stitches and he was on crutches for eight weeks.

Almost four years later, high school coach Murl Dodson took the same unfortunate boy to Tulare to watch the incomparable Mathias break the world record in the AAU decathlon championships.

When the excitement was over, the boy thought about the 26 contestants in the decathlon and said, 'I could have beaten most of the guys in that meet.'

And so Rafer Johnson decided to be a decathlon man.

One of five children of a family which knew real poverty, Rafer Johnson liked sports and he was good at them. After his visit to Tulare he began to work four hours a day at whichever events he fancied.

Two years later, Johnson was giving Kingsburg something to talk about with Tulare. Johnson was a football star, averaging more than nine yards per carry for Kingsburg High. In basketball, he averaged 17 points per game. In his one season of baseball, he batted a phenomenal .500. In track, he lettered all four years and won the state high hurdles championship in 14.3, almost won the lows in 19 flat, and broad jumped 23' 1".

Already recognized as a fine prospect, he went south to Pasadena and won a high school decathlon for the second year. He ran 14.3 over the high school hurdles and threw the high school weights 51' 10¾" and an eye-opening 174' 4¼", only ten feet behind Oerter's national record. He bettered Mathias's 1948 marks with an 11 flat 100 meters, a 22' 10½" broad jump, and a good

6' 3" high jump. He was weak only in the vault, javelin, and 1,500 meters.

He traveled across the country to Atlantic City, New Jersey, for the national AAU decathlon, July 2 and 3. He improved in his three weak events, raising his vault to 11' 4", but he slipped in other events. His score was only 5,874, good for third place.

Of all the colleges to seek his services, he chose UCLA. After freshman basketball, he began a great 1955 season. He trained as a hurdler and worked on two or three field events every day.

At 6' 3", with the slim legs of a sprinter and the agility of an all-round athlete, Johnson had the makings of a great hurdler. He ran his heat in the West Coast Relays in 14 flat, tying the U.S. freshman record. He won the Compton Invitational low hurdles in 22.9, fastest time in the world for 1955. In the AAU meet at Boulder, Colorado, he was narrowly eliminated in the highs, but he almost won the lows. Running the unfamiliar curve race, his time was 23.6 in fourth place to 23.5 for the winner.

Meanwhile, he was improving in other events. In a dual meet on March 25, in which he won six firsts, he raised his best marks in each throwing event to 46' 3", 145' 3", and 191' 11". Later, he threw 154' 11" and ran a 220 in 21.5 and a relay leg in 48.5.

But his true love was the decathlon. He once said, 'The decathlon is easier than some other meets,' and with the exception of the 1,500 meters, it was. On February 18 and 19 at Occidental College, in the Southern Pacific AAU decathlon, he hoped to qualify for the Pan American Games.

He improved tremendously over his third place in the 1954 AAU. He ran 100 meters with the wind in 10.6 and broad jumped 23' 11½". He cut his 400 meter record to 49.3. His second day was weaker, but his total was 7,055 points, ninth on the all-time list.

The 1955 Pan American Games were held in Mexico City one month later. Johnson's marks for the first day were disappointing, 147 points below his wind-aided marks at Occidental, and he was expected to lose to Bob Richards.

Johnson came through like a champion on the second day with personal records in the first four events, and he won with 6,994.

On June 10 and 11, Kingsburg (with a 1950 population of

only 2,303 people) tried to rival nearby Tulare by holding the Central California AAU decathlon.

Johnson ran 100 meters in 10.5, great time for a 200-pound non-specialist. He raised his broad jump record to 24' 6⅞". Both marks put him in the top 20 on the 1955 world list, to go with his fifth in the high hurdles and first in the lows. He put the shot 45' 3¼", high jumped 6' ¾", and ran the 400 in 49.7. His 4,537 points gave him the highest first-day score in history.

He started the second day with a good 14.5 in the hurdles, then threw the discus 154' 10¾", only a quarter of an inch short of his best. He had gained on Mathias's world record in both events, but now he was facing his three weakest events.

In the pole vault, even experienced specialists have bad days. In the decathlon, one bad part can ruin the whole. Johnson boosted his heavy body over the crossbar time after time. He surpassed his own personal record. The small crowd became excited as he continued to clear. Finally, he was over 12' 8½", and he was still ahead of Mathias.

In the javelin, Johnson gave further evidence that he was a competitor equal to Mathias. He threw a personal record 193' 10⅜". Now he needed to run 1,500 meters in 5:18 to break the world record.

His personal best was 5:23, and he disliked the event, but he ran hard, and with the hometown crowd cheering all the way he finished in 5:01.5.

His 7,985 points bettered Mathias's world record by 98 points. At the age of nineteen, he was the world record holder. His future seemed unlimited.

In 1956, he was pointing for the Olympic decathlon, but during the college season he competed with distinction in the hurdles and broad jump. Even without any such event as the decathlon, he would have been regarded as an exceptional sophomore.

In dual meets he ran the hurdles in 14.1 and 22.7 (22.6 with wind). Against Stanford, he broad jumped 24' 10¼" and against Southern California, 25' 5¾" (sixth best in the world for the entire year). He also ran a 220 in 21 flat.

At the West Coast Relays, his 14.2 earned him fourth place. He won the broad jump at 25' 2¼". His 47.4 helped UCLA win the mile relay.

The next week, in the conference meet at Berkeley, Johnson

PARRY O'BRIEN At the start of his magnificent international career, young O'Brien competes in his first Olympics – Helsinki, 1952

BOB MATHIAS His taped leg aching, the 21-year-old veteran of two Olympics strides through the darkness of Helsinki at the end of the 1952 Olympic decathlon

RAFER JOHNSON Seldom if ever has such combination of speed, strength, and agility been seen in one body. Johnson competes at Rome in 1960

A great long jump prospect in 1956, injuries hobbled Johnson. Here, in the Rome Olympics of 1960, he tries desperately to beat C. K. Yang

lost the 100 yard title by an inch. Trying to hurdle only ten minutes later, he ran into the same trouble as Dillard in 1948 and he finished third. He placed second to a team-mate in the broad jump without taking his final jumps. He won the low hurdles. His 16 points enabled UCLA to defeat USC for the first time in history.

Johnson won the broad jump at the California Relays. At Compton, he won the lows in 22.8 and ran 14 flat in the highs behind Davis, Calhoun, and Campbell.

In the NCAA meet at Berkeley, the low hurdles were eliminated in favor of the intermediates and so Johnson entered only two events, but his international class was evident.

In the high hurdles, he ran against Lee Calhoun, one of the greatest of all time. Johnson showed his unusual competitive ability by leading Calhoun over the last hurdle, but he lost by 2½ feet. His time of 13.8 against a wind of 1.3 m.p.h. was remarkable. Only four men ran faster in 1956 and Johnson was sixth in World Ranking. Only two hurdlers in history, Wolcott and Dillard, had faster times than Johnson in both hurdles races.

In the broad jump, Johnson competed against Greg Bell, soon to be Olympic champion. Johnson led with his preliminary jump of 25' ¼", but Bell won with 25' 9" on his first jump on Saturday. Johnson fought back with 25' 4" for second place.

Johnson's 16 points made him runner-up to Bobby Morrow for high-point honors and enabled UCLA to win its first NCAA title.

In the AAU meet at Bakersfield the following week, he tried only the low hurdles. He ran his heat in 22.7, then lost the final by one foot in 22.8.

The Final Trials followed a week later in the Los Angeles Coliseum. Overly eager, Johnson hit two hurdles early in his heat and rode the fifth one down. Even so, he missed his chance in the final by mere inches. In the broad jump, his struggle was against five 26-footers. He jumped 24' 10" in the preliminaries, good for third. He lost it to a 25' 1½" jump, but he came back gamely with 25' 1¾" and 25' 3¼" to make the Olympic team. He ranked sixth in the world in the broad jump.

Two weeks later, on July 13 and 14, he tried for the decathlon team at Wabash College in Crawfordsville, Indiana. Heavy rains

D   97 had softened the track and runways. He ran 10.6 in the 100, but his broad jump was a poor 23′ 2½″.

He came back powerfully, with a personal record of 49′ 8¾″ in the shot. In the high jump, his football knee bothered him, but he cleared 6′ 1″. Then, with darkness falling, he put on a sprint finish to catch Aubrey Lewis in the 400 meters. Their 47.9's were the fastest ever run in the decathlon.

Johnson's first-day total of 4,640 was the highest ever, and he started the second day with a fine 14.4 in the hurdles. He was on his way to a world record and a probable Olympic title.

Then came the trouble all decathlon men fear. In the discus, he reinjured his knee. He threw 149′ 5″, but he could vault only 11′ 5¾″. He threw the javelin 182′ 4½″ and ran 1,500 meters in 5:12.4. His 7,755 points, fourth highest ever, beat Milt Campbell by 196 points.

Johnson reinjured his knee practicing the pole vault in Melbourne and he had to withdraw from the Olympic broad jump.

He began the Olympic decathlon with a 10.9 in the 100, while Campbell ran 10.8. In the broad jump, Johnson tore a stomach muscle. Earlier in the season, he had said, 'The decathlon is actually not as difficult as people think,' but now he was changing his mind. A decathlon man must also contend with injuries, fatigue, long hours, and the weather.

His 24′ 1″ left him behind an improved Campbell and he was not in any condition to catch Campbell. His first-day total of 4,375 left him 191 points behind.

Dispirited, knowing he could not win with his injuries, Johnson lost his rhythm and ran only 15.1 in the hurdles. Campbell ran 14 flat and his lead increased to 525. Johnson lost more points with a poor discus throw of 138′ 4½″. Now he was 612 points behind. What was worse, he led Kuznetsov by only 266 points.

Every vault was painful. Lifting his legs tore at his wounded muscles. He struggled desperately over height after height, failing only after he had raised his decathlon best to 12′ 9½″.

In the javelin, Kuznetsov neared his best mark with 213′ 8″. Johnson responded with a personal record 197′ 9″.

In the 1,500 meters he had to run fast enough to maintain his lead over Kuznetsov. Suffering with each stride, he struggled around in 4:54.2, his best ever.

A sympathizer asked if his injury hurt during the race.

'Sure it hurt, but what was I going to do? Quit?'

He had lost the gold medal everybody thought was his, but under the circumstances he said the silver medal 'was very gratifying to me'.

Later he said, wistfully, 'I'd sure like to win at Rome in 1960.'

The year 1957 was almost lost to Johnson. He could not sprint nor jump because of his injured knee. He worked on the weights and improved to 159' 7½" with the discus and a good 228' 1" in the javelin. Early in June he was able to run a relay leg from the blocks in 48.6

He was a busy young man at UCLA. As if a decathlon man does not already have too much to do, he lettered in basketball, worked enthusiastically as student body president, spoke before youth groups, and began his acting career.

In 1958 he started as a weight man, and a badly pulled thigh muscle kept him at it. His results bore no similarity to the international class hurdler and broad jumper he was in 1956. He raised his shot put record to a creditable 54' 5", threw the discus 166' 4½", and reached 227' 8" with the javelin.

Then, on April 26, in a dual meet with Stanford, Johnson completed the greatest weight triple in the history of the sport. He put the shot 54' 11½", far enough to make the top 20 in the U.S. for 1958. He threw the discus 170' 9½", making him tenth best American. He threw the javelin 237' 10", good enough for No. 10 on the U.S. list.

At the West Coast Relays, he won the javelin at 238' 11". In the Coliseum Relays, he ran a fine 47-flat relay leg. In the conference meet, he won the javelin at 243' 10". In his first broad jump since the Olympics, running at less than full speed, he cleared a promising 24' 10" on a narrow foul. He qualified in the hurdles with 14.7, his first flight since 1956. Then a sprained ankle put him out of the meet.

The AAU meet in Bakersfield was a disappointment to him. He placed ninth in the discus and sixteenth in the javelin at 212' 11½". He qualified for the low hurdle final, but he did not finish.

Track fans were surprised when he recovered fast enough to compete in the Kingsburg Invitational decathlon the next weekend. He risked only one attempt in each of the three jumps, recording 23′ 3″, 5′ 2½″, and 10′ 11⅞″, but his other marks were noteworthy. He ran the 100 in 10.6, put the shot 50′ 5″, and ran the 400 in 48.9.

His high hurdle time was a surprising 14.2. He threw the discus 157′ 10½″, and the javelin 209′ 9″. His 5:02 for 1,500 meters brought his total to a good 7,780.

Greatly encouraged, Johnson entered the national AAU decathlon at Palmyra, New Jersey, eight days later. He had to run 5:14.7 in the 1,500 to beat C. K. Yang by 62 points. His 7,754 was exactly the same as his 1956 score.

He went to Moscow for the important meet with Russia 22 days later. On the first day, 75,000 people in the Bolshoi arena anticipated a great duel between Johnson and their new world record holder, Kuznetsov.

Johnson again ran 10.6, but Kuznetsov excited the crowd with a jump of 24′ 7″ while Johnson managed only 23′ 6¼″. Johnson was weak in the shot with 48′ 2¼″, and in the high jump at 5′ 10⅞″. After four events, to everyone's surprise, he was ten points behind.

In the 400, Johnson ran 48.2 and finished the first day with 4,529, a lead of 119 points in spite of his mediocre field performances.

The second day, Monday, was cool, and the track was heavy from an overnight rain. Johnson ran a disappointing 14.9 to Kuznetsov's 15.1.

Johnson threw the discus 160′ 11¼″ and gained a little more, but now he had to hold Kuznetsov in his strong events. Typically, Johnson came through with his best decathlon pole vault, 12′ 11½″, only two inches lower than Kuznetsov.

After two throws of the javelin, Johnson's best mark was under 205 feet while Kuznetsov had one of 214′ 6½″, bringing him within striking distance. Johnson could recapture the world record by running 1,500 meters in 5:05, but Kuznetsov could break it by running 4:47.4.

It seemed easier to improve his javelin mark. Johnson concentrated hard as he ran down the runway and whipped the javelin into the air. A mass exclamation of awe sounded from 30,000 people. The javelin was amazingly high in the air when it passed Kuznetsov's marker.

Johnson's throw was 238′ 2″. The world record was his again, even before the 1,500 meters. He disliked the 1,500, but now, with every second worth five or six points, he tried fairly hard. His 5 :05 picked up 225 points. His second-day total of 3,773 was the highest ever scored.

His total was 8,302 points, even though half his marks had been mediocre, for him. Kuznetsov kissed him on both cheeks. He was given a bouquet of flowers, and the Russians tossed him in the air while the crowd applauded. *Sports Illustrated* named him 'Sportsman of the Year'.

He had finished his college competition, although he was still at UCLA, and 1959 was a bad year. Leg trouble kept him out of the running and jumping events, although he raised his discus record to 171' 7½" and threw the javelin 240' 7". Once again Kuznetsov took the decathlon record away from him, by 55 points. Worst of all, his season was cut short just before graduation by a serious back injury in a head-on auto accident.

It was now obvious that only injuries were keeping him from being the greatest all around athlete of all time, but the winter of 1959–60 was one of suspense and despair.

He could not so much as jog until February of 1960. Then he spent two months of torturous conditioning. He walked and jogged as long as six hours a day. Not until April did he try sprint starts. When he first tried to broad jump, in June, he and Coach 'Ducky' Drake were as tense as bomb disposal men expecting that fatal explosion. When Johnson landed without strain, he began to hope again for his gold medal.

He had his best discus throw, 172' 3", and he ran the hurdles in an encouraging 14.1. He won the javelin at the California Relays with 249' 10", and at Compton with 251' 9½". His excellent throwing fell off in the AAU to a sixth-place 233' 1", and he placed only seventh in the Final Trials with 240 feet.

But to him, the only important event was the AAU and Final Trials decathlon held at Eugene, Oregon, July 8 and 9. He was threatened by Yang, the great Chinese, now a UCLA student who trained with Johnson.

Johnson began with his old familiar 10.6. In the broad jump, off a helpful board runway, he jumped 24' 9" and had a foul well over 25 feet. He put the shot 52 feet, his best in a decathlon, but he cleared only 5' 10" in the high jump. In the 400, he started too slowly and his frenetic sprint finish made it only 48.6.

His total was 4,750, better than any other first-day score, but he led Yang by only 195 points and Yang was dangerous in the hurdles, vault, and javelin.

Johnson ran over the high hurdles in 14.5, but Yang set the 4,500 spectators buzzing with his 14.1. Johnson was now only 62 points ahead.

Johnson needed a come-through, and so he spun the discus 170′ 6″. 'That really gave me confidence.'

Next, he raised his personal record in the vault to 13′ $\frac{1}{4}$″ and moved to the javelin runway. 'I worked hard all last week, and I knew I'd have to put everything into my first throw.'

He sent the silver javelin into the air and stopped his forward momentum as he watched it land far out on the turf. The crowd cheered. Delighted, he broke into a run toward his javelin. Then he stopped and knelt on one knee and offered thanks, his face wet with tears. The announcer verified the distance – 233′ 3″ – and once more the world record was his.

When he ran 1,500 meters in 5 :09.9, his total rose to 8,683, a startling 300 points over the world record. Added to his best-ever first-day total was a second-day score of 3,933, also the best ever made.

Then he encouraged Yang in his heat and supported his tired team-mate after it was over. Yang had scored 8,426, also over Kuznetsov's record.

Admiring Johnson, Oregon coach Bill Bowerman said, 'I don't think anyone doubts for a minute that Rafer Johnson is the best athlete in the world.'

At Bern, Switzerland, land of fast hurdle times, Johnson ran 13.9 behind Calhoun's world record 13.2. On August 30 he had the honor of carrying the American flag in the opening ceremony of the Olympic Games.

The Olympic decathlon at Rome included the five highest scorers of all time, with Dave Edstrom's 8,176 fourth, and Yuriy Kutyenko's 7,989 fifth. Johnson's analysis : 'I'm prepared to win, whatever that takes.' Even the jinx of having his picture on the cover of *Time* magazine did not worry him.

Competition began at 9 :00 a.m. on September 5 in the flag-decked stadium in Rome. Running in the fourth heat of the 100 meters on the red track, Johnson had to start four times. On the third false start, he ran 40 meters at full speed before the recall gun stopped him. With this handicap, he ran only 10.9, 132 points worse than his usual 10.6.

Jumping into a headwind, Johnson reached only 23′ 7¾″ on his first trial, to 24′ 5¾″ for Yang. Johnson jumped only 22′ 8½″ on his second. Alarmed, he powered his 196 pounds out to 24′ 1¼″.

Competition resumed after lunch, at 3:00 p.m. Johnson's first put thudded down only 47′ 8¾″ away. Exasperated with himself, he exploded to 51′ 10¾″. He gained 273 points in Yang's weak event. Now he had a lead of 143 points. Edstrom dropped out with a groin injury, and the two Russians were obviously not at their best. It was a battle between the two UCLA men.

At 5:45, during the high jump, Johnson and all the others received another bad break.. The clouds burst open above the stadium with a downpour which surely set an Olympic record. All competition stopped and everybody scurried for cover. The athletes waited, cooling off physically and mentally, while the downpour lasted an hour and 20 minutes. So remarkable was the drainage system, however, that competition resumed 20 minutes after the rain stopped.

Johnson had to be satisfied with a high jump of 6′ ¾″, while Yang went over 6′ 2¾″. Kuznetsov made only 5′ 8¾″ and he was no longer a threat ... if Johnson could avoid injury.

Johnson received a soothing rubdown before starting the 400 at 10:50 p.m. He wanted to increase his narrow 75-point lead, and he set a stiff pace. Yang was inspired, though, and he rushed past Johnson into the last curve and built up a five-yard lead. Desperately, Johnson fought back to within four feet. His 48.3 was not his best, but it was now fourteen hours since competition began that morning.

Wearily, Johnson returned to the Olympic Village with 4,647 points, not up to his potential. He had lost four of the five events to Yang and yet, without a weakness, he led Yang by 55 points. Somebody said, 'That's what the decathlon is all about.'

'The pressure is unbelievable,' Johnson says of Olympic competition. 'It can really get to you. Some athletes tense under this sort of pressure. Others rise to it and perform even better.'

After an inadequate sleep they assembled at 9:00 a.m. for the high hurdles ... and near disaster for Johnson. Off to a good start, eager for a fast time, he hit the second hurdle with a sickening thud. A smaller man might have gone down, but Johnson crashed through and ran on, raggedly. 'I lost rhythm completely, same as at Melbourne.'

The big danger, especially to a hurdler who had not been able to practice much in four years, was the possibility of being so far off stride that he could not clear the next hurdle. Somehow, he regained his stride but not his speed. His time was a shocking 15.3.

Now Johnson was in a desperate situation. Instead of leading Yang by 62 points as in his world record at Eugene, he was 138 points behind – a total of 200 points worse.

When his discus throw sailed only 146' 1½" he knew defeat was more than possible. He came back with 158' 3" and 159' 1", but he was 11 feet shorter than in his great world record performance. Still, he gained 272 points on Yang and took a lead of 144. (At Eugene he had led by a comfortable 402 after seven events and he won by only 257.)

They began vaulting at 2:30, with Yang in good position to become the Olympic champion because he could vault a foot higher than Johnson. After all these years the gold medal was slipping away.

But Rafer Johnson was a great one. He simply vaulted higher than ever before. His 13' 5¼" lost to Yang by eight inches and he still had a perilous 22-point lead.

He had said, 'I hope it's all wrapped up before the 1,500 meters. I never want to settle one in that thing.'

But Yang was a fine javelin thrower. At Eugene they had both reached 233 feet. If Johnson allowed that to happen again, it would be settled in the 1,500, and Yang would win.

They had to use the yellow Seefab javelin, unfamiliar to them. Johnson, with a best of 251' 9½", suffered the most loss, but his first throw stuck in the turf at 228' 10½". Yang threw 223' 9½" on his second throw. Johnson did not improve, and he watched tensely on Yang's last throw.

Yang did not improve, but Johnson had a lead of only 67 points. He had to stay within ten seconds of Yang to win. Yang had run 4:36.9, 17.3 seconds faster than Johnson's best. And Johnson's best had been forced out of him at Melbourne when he went all out to retain second place.

At 9:20 p.m. the tension rose as they started the last heat

together. Up in the stands, their coach, 'Ducky' Drake, was asked how it would come out. He could only praise Johnson's courage.

And that was what Johnson needed now. Doggedly, he followed Yang at a pace he had never run before. He held on, with all his strength and courage and pride. Into the homestretch he was still on Yang's heels. 'I wavered in the stretch.' He finished six yards behind, losing only nine points with a time of 4 :49.7, by far his best ever.

He won the gold medal he wanted so much by 58 points, with a score of 8,392. In the locker room, he was mobbed while Yang sat alone and wept. Yang had made a glorious effort, but Rafer Johnson was not to be beaten. Yang struggled to his feet and clasped Johnson's hand. 'Nice going, Rafe.'

Johnson said, 'Tonight I'm going to shower and then just walk for about four hours and look at the moon. I don't know where – just walk, walk, walk. I've got to unwind. I'm through, man. I'm through.'

He was voted Track & Field Athlete of the Year, and he won the Sullivan Award. No athlete has been more deserving, for in addition to his unsurpassed achievements in track, he has led a life of service to humanity. (His goal : 'Eventually, I'd like to work for the state department'). The Reverend Louis Evans said of him : 'This is a most remarkable human being.'

Certainly he was a most remarkable athlete. Although handicapped by injuries throughout most of his career his achievements in a wide range of events bordered on the fantastic :

Sprints – 10.5 for 100 meters and 21 flat for 220 yards. He came within one inch of victory in the Pacific Coast Conference 100 yard championship. In an 880 relay, he ran surprisingly close to international sprinters with a 20.7 leg.

440 – He ran 47.9 for 400 meters in a decathlon and ran a 440 relay leg in 46.9.

High hurdles – he was a rousing second in the NCAA behind eventual Olympic champion Lee Calhoun with a time of 13.8, truly outstanding against the wind. He was No. 6 in World Ranking in 1956, his one year of hurdling.

Low hurdles – in 1956 he ran under 23 flat five times, won at Compton, and placed second in the AAU. His 22.7 was the fastest time in the world.

Broad jump – in his one year before injuries stopped him, he bettered 25 feet five times. He placed second in the NCAA, was successful in making the Olympic team, and ranked sixth in the world.

Shot put – his 54′ 11½″ put him among the twenty best on the 1958 U.S. list.

Discus – he threw 170′ 9½″ in 1958 as part of the greatest weight triple of all time, and he made the U.S. top ten. He threw 172′ 3″ in 1960.

Javelin – his victories included the 1958 West Coast Relays (238′ 11″) and Pacific Coast Conference (243′ 10½″), and the 1960 Mt. San Antonio Relays (236′ 11″), California Relays 249′ 10″), and Compton Invitational (251′ 9½″).

Decathlon – after losing in the national AAU as a high school boy in 1954, he triumphed in all except one other decathlon out of a total of 11. His 'failure' came in the 1956 Olympics while badly injured. He surpassed Mathias's world record at the age of 19, and he raised the record twice more.

One track enthusiast summed it up when he said simply, 'No other man ever had the all around ability of Rafer Johnson.'

Russian head coach Gabriel Korobkov said, 'America has so many great ones to choose from, but I think Rafer Johnson was the best I've seen.'

9 DAVIS

Great champions are a special breed. The proof of their greatness is in rising to new heights in the face of ruthless competition, and rare is the man who does it consistently.

Such a rare man was Glenn Davis.

His first significant test was witnessed by 34,000 enthusiasts in the Los Angeles Coliseum, on the warm evening of June 29, 1956. This meet to choose the U.S. Olympic team was the greatest track and field meet yet contested, and Glenn Davis was up against the fastest 400 meter hurdlers ever assembled in one race.

Davis, a muscular six-footer wearing the red and gray of Ohio State University, had raced a full circuit of the track while leaping over ten dangerous hurdles for the first time only two months before. Until his name appeared in headlines three weeks before this meet, he had never aroused interest as a possible Olympian.

As a high school boy he liked to compete, and in 1954, despite a brace for his dislocated shoulder, he sped victoriously down the track in 9.9 seconds for 100 yards and 21.1 for 220. He chopped pugnaciously over the high school hurdles in 14.7 and 19.1. He flung his body over a crossbar six feet above the ground. He landed in a sand pit an exhilarating 23' 6" beyond the white takeoff board. He caused a sensation by winning the Ohio State meet all by himself, but his best 440 time was only 52 flat and he received more acclaim as an all-state football player.

As a freshman, in 1955, he was more concerned with his books than track, but in the early 1956 season Davis swarmed eagerly over the track and field for Ohio State. He stopped the watches at 9.7 and a fine 20.9 in the sprints, and 23.3 in the 220 yard low hurdles. He ran his first intermediate hurdles in an unpromising 54.4. Six days later, on April 27, at Franklin Field in Philadelphia, he won at the famed Penn Relays in 52.3. He spent most of May running in dual meets, and in the Big Ten meet

107

on May 26 he flashed around a curve full of low hurdles in 23.5 to equal a conference record good enough to last twenty-three years. He also earned thirds in the 220 and long jump and fourth in the hundred.

He did not excite international interest, however, until the Central Collegiate meet on June 9 in the hot, humid climate of Milwaukee, Wisconsin. He barely reached the safety of the tape ahead of another sophomore, Aubrey Lewis of Notre Dame. Davis's 50.8 was impressive as the fifth fastest ever, only four tenths off the world record, and both sophomores became exciting prospects in that Olympic year.

A week later, on the grey track at Berkeley for the National Collegiate championships, Lewis caught Davis off stride at the last hurdle and beat him by three yards in 51 flat. Six days after that disappointing 51.5, Davis showed another flash of potential might by winning the AAU in 50.9 with Lewis absent.

Now, in the Final Trials, he was cautious while taking his marks in the sixth lane. Lewis had hit the last hurdle in his heat and was out of the final, but this only intensified Davis's awareness of the hazards of those three-foot hurdles. He, himself had lost the NCAA race at that last hurdle and he knew the danger.

Eddie Southern was to his left in lane five. Southern, only eighteen, had frightening talent. In lane seven was Josh Culbreath, the amazing little Negro marine who had never lost a race until this year when he began his training late. Culbreath had won the AAU three years in a row, plus the Pan American title in 1955.

As the gun sounded, Davis was off his blocks fast, hurdling left leg first. At the third hurdle he saw Southern's dark hair and white shirt already even with him. Startled, he increased his speed, but the young Texan gained another yard around the last curve. To an apprehensive Davis it seemed as if Southern was the one touched with greatness.

But Davis had that special desire champions use to tap an extra reserve of strength. He dug desperately into this reserve, running not smoothly but with great power, and he began to gain precious inches on the white shirt. Into the homestretch he was still two yards behind, and he was reduced to seventeen strides between hurdles.

At the last hurdle his superior power pulled him even. Southern was running hard, far faster than any previous runner in history, but Davis crushed him in the last 40 yards. As he hit the white yarn five feet in front, he was smiling.

When the announcement came, the crowd roared with amazement. Davis wiped his eyes, hung his head, and smiled. He had run 49.5, almost a second under the world record. The stamp of greatness was on him.

Five months ahead, in Melbourne, were the Olympics – the Holy Grail of track athletes. Davis wanted to keep in shape, but an Achilles tendon injury slowed him ominously. In the first meet after the team assembled in Berkeley, six weeks before the Olympics, Davis limped a pitiful 54.2, almost out of sight behind Culbreath's 51 flat.

A week later in Ontario, California, Davis barely won by the width of his chest in 51.1, and the following week he ran only 51.9. In the final tune-up meet, he lost to Culbreath by three yards, tying up dismally in 52.1.

In Melbourne, his legs sore and tight, Davis expected serious competition from Southern and Culbreath, plus impressive Yuriy Lituyev, an undefeated Russian who had equalled the pre-Davis world record.

Davis breezed through his heat in 51.3, but Culbreath looked formidable in 50.9. In the semi-finals, early the next afternoon, Southern struck fear into Davis with a strong 50.1 while Davis had to struggle to finish second in 50.7. Culbreath seemed perilously effortless in winning the second semi in 50.9.

Two and one half hours later they were on the track again, with the tension mounting, before 100,000 in the round, three-tiered stadium of the Melbourne Cricket Grounds. Davis felt nervous in lane four, between the all-green of South African Gerhardus Potgieter and the red-shirted Lituyev.

Afraid of Southern, Davis started too fast, and he had to chop his stride at the second hurdle, but fear made him hurry and he was only two yards behind Southern over the fifth hurdle. Then he gave the cheering crowd a glimpse of his stunning power. While the others were struggling to run as fast as in the earlier semi-finals and all except Lituyev were failing, Davis used his remarkable reserve.

He ran scared until the eighth hurdle. With a small lead over

Southern, he kept driving his powerful legs in a frenzy. He led by two yards at the ninth hurdle, by three at the tenth, and he hit the tape an impressive five yards ahead in 50.1.

In his first year as an intermediate hurdler he could take pride in being both the world record holder and Olympic champion. When he crossed the line he looked toward the sky and said, 'Thanks.'

After such a year, 1957 was a great disappointment. He competed in five to seven events in each indoor meet, but a bad case of bursitis in his left thigh bothered him all spring, and he could not run in the National Collegiate championships because Ohio State had been banned for overzealous recruiting.

By such misfortune he was limited to two major meets. On June 8, at the Meet of Champions in Houston, Texas, he triumphed in his first important 440 yard race, reaching the tape ahead of Southern in 46.8. Then he hurried over the low hurdles in 22.7. His times in that admirable double were fifth and sixth fastest in the world for 1957.

In the AAU championships, held in Dayton, Ohio, Davis wanted to defend his championship, but he had not practiced since the Olympics and he missed his step shockingly in his heat.

In the final, he was yards behind Culbreath on the poorly lighted backstretch, but once again his desire pulled him through. A foot behind at the last hurdle, he hit the tape 2½ yards ahead in typical all-out effort, head twisted high to the right. His 50.9 was a new American record for 440 yards, and he was honored as first in World Ranking again.

The next night, on a dark straightaway, he finished his competition for the year with a close fifth place in the low hurdles against the fastest field ever assembled. He was still troubled with bursitis in his leg when the 1958 indoor season began, but he wanted to compete in every event possible. In one dual meet, he took only one high jump, and cleared 6' 2", tying for second. He also achieved enough in the long jump to rank eighth in Indoor Ranking for 1958.

But his main triumphs came in the hurdles. Running from one event to another, he managed to win enough hurdle races to rank third in Indoor Ranking in 1958. On March 21, Davis met the celebrated Hayes Jones in the 50-yard hurdles at the Cleveland K.C. Games. Jones was a 13.7 hurdler, destined to be best in the world for 1958, but Davis's big chest hit the tape first in an amazing 6.1 victory.

Then, outdoors at the Quantico Relays on April 11 and 12, after winning the 440 hurdles and long jump on Friday, Davis met Elias Gilbert in the highs on Saturday. Gilbert had run a fantastic 13.4 at Compton last year, but Davis beat him in 14.3.

He lost races to both Jones and Gilbert later, but now he was interested in converting to the 440 flat race, and on May 14, in a dual meet with Ohio Wesleyan, he circled the track in collegiate record time of 46.1, completing a fine double with a 21-flat 220. In the Big Ten meet at Lafayette, Indiana, on May 24, he ran a sensational 440 against the speedy West Indian, George Kerr, and he stopped the watches on the world record time of 45.8.

The National Collegiates did not schedule the intermediate hurdles then, and so Davis sought his first NCAA championship in the 440. In the meet at Berkeley he was up against Eddie Southern, who was undefeated with a pair of 45.9 times to his credit.

Taking his blocks, Davis worried about Southern once more and he knew he must run his best to win. In lane eight, he could not see his opponents, and so he ran in blindness and suspense, reaching the 220 in 22 flat. Around the last turn he ran powerfully but as they rounded into the homestretch he was dismayed to see Southern's black hair to his left. For a moment the issue was in doubt, but then he began a powerful drive which all but destroyed Southern. Davis's red-clad barrel chest reached the tape five yards ahead in world record time of 45.7.

Later, Davis said, 'I had a lot left.'

Someone asked Southern, 'Have you ever tied up like that before?' His grim answer was, 'Yes ... the last time I ran against Glenn Davis.'

In the AAU meet in the hot California valley city of Bakersfield, six days later, Davis left the 440 to Southern, who won in 45.8. Davis wanted to run the intermediates against Josh Culbreath, the world record holder, and he ran with the marvelous power of a panther. He led Culbreath by four yards into the homestretch and he won by five yards in 49.9, his third world record.

The next night, a confident Davis took on the world's best 220 runners. He won his heat and semi-final, both in 21.4, but before the final he asked coach Larry Snyder, 'Do you think those guys are as tired as I am?'

Davis sped around the curve and finished powerfully, as usual, only two yards behind Bobby Morrow, then the world's most acclaimed sprinter. Davis's second place beat out such favored sprinters as Ed Collymore and Ray Norton, who had finished one-two in the previous week's NCAA and who were good enough to rank third and fourth in the world for 1958. Davis ranked seventh. If you add a surprising 100 meters he ran later in 10.3, you can make an interesting case for Davis as a world class sprinter.

In truly astonishing condition, Davis went to Europe for a series of triumphs which proved his greatness beyond all doubt. After some comfortable warm-up races came three weeks of the most sensational 400 meter running ever seen, with and without hurdles.

At Oslo on July 17, Davis raced around 200 meters in 21.1 and over the 400 hurdles in 49.8. Not content, the next day he ran his 10.3 100 meters and a 45.6 400 meters, and the excited Norwegians made him jog a lap of honor.

In the dual meet against Russia, Davis impressed the Moscow crowd with 45.6 and 50.4 on a wet track. At Warsaw, Davis flashed across the line a full second ahead of Southern in a stirring 45.5, second fastest 400 ever run. The next day he hurried around the track twice more, over the hurdles in 49.8 and on a 45.1 relay leg.

He completed his glorious string on August 5 and 6 at Budapest in the meet with Hungary. The first day he squished around a disappointingly wet track in 45.6 and commented, 'If it had been dry, I think I could have clocked a time of 45.2.' Even so, he could smile with pride at having run seven of the thirteen fastest 400–440 races ever run.

The next night, in the hurdles, a determined Davis started like a sprinter, but he was thwarted by hitting the last hurdle and he lost valuable yards. Still, the watches showed 49.2, three tenths under his own world record, and he grinned about his third record of the year.

He lost a slow, careless 400 to Southern on the sharp-cornered track in Athens for his only 400–440 loss of the year. He was paid homage as first in World Ranking for that event, plus the intermediate hurdles, an unprecedented honor. Add his seventh in the 200, his tie for seventh on the 100 meter list, and his early triumphs over Hayes Jones and Elias Gilbert in the high hurdles, and it was a gratifying year of unparalleled achievement in quantity, quality, and versatility.

The 1959 season, however, was a disaster for Davis. A chronic back injury hurt him and his doctor cut his season short. Running in the AAU at Boulder, Colorado, Davis missed his step miserably over the first four hurdles. He pulled up within a tantalizing yard of Dickie Howard with 20 yards to go but his effort had depleted his entire reserve and he lost in 50.9 to Howard's 50.7. It was his first loss in his specialty in three years, but even in such deplorable condition he ranked fourth in World Ranking for 400 meters and sixth for the hurdles.

Now a school teacher, Davis began 1960 in poor condition. In three frustrating 440 races he saw a different runner finish ahead of him each time. Then he began to run himself into shape. In the Coliseum Relays he edged his barrel chest ahead of Howard in 51 flat, and he beat him by two yards in 50.3 at the Meet of Champions. In the AAU at Bakersfield, he needed his rousing finish to beat Howard by five feet in 50.1.

A week later, July 1, at Stanford, California, Davis took his blocks for the Final Olympic Trials, his most important race since the 1956 Olympics. He was in the slow curb lane, threatened by the fastest field of hurdlers of all time. Once again it was a test of true greatness.

He ran satisfactorily around the curve and down the backstretch, but others were ahead of him. Not until the 8th hurdle was he within striking distance of Southern. Resolutely, Davis began his powerful drive and nobody could resist him. He hit the tape in 49.5 while a shocked Southern ran 49.9 and lost to Davis, Howard, and young Clif Cushman.

In significant tune-up meets before the Olympics, he outpowered future Olympic 400 meter champion Otis Davis in two out of three races, including a notable 45.5. He was ranked fifth in the 400 meters for 1960. Then, at Bern, Switzerland, in chilly twilight, he raced furiously around a curve to equal the official record of 22.5 for the 200 meter low hurdles. The next night he won the intermediates in 49.7. He was ready for the Olympic test.

On September 2, in Rome, Glenn Davis walked uneasily through the dark tunnel from the warm-up track in the Marble Stadium into the bright sunlight of Stadio Olimpico. Proudly wearing the deep blue of the U.S.A., Davis was the sixth runner in single file, marched in by gray-clad officials like doomed gladiators in ancient Roman times.

Davis was fearful. He knew the possibilities of losing and it was on his mind when he knelt on his blocks in lane six. The orange-coated starter raised one of his two pistols and called, 'Via.' Davis rose to the set position. Then the gun sounded and he was running wildly, afraid of what might happen in this last and greatest test.

He led over the first hurdle but in his tension he was overstriding and he missed his step at the second, losing precious yardage. To his dismay, he could not regain his step, and after the fifth barrier his worry increased. Then, with the poise of a true champion, he regained his step.

He had to drive hard, but he gained satisfactorily on the curve, and he moved to second place in the homestretch. At the last hurdle he caught Howard. Only then did he feel confident. His powerful legs pounded viciously down at the track and he won by almost three yards in 49.3.

On the victory stand, between Howard and silver-medalist Cushman, a jubilant Davis received his second Olympic gold medal from the 1928 champion, David Burghley, Marquis of Exeter. They turned and watched with feeling as three American flags ran up the poles behind the Olympic torch. A happy group of Americans in the crowd sang their national anthem and Davis nudged his teammates and they smiled and waved. Davis said, 'This is a greater thrill than winning at Melbourne.'

Davis's track glory was almost ended, for he signed a professional football contract the next month, but he had still to run the third leg on U.S.A.'s 1,600 meter relay team. He took the baton barely ahead of Germany's dangerous team and then waited coolly until the homestretch before turning on his power. In the stretch he gained four precious yards, exactly the winning margin, and he collected his third gold medal and fifth world record as the U.S. team ran 3 :02.2.

In his remarkable career, Davis lost only four out of forty intermediate hurdle races. One loss came in those uncertain first two months, and the other three when he was out of condition – two of them in unimportant races. When his career ended he had to his credit six of the nine fastest intermediate times ever run. He bettered 49.9 ten times. No man has ever had such a superb record in this event, and few, if any, have proved such astonishing versatility on the track. Above all else was his rare ability to win.

The highest possible tribute came from Larry Snyder of Ohio State, who coached them both : 'Glenn Davis is possibly a greater talent than Jesse Owens.'

10 OERTER

Among the people who like track and field athletics, an argument rages: Which is more desirable, a world record or an Olympic gold medal?

One athlete who favors the gold medal is Al Oerter.

Breaking a world record, he says, is like 'trying to catch leaves'. Records fall unexpectedly, to discus throwers who happen to be at the right 'wind alley' at the right time. But when Oerter talks about the Olympic Games his green eyes light up with a glow unusual in this big, shy man.

'The Olympics are unique, a world community... what men have been trying to achieve for centuries. There is no job, no amount of power, no money to approach the meaning of the Olympic experience. It's unfortunate they only happen once every four years. They are so special....'

Al Oerter is two men in one. He is the solid citizen who does a difficult job well, who loves his wife and two daughters, and whose values are the kind the world needs. On the other hand, he is a soaring, creative, competitive genius, the like of whom has seldom been seen at any time, or any place, in any sport.

The remarkable story of Al Oerter's experiences at the Olympic Games breaks down neatly into four acts.

ACT I, 1956: The scene was the Melbourne Cricket Grounds on Tuesday, November 27. The curious shape of the round field left huge half-moons of grass on either side of the track, and the triple-decked stands, built piecemeal at various periods in the past, were filled with 100,000 enthusiastic Australians.

Young Al Oerter was nervous. Barely 20 years old, the 6' 3½", 220-pounder with a bushy blond crew-cut hoped for an Olympic medal, but his competition was strong and he was so tense that failure would be only natural. Sitting on the bench or keeping limber, he watched his opponents.

116

First, he watched Adolfo Consolini of Italy who was Olympic champion in 1948, long before Oerter wanted to throw the discus. Consolini was second in 1952, the year of Oerter's first interest in the high school discus. Now thirty-nine Consolini had a fine practice throw of 194 feet a few days before, but a cut on his index finger threatened to hamper him. His first throw went only 170' 4".

Next, Oerter watched dependable Ferenc Klics of Hungary, thirty-two years old and fifth in the last two Olympics. The discus throw is a good event for older athletes, and young Oerter knew he had a lot of improvement ahead of him. He watched Klics throw 169' 9"

Next, Oerter feared Gordien. Fortune Gordien, thirty-four, was bronze medalist in 1948 and fourth in 1952. He broke the world record in 1949 and raised it to 194' 6" in 1953, a year when Oerter could manage only 153 feet with the high school discus. In 1954, Oerter set a high school record of 184' 2¾", but Gordien surpassed that by eight feet with the heavier discus.

In 1955, while Oerter threw the heavy discus to a freshman record 171' 6" in a postal meet, Gordien let down to 180' 11". But this year Gordien was coming back strong. He threw a frightening 198 feet in practice at the Olympic Village and Oerter did not expect to beat him even when Gordien's first throw sailed only 179' 7½".

The important thing was to throw his best. His previous best, at the moment when he stripped off his blue USA sweat suit and stepped onto the concrete circle, was 183' 5", made with the help of a wind. After that he was only fourth in the NCAA and an unpromising sixth in the AAU. But he had made the team with 178' 7½" and he had four throws over 180 feet in tune-up meets, and he had a chance for a medal if he did not tie up.

'Everything built up inside me. I really was keyed up and inspired.'

He looked out toward the flag marking the Olympic record of 180' 6½". Then, carefully, he went into his windup, spun powerfully, and sailed the discus up the center.

That was a moment to remember. Nervous and inexperienced as he was, he came through with a personal record of 184' 10½", a new Olympic record. About 100,000 people roared approval.

117

'I don't know how I did it. Somehow or other everything just went right and this throw came out.'

Now he was even more tense. 'I had a hard time even raising my arm after that.' Still, he managed two more throws over 180 feet.

All he could do was watch Gordien. None of the others came close, but Gordien was always a threat. 'Naturally, I kept my fingers crossed. I was always afraid Fortune would beat me. I knew he could.'

Gordien's last throw made Oerter hold his breath, but it slapped down at 179′ 9½″. Oerter, aged 20, was the Olympic champion. The three Americans threw their arms around each other and they stood on the victory stand and watched their flags and heard their music. Oerter liked it. Quietly, he started thinking about 1960.

FIRST INTERMISSION: In 1957, Oerter showed unsatisfactory improvement. He was badly beaten in the Coliseum Relays and the Compton Invitational, and he had only one throw beyond the 180-foot line prior to the esteemed NCAA meet. Characteristically, he came through as collegiate champion with his longest throw yet – 185′ 4″. The next week, in Dayton, Ohio, he threw 181′ 6″ to win his first AAU victory. Then he lost four times in Europe and ranked only fourth for the year in the world rankings.

1958 was not much better. After Rink Babka shocked discus throwers everywhere with a throw over 200 feet on March 22 only to have it ruled invalid because it landed in a ditch, Oerter threw 202′ 6″ into a good Arkansas wind on April 5, but a slope of 2½% ruined his chance for a record.

Oerter raised his personal record by 3½″ at the Drake Relays and to 188′ 2″ at the Central Collegiates. In the NCAA, his good 186′ 2″ was tied by Babka, who beat him soundly for the AAU title a week later. Oerter lost to Babka a second time in Moscow in late July, and he ranked second in the world.

Oerter was a promising shot putter, too, with a best mark of 56′ 11″ in 1959, when only four men were over 60 feet. He renounced the shot because the lateral hip shift confused his training for the hip twist in the discus.

In 1959, Oerter was out of college, working for Grunman Aircraft in data processing. Most athletes are unable to handle the pressures of job and family in addition to training, and so they surrender their chance for success, but Oerter was well organized. He alternated weight training with throwing practice, and he competed in only a few meets, but he improved noticeably.

He won the AAU at 186′ 5″, raised his personal record to 188′ 9″ against the Soviets in Philadelphia. He improved again, to 190′ 8½″, in his Pan American Games victory at Chicago. He was first in World Ranking for 1959.

ACT II, 1960 : The scene, on September 7, was Rome's beautiful, flag-rimmed Stadio Olimpico with its background of hills and monuments. Oerter had a good season behind him with most meets over 190 feet and a new personal record of 194′ 1½″, but he was afraid.

The reason for Oerter's fear was big Rink Babka, now weighing 267 pounds, with an awesome practice throw over 200 fee. Babka had given Oerter his first downfall in two seasons at the Final Trials in Palo Alto. And on August 12, Babka had sailed the platter to an impressive record of 196′ 6½″.

Oerter had made an exciting warmup throw around 198 feet the day before, and then he qualified easily with an Olympic record of 191′ 8″, but none of that counted. Only the gold medal counted and Babka threw 190′ 4″ on his first attempt.

Oerter stepped onto the concrete circle determined to win it right away. As he spun, his foot slipped and his plan failed. Even so, his throw went 189′ 1″. On his second throw, he reached only 186′ 1½″, and his tension grew. Babka, too, failed to improve and nobody else had a chance. Oerter threw only 185′ 5½″ and he became more nervous. His fourth throw landed at 186′ 1½″ again.

'I was so tense I could barely throw.'

He entered the ring for his fifth throw. All his hopes and dreams were going for naught unless he could control his tension. A champion must, most of all, control himself when the pressure is on. He had done it in 1956, and now it was necessary again.

He spun slowly, carefully, powerfully. His hip came around first, then his body untwisted ahead of the discus. Last came his hand, whipping the discus around violently and spinning it off into space. It rode high and kept sailing, floating down reluctantly. It bit into the turf 194′ 2″ away.

Once again he had come through with a personal record where

it counted most. And after Babka's threat ended, Oerter mounted the top step of the victory stand again.

INTERMISSION : Oerter had another good throw, 194′ ½″, against the British Commonwealth in London, September 14. Then, true to his philosophy, he became semi-retired in 1961. He threw the steel-rimmed platter in only four meets. His best mark of 190′ 5½″ came, typically, in the AAU meet, but he lost to Jay Silvester.

Silvester raised the world record to 199′ 2½″ on August 20, 1961. Not satisfied with himself, Oerter worked harder on his strength and built his weight up to 250 pounds for the 1962 season. He began with his best ever throw, 198′ 6″, at the Mt. San Antonio Relays.

In the Los Angeles Coliseum Relays, throwing at night under bright floodlights, Oerter set out to better 200 feet. On his second throw he sailed the discus 198′ 7½″ for a personal record, but he was still dissatisfied.

On his fourth throw, 'The ring was so slippery I nearly fell,' but the discus hit the green turf 200′ 5½″ away, first official throw over the glamorous 200-foot mark.

Asked to compare this world record with his Olympic championship, Oerter answered in the glow of the moment, 'This is more satisfying because it was so long in coming.'

Seventeen days later, he lost his world record to Russian Vladimir Trusenyov's unexpected 202′ 2½″. Seventeen days after that, in the AAU meet at Walnut, California, June 23, Oerter put on the greatest exhibition of throwing to date. His first throw sailed 200′ 3½″. His worst was 195′ 5″. His best was 202′ 2″, only half an inch short of the world record.

On July 1, Oerter was supposed to compete against Poland in Chicago, but on Monday he strained a muscle lifting weights. He tried diathermy treatments and on Saturday he flew to Chicago, determined to compete against former world record holder Edmund Piatkowski, undefeated since 1960.

Oerter's second throw spun through the air for a long time and when he saw it land he raced after it to watch the measurement. It was 204′ 10½″, a world record.

'I had to get it early because I didn't feel strong. I really didn't expect to do it. The wind wasn't really the way I like it.'

Three weeks later, at Stanford University's huge bowl, a crowd of 81,000 watched the dual meet with Russia. Oerter was up against Babka and the only other 200-footer, Trusenyov.

Oerter threw 199′ 8½″ on his first throw, and he won overwhelmingly, with a best of 200′ 1″. He now had made five of the six throws in history over 200 feet. Undefeated, he was an easy choice as first in the world for the year.

In 1963, his first meet was the Mt. San Antonio Relays in Walnut, April 27. He said : 'Because of my job I got a late start getting into condition. I planned it that way because I didn't want to be burned out and stale for next year. I have been working out off and on since January. Mostly off. Only the last two weeks did I get down to some serious work. I still am not in top condition.'

In such deplorable condition it is small wonder he failed to better 200 feet on one throw. His series was incomparable : 201′ 5″, 205′ 5½″, 199′ 3½″, 204′ 1½″, 203′ 3″, and 202′ 10″. He had raised the world record a third time and increased his 200-foot throws to ten.

'I was the most surprised man at the Mt. San Antonio Relays. I'm not in very good shape.'

Jay Silvester became a strong threat, with a warmup toss of 215 feet and a foul of 207 feet, but Oerter came through when it counted. 'The more you strain, the less distance. It has to be a very relaxed type of motion.'

Silvester said, 'When you throw against Oerter, you don't expect to win. You just hope.'

Nevertheless, Oerter beat Silvester by an insecure foot with 202′ 11″ in the California Relays, and his 202′ 8½″ lost to Silvester's 204′ 4″ at Compton. But Oerter was suffering from a slipped disc and he could not enter the AAU meet. Every throw caused a pain to shoot down his left arm.

Back at the Mt. San Antonio Relays in 1964, Oerter was not at his best but a wind, strong enough to force him to throw wearing a ski jacket, held his discus up for the two longest throws of all time. His first sailed 206′ 6″ and his sixth was 206′ 4″.

This was gratifying in more ways than one, for Oerter's attitude toward his sport is more amateur than most. He believes some athletes do too much training.

'Technique and strength can be maintained over prolonged periods of time with minimum effort. As I become older, it becomes more satisfying to be able to maintain a world class condition while having a wife and family and a job that's rather demanding.'

Now weighing 260 pounds, he went to the AAU meet at New Brunswick, New Jersey. He threw with a homemade brace around his neck, made with two towels and a belt. This helped stop a whiplash action of his head, which pinched a nerve and hurt in his left arm. His first throw was a winning 201' 1½" and he had two others over 200'.

The next week he insured his place on the Olympic team by winning the semi-final trials in New York with 201' 11". In spite of his neck brace, he said, 'I'm throwing better than ever.'

He won against the Soviets in Los Angeles with a throw of 200' 5½", but then things began to go wrong.

'My neck still bothers me. I tried to throw without the brace but it still hurt, so I put it back on. I'll have to live with it for awhile, I guess.'

Next, Ludwig Danek of Czechoslovakia broke Oerter's world record with an amazing throw of 211' 9½" on August 2. Then Oerter threw poorly in the Final Trials. His 193' 4" lost to Silvester.

'Honestly, I couldn't get up for this meet. There was every reason to be high, but subconsciously I didn't have it. I've always advocated the team trials should be settled in just one meet.'

ACT III, 1964 : The scene was Japan's National Stadium in Tokyo, filled with 75,000 attentive spectators and rimmed with flags of all nations. Oerter could hear a peculiar metallic rhythm as wind whipped the ropes against the tall flagpoles.

Oerter was in trouble on the concrete circle. He wore no neck brace, for the pain from that injury was nothing compared with his new problem. Six days ago he had torn some cartilages in his lower rib cage. He had to stop exercising. His ribs were heavily taped. His right side was periodically packed in ice to prevent internal hemorrhaging. Doctors told him to rest for six weeks to heal his wounds.

But to Al Oerter, the Olympic Games are too important to consider quitting. Now he spun slowly in a warmup throw. The pain cut into his side like a knife and he doubled over. 'I was thinking of dropping out.'

He only thought it, though. When his turn came, he was in the circle, trying for his third gold medal. He spun around and let go, grimacing with pain. 'It felt like somebody was trying to tear out my ribs.'

The discus went only 189' 1½''. Danek, the tall, lean record holder, threw 195' 11½''. Oerter's second throw hurt again and he improved only to 191' 5'' while big Dave Weill moved ahead of him to second place with a throw of 195' 2''.

The nightmare contined, with the wounded champion spinning the discus only 180' 9½'' and 178' 4½''. Danek moved nearer to victory with 198' 6½'' on his fourth throw. Oerter watched helplessly as Silvester knocked him back into fourth place with 193' 10½'' on his fifth throw.

Of his own fifth throw, Oerter says, 'I was using a slow spin and trying to stretch the tendons to get a little higher. I had been throwing too low and I was trying a very easy turn to correct the problem. The sixth was to have been my best effort with a faster turn.'

He spun easily and lifted the back of his hand high, looking toward the sky as he whipped the discus into its whirling flight. Spectators held their breaths, watching the discus settle toward the grass. Then a mighty roar rose from the stadium. Oerter's throw was 200' 1½''. He had done it again.

A stunned Danek failed on his last throw and Oerter passed. He was still champion.

He was praised all over the track world. Coach Payton Jordan called it the gamest performance he had ever seen. Track fans noted that no man since 1908 had won the same Olympic event three times. But Oerter could throw no more. He had to rest his injuries if he expected to defend his title in 1968.

INTERMISSION : With no competition at all in 1965, Oerter built his strength up to its highest ever. In 1966, after a mediocre beginning because of rusty technique, he met Danek at the California Relays. Danek threw 205' 9'', and Oerter threw 207' 5'', a personal record. 'I'm so strong it scares me, but I'm a year away in technique.'

He won the AAU for the sixth time, threw 205' 6'' and 205' 7'' in two other meets, and ranked first in World Ranking for a sixth year.

Even with such success he gave three reasons why he expected to improve : (1) 'Slight changes in my technique, allowing for a better turn. (2) My mental attitude is better than it has ever been. (3) I am able to increase my strength each year without maintaining a severe weight training program.'

One secret of Oerter's longevity is that he enjoys throwing the discus. He considers physical conditioning important to him and to his family. 'Throwing is my recreation. I compete because I love competition.'

But in 1967 he had his worst year. He threw 203′ 6″ in one minor meet but all his others were under 200 feet and he placed a dismal fourth in the AAU. When 1968 began cheerlessly, it seemed as if time was bringing to Al Oerter, as it must to all men, a gradual extinction.

He did not believe it himself. Carefully, he prepared for October and his fourth Olympics. Before the AAU meet in Sacramento, he explained he was bringing himself along slowly. All he wanted to do here was qualify. He threw 194′ 6″ and finished nine feet behind Silvester. In the semi-final Olympic Trials in Los Angeles he was little better. He threw 197′ 10″ and lost by almost eight feet.

'I'm fairly satisfied. This was my fifth competition of the year and I figure that I am coming around. It just takes longer to get in shape now.'

Meanwhile, Silvester had broken the world record with an awesome 218′ 3½″ at Modesto, California, and had several other throws far longer than Oerter's all-time best. Four other throwers had bettered Oerter's 1966 mark of 207′ 5″, and his chances had all but disappeared.

Back home on Long Island, Oerter was getting ready. 'One of my games in track is preparing. I can't compete every week and be adequately prepared. You have three good workouts in between at most. It just isn't enough.'

He returned to California late in July, better prepared. Among the trees at the Echo Summit track, near South Lake Tahoe, on July 27, he threw 205′ 10″ to hand an unsuspecting Silvester his first defeat of the season. On August 10, at Walnut, he had five throws over 200 feet with a best of 205′ 9″, but he lost to Silvester by almost four feet.

After a disappointing third place at 196′ 4″ in Houston, Oerter went all out to win the Final Trials at Echo Summit. He threw

204′ 8″, but he lost to better throws by Silvester and Gary Carlsen.

A week later came the final blow. Silvester threw at Reno, Nevada, and raised the world record to an unreachable 224′ 5″ with a strong, favorable wind. In addition, Silvester had an over-powering series of throws, including 223′ 4″, 219′ 3″, and a foul of 230′ 5″.

But Al Oerter did not reach the peaks of true greatness by conceding defeat. He knew only one way to compete in the Olympic Games, and that way required an all-out effort, physically and mentally. He worked harder than ever, even though he said, 'I didn't think I had a chance this time.'

ACT IV, 1968 : The scene was Mexico City's Estadio Olimpico. Down the wide ramp onto the field marched the expectant discus throwers in their colorful sweatsuits. They broke ranks and each selected a discus and awaited his turn in the high green cage.

They were frustrated in their efforts to prepare for competition by a light rain. One by one, as the rain grew heavier, the competitors reluctantly took shelter under umbrellas at the edge of the field. Only Oerter continued to throw. He was beginning to gain on them.

'Once in the Olympic Village you can't improve on your strength or speed. The only thing still possible is to improve your mental attitude. In the weeks before an Olympic competition, I mentally simulate every conceivable situation for each throw. For example, I imagine I'm in eighth place, it's my fifth throw, and it's pouring rain. What do I do? An inexperienced thrower might panic or be thinking, "Gees, I hope I don't fall down." I know ahead of time what I will do under every condition.'

After twenty minutes, the concrete circle was hopelessly wet. They all retired into the warm dressing room and relaxed – except Oerter, who paced purposefully, keeping himself ready.

After another 25 minutes the unwelcome rain stopped and they were hurried into competition without a satisfactory warmup. Oerter was not wearing his neck brace nor his sweat clothes. With a towel around his shoulders, he paced back and forth like a caged tiger. His first throw went 202′ 8″, farther than any of his previous Olympic throws.

He fouled his second throw. He was now in fourth place, but

125

he knew he could do better. He had been throwing better than ever in practice. Now he needed the longest throw of his career.

He walked into the big cage, discus in one hand, towel in the other. He wiped his feet carefully and threw the towel aside. He stepped onto the pale green concrete.

'The circle was still wet from the rain, so I eliminated my preliminary warm-up swings. All that rocking back and forth upset my balance.'

He looked out toward his goal – the white sign marking Silvester's qualifying-round Olympic record of 207' 9½". He swung the discus back once, coiling for his throw. He started his spin, slowly, carefully, with great discipline and power.

He let it go, high and spinning. He recovered on his right foot and watched hopefully as the discus soared toward the dark sky. He knew it was a good throw and he watched the flying saucer hold a good flight position all the way down, past the markers of Silvester, Losch, and Milde, beyond his own best, beyond Silvester's Olympic record.

He heard the roar of joy and amazement from the crowd, and he felt a keen satisfaction. He had done it again.

He was careful to step out of the rear half of the circle. He picked up his towel and peered expectantly at the electric field board. The yellow lights appeared – 64.78. He had thrown 212' 4½", almost five feet farther than ever before.

Now the others could start worrying. Silvester, without a favorable wind, pressed too hard and fouled. Danek came through with his best throw of the year – 206' 5". Silvester continued to press and fail, and the others could not gain, but Oerter threw 204' 9½", 212' 4½", and 210' 1" – giving him the three best throws of his life.

That fourth gold medal was his.

Out of the myriad of praise for what is possibly the greatest feat in the history of the sport, came two concise explanations by coaches who know him well.

Bill Easton, Oerter's college coach, said, 'He has the most concentration of any.'

And head U.S. coach Payton Jordan said, 'He's all heart and guts.'

Or, as Silvester once said, 'He's the toughest man to beat in track and field.'

The Al Oerter story is really a drama in five acts, but the last act has not yet been written. Long ago, after his first Olympic triumph, he made what he now calls a 'silly statement' – a goal of five gold medals.

He smiles about it now, but much of the character of Al Oerter is revealed in his little comment: 'I'm 80% there.'

11 ELLIOTT

Few men are born with the natural ability of Herb Elliott. Still fewer punish themselves so hard in training. And nobody ever had a greater will to win.

The result? : A short, brilliant career as the greatest miler of all time, ending at the age of twenty-two.

Elliott's prodigious talent was in evidence from the beginning, in Perth, Western Australia. His parents valued physical fitness highly, and at an early age he liked to run, row, swim, cycle, and play football and hockey. While he was still eight, he won age-group sprint championships.

He triumphed in his first half-mile race, from handicap, at the age of ten. At fourteen, he ran his first mile, in 5 :35. He lost only once in the mile, an unfair match against a boy three years older. At fifteen, he won the state schoolboy 880 in 2 :10.4.

At sixteen, he was phenomenal. He won the junior national 880 by inches in 1 :55.7, an Australian junior record. Two days later, he crushed Ron Clarke by 20 yards in 4 :20.8, another junior record.

At seventeen, a greedy Elliott won six events in his school sports : 100 in 10.6, 220 in 23.4, 440 in 51.0, 880 in 1 :59.4, mile in 4 :22.0, and the broad jump at 19′ 7½″. One impressed witness was a skinny, tanned, white-haired man named Percy Cerutty. The famous coach told Elliott :

'There's not a shadow of a doubt that within two years you will run a mile in four minutes.'

That was in October, 1955. Later in the month, a willing Elliott won the state mile in 4 :20.4. In December, he let a piano fall on his foot, breaking two metatarsal bones, and he missed the 1955–56 season. Discouraged, he did little training and smoked thirty or forty cigarettes a day.

Then, with another great prospect about to go under, Elliott's parents took him across Australia to the Olympic Games in Mel-

Above: GLENN DAVIS Fighting for victory at Rome, Davis clears the last hurdle of his brilliant career. *Below:* The last tape in a remarkable career: Davis coasts the last stride in Stadio Olimpico – Rome, 1960

AL OERTER Watching another long one sail away, Oerter balances delicately. 'The Olympics are unique . . . They are so special'

bourne. Inspired by Vladimir Kuts in the 10,000 meters, Elliott's interest rose again. He spent three hours in Percy Cerutty's little house and the enthusiasm of the coach ingited Elliott's will to run.

They visited Cerutty's training camp at Portsea, and Elliott says: 'I took one look at glorious, God-kissed Portsea and wanted to run through the sand from sheer joy and exhilaration.' After the Olympics, Elliott joined Cerutty at Portsea and began to work.

Cerutty ran Elliott around the dirt trails through the trees and up steep sandhills until Elliott dropped. He shamed Elliott into lifting heavier weights. He force-fed Elliott his own philosophy, such as: 'Thrust against pain. Pain is the purifier. Walk toward suffering. Love suffering. Embrace it.'

Elliott did as he was told, including fixing a goal: 'I wanted to be the best miler in the world.'

He had only two months of such intense work on his still painful foot, plus one 880 race, when he entered the mile at Olympic Park Stadium on January 12. He ran a startling 4:06.0, breaking Clarke's world junior record, and John Landy commented: 'Elliott is the most fantastic junior I have ever seen. He looks as though he's been running in top company for years.'

The next day, Elliott exhausted himself in a long run on the Portsea golf course. 'Most athletes imagine themselves at the end of their tether before they're even 75 per cent exhausted. I was so determined to avoid this pitfall that if at any time I thought I was surrendering too soon to superficial pain, I'd deliberately try to hurt myself more.'

In the next few weeks he started the track world buzzing by breaking all world junior records from the 880 to 3 miles. His 880 in 1:50.8, mile in 4:04.3, and 2 miles in 9:01 were especially noteworthy.

On February 25 he had his nineteenth birthday and ceased to be a junior. He was thrown to the lions at the Australian Championships against Merv Lincoln, an experienced 4:01.8 miler on his way up. Elliott trailed for three laps, then burst into the lead.

'I felt like a frightened bunny running for dear life.' He led Lincoln by five yards at 1,500 meters and dazed him by 15 yards in 4:00.4.

Two days later, Elliott added the 880 title to his collection with a topnotch 1 :49.3. His season was over. Barely nineteen, he ranked sixth among the world's best milers for 1957. He had succeeded without sufficient background, but on May 1, he began his preparation for 1958. During the Australian winter and spring he ran 2,500 miles and lifted tons of weights.

His first mile race of 1958 came on January 25 in Melbourne. He ran 3 :59.9, but it did not excite him. He had bigger goals in mind.

The next day he saved a girl from drowning in the rip tide at Portsea, his second rescue. Four days later he raced Lincoln at Olympic Park. Lincoln was favored, off his best time of 3 :58.9, and Elliott did not shake hands.

'To shake hands with one's opponents before a race and wish them luck is hypocritical. I don't want to talk to them and the last thing I want to do is shake their hands because it would break down my purposefulness.'

Elliott took the lead after the half and led at the bell in 3 :02.6. He poured on all he had over the last lap, but Lincoln came up to his shoulder in the homestretch. Elliott fought him off to win by two yards in 3 :58.7.

Elliott barely survived in his next race as his desperate sprint barely caught Lincoln at the tape in 3 :59.6. He broke the Australian 1,000 meter record with 2 :21.0, then ran in the Australian Championships in Brisbane. He sped the last lap in 52.8, last 880 in a stunning 1 :52.8, to win in 4 :08.8. Once again, he completed a fine double by winning the 880 in 1 :49.4.

His Australian season was over, but 1958 was to be a four-part season. Before the second phase began, he created a sensation by rescuing Cerutty from drowning in the Portsea surf.

Still regarded as an exciting prospect not yet arrived, he was invited to California in May for a series of four races. When he announced he would not go without his coach, Cerutty was invited along.

He lined up for his first race, in the Coliseum Relays at Los Angeles, a strong, lean, 5' 11½", 150-pounder with a hawk nose broken in three varied violences. He took the lead in 3 :00.3 and then turned on his amazing speed. For half a lap it looked like a world record, and 34,000 fans cheered him on. But he won by only 20 yards.

'My last 50 yards were my poorest, but that may be due to the fact that there was no one at hand to push me.'

His time was 3 :57.8, faster than the official world record and second only to Derek Ibbotson's pending 3 :57.2. Elliott went sightseeing, trained, and played golf. His next race was in the California Relays at Modesto, May 31.

When he first saw the hard clay track, he exclaimed, 'Gor blimey, it's like a bloody brick.' Nobody pushed the pace, and he won easily in 4 :02.7. He said, 'Some nights you have it, others you don't. Cerutty's comment was made with fingers delicately patting a yawn.

The next weekend, Elliott was in the little stadium at Compton for the Compton Invitational. He led at three-quarters in 3 :01.8 with Olympic champion Ron Delany on his heels all the way. Now Elliott turned on his dazzling speed, his elbows flying like a sprinter's.

On the backstretch he was four yards ahead and Delany had to let him go. Elliott ran his last 120 yards in an eye-popping 14.7 to win by 15 yards in 3 :58.1.

Delany came up and said, 'Well, me boy, you may have beaten me here now, but sure I'll thrash the pants off you in Dublin town.'

Two weeks later, Elliott ran in the U.S. AAU Championships in Bakersfield. Jaded from his social activities but full of run, he sped an unnecessary 4 :01.4 in his heat.

In the final, he pushed hard on the last lap and won by four yards over Lincoln in 3 :57.9.

'I have never been in such bad physical shape in my life. I felt weak. I haven't eaten well and I ran too fast last night.'

With his U.S. season ended, he had five weeks before the most important meet of the year – the Empire Games in Wales. He did more sight-seeing and 'indulged my long-neglected taste for high living.' He relaxed his training, and placed only third in the British AAA 880.

Preparing to meet Brian Hewson again in the Empire 880, he practiced sprints and ran 100 yards with a running start in a lively 9.6.

The Empire 880 championship at Cardiff came on July 22. Elliott allowed a slow pace, trying different tactics on Hewson. They passed the 440 in 58.8. Suddenly, Elliott sprinted and opened a gap. Hewson recovered and sprinted after him. In the stretch, Hewson came dangerously close, but Elliott gave a little more and he won by two yards in 1 :49.3.

Four days later, in the rain, he triumphed over Lincoln by almost 20 yards in 3 :59.0 to complete his Empire double. Delany had promised to 'Thrash the pants off' him at Dublin on August 6, but Elliott enjoyed champagne and rich food, and he spent his time sight-seeing.

On August 4, when he should have been concentrating on the Dublin mile, he ran a remarkable half mile in London's White City stadium. He felt no seriousness about the race, but he led Hewson and Rawson, who had beaten him in the AAA. On the second lap he suddenly felt invincible. At the peak of condition, his mighty kick beat Hewson by ten yards in 1 :47.3.

Then, on the same day, he had to run another half mile. With Cerutty loudly cheering his opponent, Elliott came from behind on the last curve to win in 1 :50.7. Added to his Australian and Empire victories, this day's work earned him first in World Ranking.

Two days later, Elliott rode a bus with Lincoln through the gates at Santry and into a crowd trying to buy seats in the low stands already packed solid with 20,000 people. Elliott dressed with the others in a strange mood.

'No butterflies, no tingling. Nothing. I'm dead.'

He jogged and talked with Alby Thomas, the 3-mile record holder, then rested until half an hour before the race. He put on his spikes and began his serious warmup. The air was moist and cool from rain and there was no wind.

When the runners lined up on the red track it was raining. Elliott was in the third lane, next to Delany, and somebody in the partisan crowd shouted, 'Do him, Ronnie.'

At the gun, Thomas, a 5' 5", 126-pounder, set off at a fast pace. Lincoln followed, five yards back. Elliott was fourth, behind black-shirted Murray Halberg. 'They got off a little too fast for me.'

Chesty little Thomas passed the 440 in 58 flat and the crowd roared. Elliott passed Lincoln and ran up to Thomas's shoulder, but the little man kept going. He passed the 880 in 1 :58.0 with Elliott on his heels. Elliott thought, 'I don't even feel I've been running.'

With a record in mind, Elliott charged past Thomas on the backstretch. 'I knew I was running the fastest race of my life.' Into the curve he heard foosteps and Lincoln shot past. 'I was thunderstruck.'

Elliott followed Lincoln down the homestretch. The bell sounded its warning, in 2:59, and Elliott ran past Lincoln into the turn. Three others were threatening behind Lincoln. To the screaming Irish crowd it was still anybody's race, and their boy Delany was still in it.

But Elliott had that invincible feeling again. He could hear Lincoln behind him, with all the frenzied uproar, and he drove hard down the backstretch. On the turn he was timed in 3:39.6, second best ever for 1,500 meters. He sprinted home ten yards ahead of Lincoln.

An excited timer rushed to Elliott. 'Fantastic,' he said. 'It's just fantastic. Your time is 3:54.5.'

Lincoln, who ran 3:55.9, asked Delany if he felt like taking up tennis. Delany, third in 3:57.5, was violently ill, but he said later, 'There is only one way to beat Elliott. That's to tie his legs together.' Halberg kept shaking his head and muttering about running 3:57.5 and placing only fourth. And Thomas, fifth in 3:58.6, was exuberant.

Elliott went to a pub, phoned his fiancee in Australia, 'and then I sat down and got a little drunk.'

The very next night, Elliott helped Thomas in his 2-mile race. He set the pace until the sixth lap when Thomas went past and kept pulling away. 'It was hopeless.' Thomas set a world record of 8:32.0. Elliott's 8:37.6 was bettered by only two runners before this race.

Thus ended the third phase of Elliott's magnificent year. He was due in Stockholm in eighteen days. Denied expense money by international rules, he joined other carefree athletes in driving Gordon Pirie's Volkswagen bus to Sweden. They camped out nights and relished large quantities of beer and ale. They trained sporadically along the way. 'It provided the relaxation that was desperately needed before I could train intensely again.'

He was a spectator at the European Championships and stayed at an athletic camp outside Stockholm. Refreshed and enthusiastic again, he trained hard with Ibbotson for several days.

On August 25, at the 385-meter Stora Mossan track, he ran

his first 1,500 meter race, winning easily in 3:41.7. Three days later he was in the new stadium at Göteborg, running 1,500 meters against a great field.

The race started at 7:24 p.m. with world record holder Stanislav Jungwirth setting a mad pace of 56 for the first 400 meters. Elliott was seventh, in 58 seconds. Thomas took over the lead, but Elliott caught him in 1:57.5. 'Suddenly my limbs and lungs were being tortured no longer. I felt strong and confident.'

He ran the third lap in an awe-inspiring 58 flat, scattering the great field of runners behind him. He increased his pace in a long hard drive to the finish. His last 400 meters took only 54 seconds and he won by 18 yards. His 3:36.0 broke the world record by 2.1 seconds.

The crowd of 35,000 continued to applaud for a full minute after the race. Elliott was given a bouquet. He jogged a lap of honor, then tossed the flowers to the crowd.

He was scheduled to run a mile the very next night in Malmö. He objected strenuously to plans for a sub-four-minute race. 'I'm not a machine that can be wound up every day.'

Cerutty calmed him down and raised his confidence in his fitness. Elliott followed the 3:02 pace, feeling tired, but when he turned on his power he ran the last lap in 56 and beat Dan Waern by 25 yards in 3:58.0.

He was tired of racing again, after nine months, but he agreed to run an invitational mile in London's White City on September 3. In a daze, he did not realize his time for three laps was 2:59.8. Hewson was at his shoulder and he was having a crisis, but he would not quit. On the backstretch he pulled away and broke Hewson, but he pushed himself all the way to the tape.

He celebrated at a night club that night, got to bed at 3:30 a.m., and did not hear his good time until the next noon. It was 3:55.4, second best ever.

He flew to Oslo, feeling listless. On September 5, in Bislet Idrettsplass, he ran his last race of the year. After 800 meters in 1:59, he tried to run away on the third lap. His lap was a fantastic 56.5 and put him 30 yards ahead of an astounded Halberg.

Elliott was 'flagging badly at the end.' He lost 20 yards of his lead. His head throbbed and his whole body ached. His time was 3:37.4, second best ever, and yet the crowd of 33,000 applauded only mildly. 'I'd strained my body to the bounds of endurance and running had become a nightmare.'

And small wonder, for in the past nine days he had run four quality races against the best runners of Europe and Australasia, outclassing them completely. His four races included the two fastest 1,500 meters ever run, the second fastest mile, and another mile in 3 :58.0, tenth fastest of all time. No other man had ever run such fast races in a lifetime. No other man has ever run so close to his best so many times in so few days.

Within the past thirty-two days he had also run his 3 :54.5 mile, the fourth fastest 2-mile in history, and the third fastest 880.

In 1958 he ran under four minutes a total of ten times, plus three 1,500 meter races of equal value. He ran six of the eleven fastest miles ever run, plus the two fastest 1,500s. He richly deserved the title of History's Greatest Miler.

And he was only twenty years old.

To prepare for Cambridge, he began a first year science course at Melbourne University and crammed four years of Latin into nine months. On May 2, 1959, he was married. He also spent time talking to groups of boys. The result was a lack of training.

'The old dedication to running had vanished.' Sometimes he played golf at Portsea instead of running.

He raced only a little in 1959. 'I was amazed that I continued to win races, though only half fit.'

His most severe test of that short season came on March 14 in Brisbane. He rode with Lincoln of the five-hour journey. Carelessly, he drank a bottle of beer and smoked several cigarettes.

Lincoln's hopes were aroused and he pushed the pace on the grass track. He passed three quarters in 3 :01 and gave it everything he had into the last curve. Suddenly, Elliott exploded and ran away from him. Lincoln, beaten by 30 yards in 3 :58.9, saw Elliott dry-retching. Completely shocked at this burst from a man obviously out of shape, Lincoln never ran well again.

As 1959 ended, Elliott realized the Olympic Games would be held in eight months. 'On 26th December I stopped smoking and started serious training at Portsea.'

So great was his natural talent, however, in spite of two losses in shorter races, he ran 3 :59.8 on Bendigo's grass track, and won the Australian Championship at Perth in 4:02.1, distressed by the heat.

'The pain was excruciating. My stomach was convulsing and I felt every moment that I would vomit.'

He won the 880 title from Blue and beat him again in April. On April 2, at Bendigo, he ran 5,000 meters in 14:09.9. At the end of the month he punished himself in a 33-mile run. In May he went to California for three races.

He won the Coliseum Relays 1,500 in a lazy 3:45.4. Then a sore knee developed and doctors advised him to withdraw from the California Relays. At the last moment he told meet director Tom Moore, 'You'll have to count me out, Tom.' Depressed, he broke into tears.

But at the Compton Invitational on June 3 he was able to win in 3:59.2. He returned to the Australian winter, knowing he had to improve in the three months remaining. 'There were days when I was filled with self doubt.'

For a few weeks he ran before daybreak in the streets of Melbourne. He cut short his lunch hour so as to train earlier in the afternoon, but darkness caught him. Twice a week he lifted weights instead of eating lunch, and he listened to Cerutty now.

'He is like an oasis in the desert of my lost enthusiasm.'

On July 23, his wife and baby son left for Rome. Elliott received a leave of absence from Shell Chemical and joined Cerutty at Portsea. 'I needed Percy's inspiration more than I could remember needing it when I was a young and dedicated athlete.'

He trained hard once more, but he ran two bad races, and he arrived in Rome far from confident. On September 3 he could not restrain himself from winning the fastest Olympic heat – 3:41.4 – and now he felt confident. But the next day his throat was sore and his glands swollen. It took all his effort to obtain a penicillin shot.

On the morning of September 6, he attended early mass. Then he ate breakfast and tried to sleep, but the prospects of an Olympic final were too exciting. He tried to read, but he could not concentrate. For an hour and a half he considered race tactics. At 11:30 he went out and jogged easily on grass. He ate a light salad and tried to sleep. He lay awake, with his eyes closed, until 3:00 p.m.

'My nerves and muscles were screaming for action.'

He rode a bus to Stadio Olimpico and went to the dressing-room. He still had half an hour before his warmup. 'Even the worst pain of a mile race is preferable to the two hours anxiety experienced beforehand.'

It was a relief to start the race. He bungled along in the midst of eight other runners. At 300 meters : 'I feel as though I've run two laps already. I'm more tired than I should be.'

He ran wide around the curve. Michel Bernard, in the blue of France, led the pack in 58.2. Elliott ran down the backstretch in sixth place. Around the bend, he moved to fourth, breathing hard. 'I shouldn't feel as tired as this.'

At 800 meters he was a close fourth behind Bernard's 1 :57.8. He had wanted to make his break here, but now he felt too tired. Only his long practice at punishing himself enabled him to try. They had been averaging 14.7 seconds for each 100 meters. Suddenly, he ran the next 100 in 13.2 and he was ahead of a strungout line of discouraged runners.

He eased up a little for the next 200 meters, running 28.8 with Rozsavogyi and Jazy on his heels. The bell sounded with a long clanging and he spurted. He ran the curve 100 meters in 14 flat. His crushing lap had taken only 56 seconds and now there was a three-yard gap back to Rozsavolgyi.

To Elliott, running scared, three yards were not nearly enough. On the backstretch 100, he punished himself to 13.6 and his lead became eight yards.

There, on the edge of the track, was Cerutty, wildly waving a white towel, his signal to sprint. Not knowing how close his pursuers were, Elliott forced his protesting body around the curve 100 in 13.6, increasing his lead to 15 yards.

He began to tie up slightly. Try as he might, his last 100 meters slowed to 14.4, but he won by an overwhelming 20 yards in world record time of 3 :35.6. His last 800 meters was in 1 :52.6, truly astounding after a fast start.

On the victory stand, seeing his flag and hearing his national anthem, his sophistication gave way to pride. 'The tears welled up. . . .'

Outside the stadium, he saw Kuts, who had inspired him four years before in Melbourne. The Russian champion spoke in halting English : 'It was a wonderful run.'

After the Olympics, Elliott ran eleven races in nineteen days, losing only in an 880 race behind Peter Snell, Delany, and Blue. He ran four good mile races with times from 3 :59.8 to 3 :57.0. He barely beat Waern in two races, including a fine 3 :38.4 1,500. His last race was at 1,000 meters against Waern, the official world record holder. Elliott powered ahead to win by two yards in 2 :19.1, seventh fastest ever run.

Elliott completed the year having run the three fastest 1,500's of all time. He ran under four minutes in the mile seventeen times, plus six 1,500s better than a 4-minute mile. His 1,500 meter record lasted nine years.

Although he made a half-hearted effort to run in 1961 and placed fifth with a 1 :52.5 half-mile, he actually retired as a miler at the age of twenty-two with the best possible competitive record – undefeated.

12 BRUMEL

There is a wonderful moment in the life of each great athlete when his superiority shows through the darkness of past struggles and frustrations with the suddenness of a flash of lightning.

Such a moment in the life of Valeriy Brumel came near the climax of the high jump competition at Moscow on August 13, 1960.

Only eighteen years old, Brumel had been selected to the Soviet Olympic team in spite of a disappointing season. Only the confidence of his coach, Vladimir Dyachkov, had secured Brumel's place on the team in discussions within the council, and there were many who criticized Brumel's mediocre record. True, he had cleared the bar with a personal record in each of the first three meets of the 1960 season, reaching 6' $9\frac{7}{8}$", but then a hip injury set him back and he jumped a poor 6' $6\frac{3}{4}$"in the two big meets.

Now he had two misses and he stood with Dyachkov, eager for advice. Dyachkov, his eyes always calm behind his spectacles, said, 'Technically, everything seems to be correct.'

Then he gave Brumel the advice which brought the boy to his moment of break-through into greatness: 'You are too strained at the start. Run in more freely . . . don't tense up.'

Good advice to any athlete, but Brumel proved himself to be one of those rare ones who can do it. He ran relaxed, and he jumped relaxed, and his third jump was good. The height was a new European record of 7' $1\frac{1}{2}$", an astounding improvement.

Brumel's next effort was in Rome's Stadio Olimpico, wearing one blue shoe and one red shoe. In the gathering dusk, he no longer read the mystery story which occupied his time during the long competition. He had cleared the bar satisfactorily at 6' $10\frac{1}{4}$" and now he watched the bearded Swede, Pettersson, miss on his third attempt.

After a miss by the crippled defending champion, Charley Dumas, Brumel was now fourth. Only his two red-shirted teammates remained, along with the tall American world record holder, John Thomas. Brumel did not expect to win, but he had hopes of beating his teammates for the silver medal.

At 6' 11½" he tumbled the bar into the pit. Sick at heart, he watched Bolshov straddle easily over the bar. Next came mustachioed Shavlakadze, wearing white bandages on his right calf and wrist. Shavlakadze floated over on his stomach with dismaying ease.

Thomas passed. The confidence of the giant American was formidable. Brumel knocked the bar off again. One more miss and he would not win a medal. He concentrated on relaxing for his last attempt.

He ran hard toward the pit, kicked into the air, and folded himself over the crossbar and into the pit full of shavings. He was saved, for the time.

The bar was raised to 7' ¼". He had to jump first again, and he hit the crossbar too hard. Only Shavlakadze cleared on his first jump.

Carefully relaxed, Brumel cleared on his second trial and grinned as he ran out under the crossbar. Thomas sailed over, spread out like a huge bird. The bar was raised to 7' 1", and Brumel had to clear it or he would win no medal.

It was now too dark to see well, but he made the effort and missed. Bolshov also missed, and now the lights were turned on. Shavlakadze seemed calm as he floated over the bar, but Thomas missed badly.

Once again, Burmel concentrated intently on the paradox of exploding with all his strength and yet relaxing all unnecessary muscles. Somehow, he did it, clearing the bar at 7' 1".

He saw Bolshov miss and he was suddenly third. Now he watched Thomas. The tall, blue-clad Negro looked worried and he dragged the crossbar off with his left leg.

Brumel was now second. He saw Bolshov and Thomas miss a third time, but he did not dare show his joy. The bar was raised to 7' 1¾". He had to clear to win, but he could not come close. He had second place already, and that was enough for an 18-year-old.

He stood on the victory stand alongside Shavlakadze and received his silver medal. He listened to their national anthem. He marched solemnly off the field, hiding his pleasure. Then, inside the tunnel, Bolshov and the others were there and he jumped with sheer joy and there was much hugging and grinning and excited talk.

This was the first tangible reward for all the truly hard work – the heavy weight lifting, springing from his toes while carrying heavy weights, the sprinting, the gymnastics, the dull hours developing rhythm in the runup and takeoff. 'Speed-strength', Dyachkov called it, and Brumel agreed.

'The higher the jump the more speed is necessary, and the more strength.'

For an 18-year-old boy, an Olympic silver medal is a rare achievement, but Brumel did not bask in his glory. On September 17, in Odessa, he raised his European record to 7' 1⅞". He had them raise the bar a centimeter higher than Thomas's world record of 7' 3¾" and he came surprisingly close.

Now his confidence grew, but he cleared only 6' 11¼" and 7' ⅝" in his next meets. At Lugansk, on October 9, he cleared 7' ⅝" without a miss. Then, on his second trial, he cleared 7' 2¼", his third European record since August.

On October 15 at Kiev, he proved he was only human, losing to Shavlakadze and Bolshov. At Uzhgorod, on October 23, he cleared only 7' ⅝", but two days later in the same city, he improved his record to 7' 2¾".

He travelled to China and jumped 6' 10⅝", 7' ¼", and 7' 1⅜" in three meets. Back home, he prepared for the indoor season. On January 28, 1961, he was in Leningrad's glass-roofed Winter Stadium. He was jumping from a dirt takeoff, using his regular shoes, and he had never felt so strong.

The bar was raised to 7' 3", higher than he had ever cleared, and he missed. On his second attempt, he cleared, and the bar was raised to 7' 4⅝". It was an unrealistic height, but he felt no concern.

'I just wanted to jump like the devil.'

He cleared on his first attempt.

It was the highest jump ever made. He was so excited he could not sleep all night long. To be the best in his event in the entire history of the world at the age of eighteen was more than he, or any other mortal, could comprehend.

'It did not feel like anything really great. It was just like any other jump. I expected to make it.'

Thomas still threatened, having cleared 7' 3'' that same night, in Boston. Brumel flew to New York for a series of three summit meetings.

They met first at the New York Athletic Club Games in Madison Square Garden. Unused to a board takeoff, Brumel warmed up with graceful ballet leaps, then missed once at 6' 8'', carelessly. Then he made every height until he won at 7' 2''. He missed twice, then dove over 7' 3''. At 7' 5'', all three jumps were good misses.

A week later, they met again in the AAU meet. Brumel had hurt his toe, but he won at 7' 2''. Their third meeting, on March 3, came in the Knights of Columbus meet, and Brumel established himself as superior with a new American indoor record of 7' 3½''.

He went home and trained hard and he did not jump again until after his nineteenth birthday on April 14, 1961. In his first outdoor meet, he leaped higher than Shavlakadze and Bolshov with 7' 1⅝'' and he had a good jump at a world record.

On June 18, in Moscow, Brumel seemed hopeless, missing twice at 6' 9⅞''. Then he succeeded at five heights without a miss. The last clearance was 7' 4'', a new world record. He tried 7' 6½'' three times, with one good effort.

Brumel's intense competition with Thomas was resumed in the dual meet with USA at Moscow's Central Lenin Stadium on July 16. Brumel was superb, clearing 7' 2¼'' without a miss, but Thomas also cleared. The bar was raised to a world record 7' 4¼'' and rain began to fall. Thomas came startlingly close on his third attempt. Then Brumel dove over, elbows held high behind him, his mouth wide open, and a crowd of 70,000 thundered approval.

'The thing you have to understand is that I have been working very hard at this jumping – longer and harder than Thomas. You may not have heard of me until Rome, but it has been a long time for me.'

In Sofia, Bulgaria, at 6:40 p.m. on August 31, Brumel stood with his back to half a dozen rows of curious people in front of a large building. He had missed twice at 7' 4⅝'', but now he ran fast and twisted successfully over the bar for his third world record jump of the year.

He used excellent jumps of 7' 3'' against Great Britain, 7' 3⅜'' in the USSR Championships, and 7' 2½'' in Tokyo to finish the season undefeated. Somewhat incidentally, he had a good broad jump of 25' 1¼" in the qualifying round of the USSR Championships.

Brumel, who had made only 362 practice jumps in all of 1961, gave up jumping for the winter and worked for 'speed-strength.'

'The barbell and I are particular friends. Weightlifting develops practically the same muscles which send a jumper up.'

In April of 1962, when he took his first jumps, his sense of timing was off and he was discouraged. In his first meet, on May 21, he jumped only 6' 9⅞" and Bolshov beat him with fewer misses, but in June Brumel was better, sailing over seven feet in all three meets. Before their trip to Palo Alto, for the dual meet with the United States, Dyachkov told him, 'Now you are ready for a new record.'

The esteemed meet was held in Stanford's huge stadium and Brumel jumped before 81,000 people from the same grass takeoff where Thomas had set his world record of 7' 3¾". Brumel had been swimming that morning, but he won with flawless jumps through 7' 1". He missed once at 7' 2", but he cleared 7' 3" on his first attempt with apparent ease. The bar was raised to 7' 5", a record height he had missed many times.

Now he hesitated. The crowd grew silent, wondering at this slim, dark-haired youth in red vest and blue shorts who could seriously attempt to throw his entire body over a crossbar almost a foot and a half above his head.

He started walking toward the bar, casually relaxed. Then he jogged a few steps. Suddenly purposeful, he crouched and ran fast in an awkward way, his elbows leading his armswings. Smoothly, he leaned back, stretched his left foot forward, and kicked his right leg with savage power.

He shot upward, legs spread. His right arm and leg went over easily, then his head. He dipped his head and tucked his left arm close to his side, safely out of the way. He twisted over the bar, hitting it hard enough to make it move. Recoiling with a fright reaction, he thrust his left leg high toward the sky and dropped into the pit.

He thought, 'Will it stay up?'

Before he could look, a tremendous roar of pleasure from 81,000 Americans told him the bar was still there.

'I was filled with inexpressible joy.'

He bounded to his feet and faced the nearby crowd. He threw both arms straight up and grinned. Bolshov kissed him. Thomas hugged him. 'This was a marvelous moment for me.'

Nine days later, in Helsinki, he barely missed 7′ 5⅜″. He won the USSR Championships at 7′ 3½″. Suffering from a cold, he won his greatest title yet, the European Championships, at 7′ 3″.

On September 29 in Moscow, Brumel, who likes books, plays, and chess, visited an art gallery in the morning before an unimportant meet for physical education students. He did not jump as well as usual. He missed once at 6′ 8¾″ and at 6′ 11½″. He missed twice at 7′ 3″ and so an attempt at 7′ 5½″ was not seriously regarded. It was something of a surprise when he cleared cleanly on his first jump.

At the end of his 1962 season, Brumel had made the six best jumps of all time and twenty-one of the twenty-three highest ever.

He cleared 7′ 2¾″ indoors in Leningrad. Then he left his wife Marina, a gymnast, and flew to New York to challenge Thomas in the 1963 indoor season. On February 1, he cleared 7′ 2″. On February 9, in Los Angeles, he injured his foot and jumped in great pain. He cleared 7′ ¼″, same as Thomas, but he lost on more misses. On February 15, he raised his board record to an excellent 7′ 4″, and he won the AAU at 7′ 3½″.

He was apparently not at his best in the dual meet with the USA at Moscow on July 21. He disappointed once at 7′ ⅝″ and he missed twice more before diving over 7′ 3¾″. The bar was raised to 7′ 5¾″, but his first jump was poor and his second was only fair. On his third attempt he flopped over for his third world record made in meets against the USA. The huge crowd, including Premier Khrushchev, were delighted.

He had cleared the bar at a height more than 16 inches above his head. This recalled a conversation when he was fourteen. A coach asked why he was so anxious to high jump and Brumel answered :

'I read somewhere that there are people who can clear the bar raised higher than their own height. I'd like to do the same thing.'

Brumel was undefeated outdoors, but no other jumps were higher than 7′ 1¾″, almost a mediocre height for him.

He started out in 1964 as if he would continue in triumph indefinitely. He won at 7′ 3¾″ and 7′ 3¼″ in June. In July, he won against the USA in Los Angeles with 7′ 3½″, but he missed badly at 7′ 6″. He flew over 7′ 4¼″ at Kiev on August 8.

Then came a decline which neared disaster. No word of an injury leaked out through the iron curtain until the next indoor season, but suddenly Brumel was no longer the super athlete. In the five meets before the Olympics he lost twice to Shavlakadze at 7′ 1½″ and 7′ ⅝″.

At the Olympic Games in Tokyo, he was obviously off form, although his injury was never mentioned. In the qualifying round on October 20 he had two shocking misses at 6′ 9¼″. In the final the next day he had some shaky takeoffs, but he cleared 6′ 11½″ without a miss and there were only five jumpers left.

On his first jump at 7′ ¼″ he again had takeoff trouble. He hardly left the ground, and he grabbed the crossbar with his hand. On his second jump, he missed badly.

Now came another moment of truth. He could not afford another bad takeoff. He could not afford the fear of imminent failure. He concentrated on form and relaxation. Everything had to be right. As he faced the bar, a whole career seemed to hang in the balance and the suspense was enough to defeat almost anybody.

Brumel approached the bar fast but carefully. His foot-plant was precise and he threw all his extraordinary power into his kick and spring. He was over the bar. He did not touch it. He was still in.

The bar was raised to 7′ 1″. He was now in fourth place, and his next jump was as important as the one he had just made. Any miss now could be the one to defeat him.

He cleared the bar on his first jump.

Now he sat quietly while the others missed. As suddenly as that he was back in first place. Thomas, again dangerous, cleared on the second round and Brumel ran over to shake his hand as he left the pit. On the third round, big John Rambo of the USA went over, but Pettersson and Shavlakadze missed, assuring Brumel a medal.

The bar went to an Olympic record height of 7′ 1⅞″. Once again, a miss would give Thomas a chance to take the lead. After Rambo missed, Brumel went about his jump with the care and precision of a jeweler. He did everything exactly right and he left the bar on the uprights.

Thomas cleared impressively on his first jump, but Rambo went out. Now there were only two of them as the bar was raised to 7' 2⅝". Now the tension reached Brumel. His cortical nerve cells were tired, and he jumped poorly, for him, limited by his mysterious disability. But Thomas could not clear either.

Even off form, Brumel won the gold medal he wanted so much.

At the end of the 1964 season, he had the ten highest jumps of all time and eighteen of the nineteen jumps better than 7' 3". He had cleared 7' 2" 43 times, compared with fifteen by all other jumpers.

He did not jump again until February, 1965, when he again tried some U.S. indoor meets. He had to withdraw from a meet at Philadelphia on February 5, and then it was disclosed he had a bad knee before the Olympic Games. Six days later, in the NYAC Games, he was successful at 7' 3", and he won the AAU at 7' 2". In San Francisco, February 26, he won at seven feet on fewer misses, then withdrew in pain.

His knee was so bad he had to miss two months of training. He did not jump in competition until July 18. Still hampered by his bad knee, he could jump no higher than 7' 2¼" in 1965. But he was good enough to be undefeated and he ranked first in the world for the fifth consecutive year.

In his five great years since his first Olympic year, no man jumped higher than Brumel in the same meet, although he suffered defeat four times, one of them indoors.

Four days after jumping 7' ⅝" against France on October 3, he was riding behind a friend on a motorcycle late at night. Going through a dangerous underpass, the driver veered sharply to make an unsuspected turn and lost control.

When Brumel regained consciousness he examined himself for injuries. Everything was all right except his right leg. He could see white bone sticking out. In the hospital it was discovered that he had two simple fractures below the knee and one multiple fracture of the ankle.

He was in surgery for five hours. At first, doctors feared they would have to amputate, because of gangrene. He ran a high temperature for three weeks.

Coach Korobkov was in tears. 'I can't believe that such a stupid accident can interrupt the career of the greatest athlete we've ever had in the Soviet Union. We were expecting even more from Brumel.'

Later, Brumel said 'I'll never give up sports. It is my passion. It is my life.'

His leg was in a cast for almost three years. He used crutches thirty-one months. He tried to exercise too soon, and the leg gave way again. He endured six operations. His leg had to be stretched to restore its proper length. Three years and eleven days after the accident, he began to walk without crutches.

He began training – gymnastics, swimming, running. Once, he ran 100 meters in 10.6; now he set a goal of 12 flat. In the early spring of 1969 he jumped 6' 7", and with characteristic determination, he intends to add more glory to a career already among the great ones.

13 SNELL

For some reason the winner of the Olympic 800 meters has always been from an English-speaking nation. Perhaps this is no more than coincidence, but athletic enthusiasts from Great Britain and her former colonies have accepted this tradition as their just due.

Thus, it was a great disappointment to these devotees when the heats and semi-finals at Rome in 1960 saw the elimination of all their hopes.

Among the six finalists who took their marks on the curved starting line forty-five minutes after Glenn Davis had won the 400 meter hurdles were some of the fastest runners of all time.

The only finalist acceptable to Anglophiles was an unknown novice named Peter Snell.

He was a muscular 6-foot, 176-pounder in the all-black of New Zealand. He had already shocked spectators at the Olympics by qualifying for the final. The day after running two heats, Snell surprised them by winning his semi-final in 1:47.2. At twenty-one, he certainly lacked experience, and his hard semi-final had probably expended all his reserves. Almost everybody picked him to finish last.

When the starter in his orange coat fired his starting gun, Snell ran hard, staying in the sixth lane around the curve. Into the backstretch, he cut sharply to the curb and found himself fourth. The pace was fast – 25.4 for 200 meters and 51.9 for 400 – and Snell had no inclination to move up. He alternated between fourth and fifth with Roger Moens, the confident world record holder.

The crowd roared so loudly Snell could barely hear the bell and he heard no lap time. Around the curve, into the backstretch, he was satisfied to stay close, but at 600 meters in 1:19.1, a wall of runners blocked him off.

He faced the choice of running extra yards around the curve

or staying inside in fifth place. He chose to stay on the pole.

'I felt this meant abandoning the chance of winning the race, but there was the hope that the front runners would split and I could get through into a place.'

Turning into the homestretch, Moens went into the lead, followed by George Kerr, whose 1 :46.4 was the fastest time of the year. Snell saw his chance and burst through alongside Paul Schmidt, a 1 :46.2 man. 'Here was a chance for third.'

Snell continued his determined drive, past Schmidt, past Kerr. Now only Moens was ahead of him, on his right.

Twenty yards from the tape, Snell fought even with Moens, between the unsuspecting Belgian and the curb. His legs pounded powerfully with every bit of strength he had. As Snell pulled ahead, Moens looked over at him in shocked bewilderment.

Snell stretched his arms out and threw back his head as he reached the tape, but he did not know he had won. 'I was so delighted with my own performance I didn't care whether I was first or second.'

Exhausted, he held onto a metal post outside the track until he recovered enough to walk back. Then Moens, who had been on his knees in despair, came over and congratulated him.

Snell was still in the stadium when the 5,000 meters was run. He cheered mightily as his teammate, Murray Halberg, gave New Zealand a second gold medal in half an hour.

Now came a deluge of interviews. Everybody in the track world wanted to know about Peter Snell :

At the age of twelve, he was successful in both the 440 and 880 in school record time. He set a junior cross country record at thirteen. He set a school mile record of 5 :21 at fourteen, and he cut his times to a good 2 :01.6 and 4 :48.4 in his last year.

All this was done casually, with no specialization. His best sport was tennis, where he was good enough to reach the quarter finals of the national under-17 tournament, but he also liked cricket, the high jump and broad jump, golf, badminton, rugby, and hockey.

One teammate discouraged even that much running, telling Snell, 'Pete, you'll never do any good. You haven't got a finishing sprint.'

At eighteen, selected to run against an Auckland team, he surprised everyone with a 1 :54.1 victory. That triumph led to a meeting with Arthur Lydiard, and he began following Lydiard's training with enthusiasm. He gave up tennis and placed third in the national championships in 1 :52.9.

When that 1958 season ended, he began full-scale training under Lydiard, although he had to spend two evenings each week at night school preparing for examinations in quantity surveying. At first, he had difficulty doing the long distance training Lydiard advocated. After his first agonizing run over Lydiard's hilly, 22-mile course, he burst into tears.

Later he cut his time from over 3 hours to 2 :40 and ran well in cross country. In the 1958–59 season he made a national reputation. He beat Halberg at 2,000 meters in 5 :15.8 and won two Auckland titles in 1 :51.6 and 4 :12.4. At the national championships, he won victories in both events.

If such progress had continued in the 1959–60 season, Snell would have been known in Rome, but after a good fourth place in the national cross country, he suffered a stress fracture of the tibia with total inactivity for two months.

By Christmas he was running again, but he lost twice and ran only 1 :53.9 in the national 880. On March 14, he ran in Melbourne against Herb Elliott and Tony Blue, a promising 1 :48.9 man, soon to run 1 :47.8. After a slow start, Snell outsprinted them in 1 :51.3.

In good practice runs at Rome, he ran three-quarters in 2 :57, an 880 in 1 :48, and 400 meters in 48. Lydiard told him, 'This is going to be a test of stamina and you are probably the only athlete sufficiently prepared to stand four races in three days.'

After his Olympic triumph, the next question in the minds of track fans concerned Snell's future. Twelve days after, he answered decisively in a 2-mile relay against the USA at London.

Snell took the baton three yards behind, ran a lap in a sensational 50.5, and finished with an amazing time of 1 :44.8. Even if his running start added a full second to his time he was far superior to the world record of 1 :46.8.

'In Rome, I realized I just hadn't appreciated my own capabilities.'

Eight days later, in Dublin, Snell ran against a crack field in a night meet at the famous Santry track. He ran away from Ron Delany, Blue, and Elliott with 300 yards to go and held on to win in 1 :47.9. The next night he ran his first good mile, in 4 :01.5, but he finished fifth behind Elliott's 3 :57.0.

Snell ended the 1960 season five days later at White City stadium in London when he smashed Kerr by 15 yards in 1 :47.5.

In November, another leg injury interrupted his training for six weeks, but by January 21, 1961, he was good enough to beat Kerr and Moens in 1 :49.0. He lost four races after that, partly from poor tactics, but he needed a rest and he did not race again until June 28 in London, where he beat Schmidt in 1 :48.4.

In Helsinki's Olympic stadium, Snell won the World Games 800 in 1 :47.6 and in Dublin he beat Kerr by a foot in 1 :47.2, fastest of the year. He ranked first in the world for the second year.

An hour after his 1 :47.2 880, his rousing 4 :01.2 anchor leg gave New Zealand the world record in the 4-mile relay. That run 'proved to me what an athlete is capable of doing in an inspired moment', and for the first time 'steered my thoughts toward more concentration on mile running'.

The next day he placed third in the mile, in 4 :10.0.

In Sweden, two days later, Snell beat Waern over 1,000 meters in 2 :20.4, third fastest of the year. After a 1 :48.8 880, he went home to rest.

It was six weeks before he resumed hard training. Then he ran four miles to work and four miles home. In November, he ran the 22-mile course in 2 :11, then a full marathon in 2 :41. The afternoon of the marathon he tried to play cricket. That evening, worn out, he went to a party where he met Sally Turner, later to be his wife.

In December he was in great shape, running ten miles every morning and doing speed work at night. 'I have several of my races on tape. When training gets tough and discouraging, it helps to go in my room and listen to the Rome 800 broadcast.'

On January 1, he lost a handicap mile, but his time was 4 :01.3, with an impressive last lap of 56.3. On January 20, he ran 1 :48.2, and four days later, 1 :47.1.

Snell's next race was to be a mile run at Wanganui on January 27. He intended to run New Zealand's first sub-four-minute mile, and he had secret hopes of bettering Halberg's national record of 3 :57.5. As for Elliott's world record of 3 :54.5, 'I shrugged the suggestions off as being ridiculous.'

On the morning of the race, he jogged for half an hour. He flew to Wanganui, had afternoon tea with relatives, and sought the privacy of a hotel. He stretched out while he ate a package of barley sugar and worried about Lydiard's prediction that he would run 3:55. At six o'clock he went out and looked at the grass track, bare in spots. At 8:55 he began to warm up, nervously. At 9:30 they lined up on the backstretch of the 385-yard track.

When the gun sounded, he started poorly. He was seventh at the 220, in 31.7. Too slow. He moved to third at the 440 in 60.7. He moved to second at the 880 in 2:00.6, then took the lead.

His goal was to reach the three-quarter mark in three minutes With nobody helping him, he reached the mark in 2:59.6. 'I was still moving comfortably.'

In the homestretch, approaching the bell, Bruce Tulloh sprinted past. Snell moved confidently to Tulloh's shoulder around the curve. Then he burst into a hard drive and ran away from Tulloh.

'At this point I abandoned the studied relaxation. This is the moment when you stop consciously controlling what you are doing and pour everything into driving out the utmost speed.'

The crowd exploded into a roar of joy and excitement. On top of his 2:59.6, this speed meant a fast mile. 'I don't think I've ever felt such a glorious feeling of strength and speed without strain.'

Around the curve he raced, and down the stretch. He was still running hard and fast when he hit the tape. The crowd poured down onto the field. After several minutes of utter confusion came the exciting announcement. His time was 3:54.4, one tenth of a second under Elliott's world record.

A week later, after an easy half-mile in 1:52.2, and two pleasant days of sightseeing, he was in Christchurch for a half-mile race before only 12,000 people. 'I was definitely going for a world record.'

Snell had the pole lane, with seven runners outside him. At the gun, he started fast, but quarter-miler Barry Robinson went out too fast. His time was 50.7 and Snell ran 51 flat. Then he saw Robinson move out to the second lane.

'I was feeling as good as or better than I had in many of my other races.'

Instead of coasting, he began to push the pace. He knew he was far ahead of world record pace, and he had the necessary courage. 'It was only a matter of being able to continue.'

All around the curve and down the backstretch, 'I felt myself travelling fast.' At the end of the straight his time for 660 yards was a fantastic 1 : 16.9.

Around the curve he fought to keep going. 'I felt myself slowing.' Now came the physical and psychological benefits of Lydiard's hard work. He was able to keep moving, but when he reached the straightaway his legs tied up and he wobbled. 'I felt that I had come to the end of my run.'

He was running much slower now, and he had to struggle against his inclination to slow down even more. He forced himself all the way, through the tape at 800 meters and on to 880 yards.

'I knew I must have gone inside the records.' Half dazed, he watched the other runners finish. Then, without knowing his time, he jogged a victory lap. He recovered quickly from his violent effort, especially after he heard his amazing times.

He had passed 800 meters in 1 :44.3, 1.4 seconds faster than any other man. His 1 :45.1 for the half-mile broke the old world record by 1.7 seconds. He was now the first man in twenty-five years to hold both the 880 and mile records, and he had accomplished the feat in eight days.

His 220 splits were an unusual 24.8, 26.2, 25.9, and 28.2. Thus, his final 120 yards took at least a full second longer than in his world record mile.

In Los Angeles, on February 10, he had his first look at an indoor track. That evening, when he appeared before his race, 13,000 fans gave him a thundering ovation for his recent records.

He led from the start. He passed the 880 in 1 :50.2, the fastest time ever run on a 160-yard track. His time of 2 :06.0 for 1,000 yards was almost two seconds under the world indoor record.

But the award to the outstanding athlete went to Jim Beatty for a record 3 :58.9 in the mile, and Beatty's prancing joy soured Snell. 'If I ever meet him on the track, it will be my pleasure to beat him.'

Back in New Zealand, he ran a mile in 3 :56.8, the sixth fastest ever run. He needed to rest, but he had more commitments.

He won the national championship on March 10, running 1:53.9 in mud. A week later, he ran in the Metropolitan Gymnasium, near Tokyo's familiar Olympic stadium. He beat Halberg in a good 4:06.7. The next night he set a world indoor record of 1:49.9 for 880 yards on the 160-yard track.

Now he was happy to rest four days. After a short period of winter training, he ran a mile in 4:00.5 on April 23. On his way to California, he stopped in Hawaii and ran 1:47.8. While there, he learned New Zealand had lost their world record for the 4-mile relay to the University of Oregon. Dyrol Burleson had anchored Oregon with a formidable 3:57.9, all alone.

When Snell learned Burleson was a late entry in the Coliseum Relays mile, he was stunned. Burleson had beaten him twice last year, and Snell was unsure of his own fitness.

They ran before 40,000 enthusiasts. Snell stayed off the 3:02.1 pace and Burleson stayed on his heels. Into the last curve, Snell started his sprint, and behind him, Burleson followed purposefully.

Burleson finished as fast as any previous miler, but Snell simply ran away from him with the fastest finish ever seen. The crowd was gasping in admiration as he ran the last 120 yards in an amazing 13.4. Nobody had ever run faster than 14.2.

He won by 12 yards in 3:56.1, fastest ever in the United States. Now he was regarded as the best mile racer of all time.

On June 5 he began training for the Commonwealth Games to be held in Perth in November. He won the Auckland cross country championship from Bill Baillie by three yards in a strenuous battle over 10,000 meters. Three weeks later, he won the national cross country title by a remarkable 41 seconds.

He suffered his inevitable slump in August. In September he broke a bone in his foot and had to rest for a month. On October 22, he ran a hard 880 in 1:56.0, losing to Philpott's 1:53.4. Unlike some champions, Snell used minor races as workouts and he did not mind losing many of them.

On November 26, he ran in the 880 final of the Commonwealth Games. After a slow pace, Kerr pulled alongside in the homestretch. Snell 'gave it everything I had', and finally cracked Kerr 20 yards from the tape in 1:47.6.

On November 29, Snell qualified for the mile final with an easy 4:02.4. 'It was just no trouble at all.'

On December 1, he ran a hard 440 in a futile attempt to qualify in the relay. In the afternoon he had to meet a dangerous field in the final of the mile.

A crowd of 45,000, including the Duke of Edinburgh, were disappointed with the pace. After three-quarters in 3 :09, Snell won by four yards in 4 :04.6.

Snell ran poorly, for him, during the 1962–63 season. His best effort was a hard 3 :58.6 mile which barely beat Davies. Then he eased off to a long, slow type of training. 'I was concerned to put something back into the bank to wipe out the overdraft on which I had been operating.'

He was married in May and left for America the next day on a honeymoon which was to include three races in California.

The first was the Los Angeles Coliseum Relays on May 17. He did not feel well, even with a 3 :06 pace, and Burleson gained on him in the stretch. Snell won by only four feet in 4 :00.3. 'The final sprint was an effort.'

Beatty, who looked great in the 5,000, apparently thought the time was ripe and he announced he would run the mile against Snell in the California Relays the following week. The publicity build-up was the greatest Snell had ever seen, and 40 million people were to watch the race on television. 'If he won, I felt, I was done.'

On Saturday morning, in Modesto, he jogged for twenty minutes, ate lunch, and sat in his room worrying. Cary Weisiger had said, 'If we can't beat this guy on his honeymoon, we never will.'

On the way to the track an hour before the race, Snell heard the opening ceremony on the car radio. The New Zealand anthem was played, and he felt emotional. He was tense and he never felt right until the gun sounded. 'I was so nervous I couldn't finish my warmup.'

Snell, wearing the New Zealand all-black, was fourth at three quarters in 3 :00.2. He moved easily past Beatty on the backstretch, then waited for Beatty to move, but Weisiger and Grelle were pulling away dangerously. Snell forgot about Beatty and went after the other two.

Suddenly, just before the last turn, he exploded into a sprint the likes of which nobody had ever seen. He flew past the astonished Americans into a 10-yard lead at mid-curve. Into the homestretch he looked back, saw a 15-yard gap, and was satisfied to ease off a little.

His time was 3:54.9 and it was obvious he could have broken the world by starting sooner. He was surprised at how fresh he felt. 'I felt like a crisp apple right off a tree.'

At Compton, on June 7, Snell was the target of all the best American milers except O'Hara. After three quarters in 2:58.7 Snell caught Weisiger at the last curve, but he slowed to stay on Weisiger's shoulder. 'I found I couldn't sprint as I wanted to.'

He trailed Weisiger past 1,500 meters in a new American record of 3:39.3. Then he surged past Weisiger and opened a gap. He was surprised his time was as fast as 3:55.0. 'I didn't have my usual kick. I had more left but I couldn't use it. It was a real hard race.'

The place times of his competitors were faster than any in history: Beatty 3:55.5, Burleson 3:55.6, Grelle 3:56.4, Weisiger 3:56.6, Bobby Seaman 3:59.1. This gave Snell three of the four fastest miles ever run.

His 1963 season ended there, and he should have started his long, slow conditioning for the 1964 Olympic Games. But the adjustment to married life, a break with Lydiard, and an understandable need for rest all contributed to a less-than-promising winter.

In October he lost twice, but on January 1, at Wanganui, he ran 3:57.7. He was rounding into shape. 'That mile put me right again.'

Another illness set him back and he lost again. Although he won the national 880 in 1:53.2, people began to believe he was through and he resolved to show them 'I was still around and still dangerous.'

In March he ran well in South Africa with a 3:59.6 and championship victories in 1:50.4 and 4:06.2. On April 11, he raced Davies at Auckland and barely succeeded in 3:58.5.

Then he settled down to serious training for Tokyo. Never before had he been able to maintain a schedule of 100 miles a week for more than three weeks but now he did ten weeks. Every Sunday night he ran the difficult 22-mile course.

Next, he labored through six weeks of hill running. His goal at Tokyo was the 1,500 meters because, 'I felt that some of my sharpness, which was necessary for 800 meters, had gone.'

He began his track work with 20 quarters averaging 62.5, and his speed work went well. For the first time in his career he trained straight through Lydiard's program the way he wanted.

Then, at Tokyo, he caught the 'flu, but he ran three quarters in 2:56 and a mile in 4:02. In an important trial against Davies and O'Hara, Snell ran 1:47.1 for 800 meters. Encouraged, he decided to run in the Olympic 800.

A week later, on October 14, he ran the first heat of the 800. Those who were uncertain of his condition saw him win easily in 1:49.0. In his semi-final the next day, he again won, with 1:46.9. He 'still had something in reserve'.

In the second semi-final, Kerr and Wilson Kiprugut of Kenya broke his Olympic record with 1:46.1. 'I was shocked.'

On the third day, Snell lined up for the final in the pole lane. The weather was perfect and he felt fine. He started fast, but into the backstretch he was third. At the bell, in 52.0, he was in a dangerous box, and he was in it all around the curve to the last backstretch. 'I was very worried. I hadn't been boxed as badly as that before.'

He dropped back, swung wide, and shot past everybody with unmatchable speed. On the curve, he gained, but down the home-stretch 'I subconsciously held just a little back for the 1,500.'

He won by four yards over Bill Crothers in 1:45.1, second only to his own world record. Considering the box he'd been in and the fast semi-final the day before, this was truly a great time.

On the victory stand he received his gold medal suspended by a ribbon of Japanese silk. He walked across the track, below the Emperor's box, and gave it to his wife.

The very next day, he had to run the first heat of the 1,500 meters. His aim was to conserve energy, and so he claimed the last qualifying spot in 3:46.8, only two yards ahead of the next man. 'The crisis was now happily over.'

He had a day of rest before he ran his semi-final. He won without trying to in 3:38.8, his fastest 1,500. The others in Snell's heat all ran slower in the final and he, too, was to feel its effects.

He had a day of rest. 'In no circumstances would I attempt to run a record. It was going to be a matter of waiting as long as possible and concentrating purely on winning.'

And in the final he did exactly that, staying off the pace of

58.0 and 2 :00.5. At the bell he was boxed, but John Whetton, 'with the manners of a true Englishman', moved aside and let him through on the curve.

Davies led the expectant pack at 1,200 meters in 2 :59.3. Snell, in third place, looked awkward, as usual, running at a 60-second pace. Dramatically, he exploded into a beautiful stride, long, fast, and powerful, and he shot into the lead before the curve. They had been running at an average pace of 14.5 for each 100 meters. Snell ran that 100 in an astounding 12.7.

The crowd's roar increased with no surprise whatever. Snell's bold move was entirely predictable, but not his speed. He shot around the curve 100 in an unparalleled 12.3 and opened a gap of six yards, and the crowd expressed amazement and admiration.

He looked back in the stretch. 'I felt that I could renew my effort if I needed to.' He saw no challenger behind him. 'My run down the straight was a little easier than it had been in the 800 meters.' His last 100 meters was only 13.6, but he pulled away to win by 12 yards.

He is the only middle distance runner who ever won three Olympic gold medals.

His amazing finishing speed, especially the middle 200 meters in 25 flat, gave him a last lap of 52.7, a last 300 meters in 38.6, and a final time of 3 :38.1.

Back home, instead of being able to rest from his strenuous efforts, Snell found himself in demand during the New Zealand racing season, and he had to do some training for his farewell appearance in Europe in 1965.

At Auckland, before 12,000 people on November 12, Snell made an attempt on the world record for 1,000 meters. At 200 meters he heard a call of '26' and he thought he was running faster than he was. He relaxed and passed 400 meters in 55. 'Immediately I had to put on the pressure.' He passed 800 meters in 1 :49.5 and barely broke the record with 2 :16.6. He now held the world record at four distances.

Five nights later he planned to break his mile record on the same track. He knew the pace was too fast but he made the decision to follow, and he passed the quarter in 56.4. The pace slowed before the 880, but 'I yielded to an urge to continue at the same rhythm.'

He led at the half in 1 :54.1. Thinking of a really fast time, he kept the pressure on, but with a lap and a half to go he could feel his legs begin 'to cry out for relief.'

He passed three-quarters in 2 :54.3. He forced himself, trying to run faster. His rhythm was gone, along with his energy reserve, his concentration, and his leg speed. All he had left was his will to fight. 'The reserves had already been expended. There was nothing there.'

With the crowd screaming encouragement, he was able to finish, but without any increase in speed. 'It was mechanical desperation running, completely without inspiration.'

His time was 3 :54.1, a new world record, but still disappointing. 'I felt really good during the fast early stages. My legs shouldn't have gone so dead later.'

He finished the year with an Australian all-comers record of 3 :57.6. He received many awards for his achievements, including an O.B.E. For all practical purposes, this was the end of his great career, for his farewell tour was a disaster.

He barely won the Compton mile from Grelle in 3 :56.4. He lost a 1 :48.4 880 to Crothers. Then, in Vancouver for a mile on June 15, he suffered from gastritis and ran last.

He recovered, somewhat, in time for the U.S. championships in San Diego on June 27. He ran a strong 3 :55.4, but he lost a bitter stretch battle with 18-year-old Jim Ryun.

Then came a series of defeats. The races came too close together to allow him to recover from his illness. Most of all, he lacked the incentive of an Olympic Games.

He retired.

Snell's phenomenal competitive record in big meets was untarnished by his last disability. In addition to his three Olympic championships and world records in four outdoor and two indoor events, he was the best in World Ranking seven times. In 1962 and 1964 he was first at both distances.

His accomplishments alone labeled him the world's greatest middle distance runner, but it was his habit of winning in such convincing style which prompted one otherwise cautious track fan to exclaim : 'When he's right, Snell is unbeatable.'

SUPPLEMENT

Ashenfelter, Horace (USA) : 1952–1956   Steeplechase
Ashenfelter won the 1952 Olympic steeplechase in 8 :45.2, fastest ever run.

Attlesey, Dick (USA) : 1950–1952   High Hurdles
Attlesey ran the first 13.5 high hurdles, at Fresno on May 13, 1950. He won the 1950 AAU in 13.6. On July 10, 1950, he ran the 110 meter highs in 13.5 at Helsinki. He ran 13.6 twice in 1951, giving him five of the six fastest ever run.

Bacon, Charles (USA) : 1908   400 Hurdles
Bacon won the 1908 Olympic 400 meter hurdles in world record time of 55.9.

Bannister, Roger (GB) : 1950–1954   Mile
Bannister ran few races, preferring to point for the important occasion while doing his medical studies. He was first in World Ranking in 1951, at the age of 22, with a best mile of 4 :07.8 in the AAA. Favored in the 1952 Olympic 1,500, he ran only once before the Games. Lack of experience plus three races in three days relegated him to fourth place. In 1953, he ran 4 :03.6 and 4 :02.0 and won the AAA in 4 :05.2 to rank third in the world.

On May 6, 1954, on the Iffly Road track at Oxford, he became history's first 4-minute miler with 3 :59.4. He won the AAA in 4 :07.6. He defeated Landy at the Empire Games in 3 :58.8. He won the European Championships 1,500 in 3 :43.8.

Barnes, Lee (USA) : 1924–1928   Pole Vault
Barnes, only 5' 8" tall, won the Olympic pole vault in 1924 as a schoolboy and vaulted 12' 11½" again in the 1928 Olympics for fifth place. On April 28, 1928, he set a world record of 14' 1¾".

HERB ELLIOTT   The strain of bitter self-punishment shows on Elliott's face
at Rome, but he never quit until he won

VALERY BRUMEL   A jubilant Brumel bounds out of the piled chunks of foam
rubber at Tokyo after clearing 7′ 1¾″

Bausch, Jim (USA) : 1930–1932   Decathlon

Bausch won the 1932 Olympic decathlon with a new world record. He won the 1931 AAU pentathlon and the 1932 decathlon.

Beamon, Bob (USA) : 1965–   Long Jump

Beamon long jumped 25′ 3½″ in 1965 and set a national high school record of 50′ 3¾″ in the triple jump. The next year, at nineteen, he improved to 25′ 7″ and 50′ 8″ and placed fourth and ninth in the AAU.

In 1967, he won the indoor AAU long jump at 26′ 11½″. Outdoors, he was third in the AAU and second in the Pan American Games, with 26′ 5¾″. He jumped 26′ 8″ with wind.

Indoors in 1968, he showed it was only a matter of time until he became the longest jumper in history. He won the NAIA with a world indoor record of 27′ 1″. He won the AAU at 26′ 11½″ again (plus 52′ 7″ for third in the triple jump). He won both events in the NCAA at 52′ 3″ and a world record 27′ 2¾″.

Outdoors, he jumped 27′ 4″ with wind, won the AAU at 27′ 4″, and leaped 27′ 6½″ with a 7.1 m.p.h. wind in the Final Trials.

At the Olympic Games, with the aid of Mexico City's high altitude, he was expected to better 28 feet. After nearly fouling out in the qualifying round, he put everything together in his first jump of the final.

A 9.5 sprinter and 6′ 5″ high jumper, he hit the board exactly right without chopping his stride. His technique was his ultimate. The wind behind him was a helpful two meters per second. The altitude aided him by many inches. His landing was excellent, with his legs extended, and yet he shot across his feet and bounced twice without stopping.

His distance was 29′ 2½″, probably the greatest single performance in the history of track and field.

Beccali, Luigi (Italy) : 1931–1938   1,500

Beccali won the 1932 Olympic 1,500 and was third in 1936. He set a world record of 3 :49.0 in 1933 and won the European Championships in 1934.

Berruti, Livio (Italy) : 1959–1968   Sprints

Berruti won the 1960 Olympic 200 in a world record equalling 20.5. He placed fifth in 1964 and competed in 1968. He ran 10.2 when the world record was 10.1.

Bikila, Abebe (Ethiopia) : 1960–1968   Marathon

Bikila had no record of note before 1960. He had won two marathons (2 :21 :23), but he had lost shorter trials. At Rome, running barefoot on the stones of the Appian Way, he pulled away at the end to win the Olympic marathon by 25 seconds in 2 :15 :16.2.

He won the 1961 Košice Marathon in 2 :20 :12 and other marathons, but lost a 10,000 to Wolde at Berlin in 1962, where he ran 29 :00.8 in his first race on a track.

In 1963, he led the Boston Marathon for 20 miles, but a leg cramp dropped him to fifth place at the end, his first loss in a marathon. In August, 1964, he ran 2 :16 in training, but in September, 40 days before the Olympic marathon, he had an appendectomy. Thus, he was not favored to win at Tokyo. In fact, no Olympic runner had ever won twice.

Running in shoes this time, he moved to the front at 20,000 meters in a swift 1 :00 :58 and pulled away. He won by over four minutes in 2 :12 :11.2, fastest marathon ever run. He appeared fresh and said, 'I could run another ten kilometers.' Ron Clarke said, 'That was the greatest performance ever in track and field.'

At the age of thirty-six in 1968, Bikila felt ready for his third Olympic championship as a high altitude runner, but he was forced to drop out with an incipient fracture of his left fibula. Early in 1969 he was partially paralyzed in an auto accident.

Bolotnikov, Pyotr (USSR) : 1955–1964   Distances

Bolotnikov placed 9th in the 1956 Olympic 5,000 and 16th in the 10,000. He won the 1960 Olympic 10,000. On October 15, 1960, in Kiev, he broke the world record with 28 :18.8. On August 11, 1962, he lowered his own record to 28 :18.2. A month later he won the 10,000 in the European Championships and placed third in the 5,000. He was first in the world in 1959, 1960, and 1962. He finished 25th in the 1964 Olympic 10,000.

Boston, Ralph (USA) : 1959–1969   Long Jump

In 1959, Boston had a best long jump of 25' 3" and placed third in the NCAA and fourth in the AAU. One year later he had improved only 4¼ inches and placed sixth in the AAU, although he won the NCAA and NAIA.

Suddenly he turned into a great jumper. His winning 26' 6¼" at the Final Trials was wind-aided, but he had a legal 26' 4¼". On August 12, at Walnut, California, he broke Owens' 25-year-old record by leaping 26' 11¼". He won the Olympic champion-ship at 26' 7¾".

In 1961 he set an indoor record of 26' 6¼" in the AAU. Out-doors, he was undefeated until injured in September. He raised his world record to 27' ½" at Modesto, California, May 27. He jumped 27' ¼" at Albuquerque, New Mexico, June 17. He won the AAU at 26' 11¼". He broke his record with 27' 2" against the Soviets at Moscow.

In 1962 he was undefeated outdoors. He won the AAU at 26' 6" and jumped 26' 9" against the USSR, with wind. In 1963, his best jump, 27' 2¾", was wind-aided and lost to Phil Shinnick's 27' 4". He won the AAU at 26' 10" and the Russian dual meet at 26' 10½". His best legal jump was 26' 11¾".

In 1964 he jumped 27' 2½" at Modesto, won the AAU at 26' 7½", and cleared 27' 5½" with wind in the semi-final Olympic Trials. He jumped 27' 3¼" on August 11. In the Final Trials at Los Angeles, September 12, he regained the world record with 27' 4¼" but his winning jump was a wind-aided 27' 10¼".

Rain and win held him to 26' 4¼" in the Olympics at Tokyo and he lost to Davies.

In 1965, he lost only in his first meet. He cleared 27' 2" with wind in Madrid. He raised his world record to 27' 4¾" at Modesto, May 29. He won the AAU at 26' 3½".

In 1966 he had an ankle injury. He lost twice and had best jumps of 26' 10" at Mexico City and 27' with wind. He won the AAU at 26' 3".

In 1967 he barely lost his AAU title, after winning six years in a row. He lost three other meets, but he jumped 27 feet in five meets, including 27' 2½" in the Pan American Games, and he was No. 1 in World Ranking for the eighth consecutive year.

In 1968 he started poorly, with a floating cartilage in his knee. He was second in the AAU at 26' 7¾" and reached 27' 1" with wind at the Final Trials. At Flagstaff, Arizona, a high-altitude site, he jumped 27′ 5½″ with wind. In the qualifying round at Mexico City he set an Olympic record of 27′ 1½″.

In the final, his first jump of 26′ 9½″ was good for third place. On his fifth jump, he had a hairline foul close to 28 feet.

Boston was talented in several other events. In the high hurdles, he was undefeated in 1961 with a best time of 13.7, and he ranked fifth in the world. In 1965 he won the indoor AAU high hurdles. In the low hurdles, he ran 22.4 in 1960 and 22.2 with wind in 1961.

He high jumped 6′ 9″ in 1960, placed fourth in the 1963 Pan American Games at 6′ 8⅜″, and cleared seven feet in practice. In the triple jump, he led the U.S. list in 1963 with 51′ 8¼″ and jumped 52′ 1½″ after the 1964 Olympics. In his 1961 conference meet, he won the javelin at 185 feet and vaulted 13 feet.

Bouin, Jean (France) : 1911–1913   Distances

Bouin set world records for one hour in 1911 and 1913 (11 miles, 1,412 yards); he lowered the 10,000 record to 30 :58.8 in 1911. In the 1912 Olympics he set a world record in the heat of the 5,000 and barely lost in the final.

Bragg, Don (USA) : 1955–1960   Pole Vault

Bragg, 6′ 3″ and 197 pounds, set a world record of 15′ 9¼″ in 1960 with a steel pole. He set an Olympic record of 15′ 5″. He set an indoor record of 15′ 9⅝″ in 1959. He won the 1955 NCAA and the 1959 AAU. He ranked No. 1 in the world in 1959 and 1960.

Budd, Frank (USA) : 1961–1962   Sprints

Budd ran the first official 9.2 in the 1961 AAU and tied the 220 straightaway record of 20 flat in 1962.

Burghley, David (GB) : 1927–1932   Hurdles

Lord Burghley set a world record of 54.2 for the 440 yard hurdles in 1927. He won the 1928 Olympic 400 meter hurdles. He was fourth in the 1932 Olympics in 52.2 and placed fifth in the high hurdles. He won a silver medal in the 1,600 meter relay.

Calhoun, Lee (USA) : 1956–1960   High Hurdles

Calhoun is the only man ever to win two Olympic high hurdles. In 1956 he lowered his best time from 14.4 to 13.5. He won the indoor AAU, the NAIA, the NCAA, and the AAU before his narrow 13.5 victory over Jack Davis at Melbourne.

He repeated his four national championships in 1957. In 1958 he was suspended for being married on television and receiving wedding gifts. In 1959 he won his third AAU title.

He won the 1960 Final Trials in 13.4. At Bern, Switzerland, on August 21, he tied the world record of 13.2. He won his second Olympic gold medal in 13.8.

Carlton, James (Australia) : 1931–1932   Sprints

Carlton ran an unofficial 9.4 in 1931. Later, in New Zealand, he won a double victory over George Simpson. On January 16, 1932, he ran 220 yards around a curve in 20.6, unbeaten for 28 years. He retired to the priesthood before the Olympics.

Carr, Bill (USA) : 1932   440

With a previous best 440 of 48.4, Carr defeated world record holder Eastman (46.4) in 47 flat for the IC4A title. He beat Eastman again in the AAU with 46.9 for 400 meters. He won the Olympic championship in 46.2, a world record, then anchored the world record relay team. His career ended with a traffic accident.

Carr, Henry (USA) : 1962–1964   Sprints

Only a 9.4 man for 100 yards, Carr ran 20.1 for a straightaway 220 and set a world record 20.3 for 220 yards around a turn in 1963. He ran eight other races between 20.4 and 20.8. In 1964 he lowered his record to 20.2 and won the Olympic championship in 20.3. He anchored USA's gold-medal 1,600 meter relay team He ran 45.4 for 400 meters and won two AAU furlong titles.

Carr, Sabin (USA) : 1927–1928   Pole Vault

Carr became the first amateur to vault 14 feet, in 1927. In 1928, he vaulted 14' 1" indoors and won the Olympic championship.

Cawley, Warren (USA) : 1959–1964   440-Hurdles

As a high school boy, Rex Cawley became the first hurdler ever to place in all three events in an AAU meet. He was fifth in the high hurdles, third in the lows, and sixth in the inter-mediates in 1959. He ran the highs in 13.9 that summer in Europe.

In 1960, he ran 50.6 for the 400 meter hurdles, placing seventh in the Final Trials. In 1961, ranked fourth in the world with 49.9, he also ran a 46.2 440 and 22.5 for the low hurdles before an injury forced him out. Injuries hobbled him again in 1962, but he moved up to No. 3 with a best of 50.6 for the 440 hurdles.

In 1963 he became first in the world with 49.6 for the NCAA 440 hurdles. He also won the AAU title and placed second in the NCAA 440 with 46 flat.

In 1964, he set a world record of 49.1 in the Final Trials and won the Olympic championship in 49.6.

Clarke, Ron (Australia) : 1956–1969   Distances

Clarke set a world junior record of 4:06.8 for the mile in 1956. After carrying the Olympic torch into the stadium at Melbourne, he ran 4:07.2 early in 1957 and retired.

He began training again in 1961 at the age of twenty-four. On December 18, 1963, in Melbourne, he broke the world records for 6 miles (27:16.6) and 10,000 meters (28:15.6).

In the 1964 Olympic Games, he led in the homestretch of the 10,000 but finished third. In the 5,000, he wore himself out with repeated 'surging' and placed ninth. He ran the marathon in 2:20:26.8 for another ninth place.

On December 3, he broke the world record for 3 miles (13:07.6), and on January 16, 1965, he lowered the 5,000 meter record to 13:34.8. He took another 1.2 seconds off that record 16 days later in Auckland, New Zealand. He went on to run an astounding number of fast distance races.

On March 3, in Melbourne, he set a world 10-mile record of 47:12.8. On June 4 in Los Angeles, he lowered his 3-mile record to 13:00.4 and his 5,000 record to 13:25.8. At Turku, Finland, June 16, he broke his 10,000 record by 1.6 seconds. On June 23, he bettered two world records – 3,000 in 7:51.0 and 2-mile in 8:24.8 – but lost both to Jazy.

After losing a 3,000 and two 5,000's, he ran 3 miles in 12 :52.4 at London, July 10. Four days later, at Oslo, he lowered the 6-mile and 10,000 record to almost unbelievable times of 26 :47.0 and 27 :39.4.

At Geelong, Australia, on October 27, he broke the world records for 20,000 meters (59 :22.8) and one hour (12 miles, 1006 yds).

In 1966 he made fast runs commonplace. On July 5, in Stockholm, he lowered the 3-mile record to 12 :50.4 and his 5,000 meter record to 13 :16.6. In the Commonwealth Games he lost the 6-mile to Temu and the 3-mile to Keino, even though he ran 12 :59.2. He dropped out of the marathon after 19 miles.

In 1967, tired of losing to faster finishers, he improved his speed. He lowered the world 2-mile record to 8 :19.8 at Vastoras, Sweden, on June 27. His only loss of the year was to Keino in Los Angeles when he was injured. He won the British AAA 3-mile for the third straight year under 13 minutes. Two days later, he ran 12 :59 to give him seven of the nine times ever run under thirteen minutes.

In 1968, he took a fifth of a second off his world 2-mile record in London, August 24, and ran under 13 :40 for 5,000 meters on nine occasions, but he lost five races before the Olympics. He could not cope with Mexico City's high altitude and placed sixth in the 10,000 and fifth in the 5,000. He announced his retirement, but he ran well enough in early 1969 to set an indoor 3-mile record of 13 :12.6 at Oakland, California.

To his credit were the four fastest 6-miles, the three fastest 10,000's, and the two fastest 2-miles, 3-miles, and 5,000's. He was first in World Ranking for 5,000 meters in 1967 and 1968, and for 10,000 meters in 1963, 1965, and 1968.

Cochran, Roy (USA) : 1939–1948   400 Hurdles

A 23.1 low hurdler in 1939, Cochran won the AAU 440 hurdles in 51.9 as a novice. On April 25, 1942, at Des Moines, Iowa, he set a world 440 hurdle record of 52.2. After the war, he ran 46.7 for third in the 1946 AAU 400 meters. He won the 1948 Olympic intermediates in 51.1, bettered only by Hardin. He won a second gold medal in the 1,600 meter relay.

Connolly, Harold (USA) : 1953–1969   Hammer

Connolly won the 1956 Olympic hammer throw with an Olympic record of 207' 3½". He competed in three more Olympics, placing eighth in 1960 and sixth in 1964.

He raised the world record to 220' 10½" and 224' 10½" in 1956, to 225' 4" in 1958, to 230' 9" in 1960, to 231' 10" in 1962 and to 233' 2" and 233' 9½" in 1965, when he had to his credit seven of the eight longest throws ever made.

In World Ranking, he was first twice, No. 2 six times, and third three times. He won the AAU hammer nine years. He set a best-ever record with the 35-pound weight in the 1960 indoor AAU and won the title twice more.

Consolini, Adolfo (Italy) : 1938–1960   Discus

Consolini placed fifth in the discus in the 1938 European Championships at the age of twenty-one and 17th in the 1960 Olympic Games at the age of forty-three. In between, he missed two Olympics because of war, won in 1948, was second in 1952, and sixth in 1956. He won European Championships in 1946, 1950, and 1954. He set a world record of 175 feet on October 26, 1941. He lost it in 1946 but regained it with 181' 6½" at Milan, October 10, 1948. His lifetime best, a European record, was 186' 11" in December, 1955, at the age of nearly thirty-nine.

Courtney, Tom (USA) : 1955–1958   880

Courtney won the 1956 Olympic championship at 800 meters. On May 24, 1957, in Los Angeles, he lowered the world 880 record to 1 :46.8. On August 9 in Oslo, he ran 800 meters in 1 :45.8, one tenth slower than the world record. After the 1957 season he had five of the eight fastest 800–880's ever run. He was first in World Ranking in 1956 and second in 1957 and 1958. He won the NCAA in 1955 and the AAU in 1957 and 1958. In the 400 meters, he ran 45.8 to win the 1956 AAU and ranked first in the world in 1957.

Craig, Ralph (USA) : 1910–1912   Sprints

Craig twice equalled the world's 220 record of 21.2 in 1910 and 1911, also winning three IC4A sprints. In the 1912 Olympics, he won both sprints.

Crothers, Bill (Canada) : 1963–1968   880

Crothers may have ranked as the greatest half-miler of all time except for the presence of Snell. Crothers' 1963 AAU victory in 1 :46.8, his second place in the 1964 Olympics with 1 :45.6, and his indoor 1,000 in 2 :06.4 were second only to Snell. He was first in World Ranking for 1963 and 1965. He ran a 46.2 440 in 1961 and a 4 :03.1 mile in 1964.

Csermák, József (Hungary) : 1952–1960   Hammer

Csermák won the hammer throw in the 1952 Olympics with a world record 197' 11½" at the age of twenty. He threw 205' 4" in 1956 and placed fifth in the Olympics. His best throw was 210' 8½" in 1960, but he failed to qualify in the Olympics.

Cunningham, Glenn (USA) : 1932–1940   800–Mile

Cunningham was fourth in the Olympic 1,500 in 1932 and second in 1936. He set a world mile record of 4 :06.7 in 1934 and an 800 meter record of 1 :49.7 in 1936. He won six AAU championships.

Danielson, Egil (Norway) : 1955–1958   Javelin

Undefeated in 1956, Danielson won the Olympic javelin with a world record 281' 2½". He ranked second in the world for the next two years and placed second in the 1958 European Championships.

Da Silva, Adhemer Ferreira (Brazil) : 1948–1960   Triple Jump

After an 11th place in the 1948 Olympics, Da Silva triple jumped 52' 6" on December 3, 1950 in Sao Paulo to equal the world record. On September 30, 1951, he took sole possession of the record with 52' 6¼". In the 1952 Olympics, he won the championship with a world record 53' 2½". He lost the record in 1953, but in the Pan American Games, at Mexico City, March 16, 1955, he leaped 54' 4" to regain the world record. In the 1956 Olympics, he won again with 53' 7¾". He jumped 53' 3¾" in 1958, but he placed only 14th in the 1960 Olympics. He was undefeated from 1951 through 1956.

Davenport, Willie (USA) : 1964–1969   High Hurdles

Davenport surprised in 1964 by making the US Olympic team. Injuries eliminated him in Tokyo, but he was first in World Ranking for the next four years. He won the AAU high hurdles three years, but injuries forced him out in 1968. He came back on August 31 at Knoxville, Tennessee, to equal the world record of 13.2. He won the Final Trials in 13.4. He won the Olympic title in 13.3. In 1969, he set several indoor records, and tied for first in the AAU.

Davis, Hal (USA) : 1940–1943   Sprints

In his first year out of high school, Davis won both AAU sprints in 10.3 and 20.4, each only one tenth off the world record. The next year, 1941, he tied the world record of 10.2 in the Compton 100 meters, but a poor start cost him his AAU title in the 100, his only loss of the year. He won the 200 in 20.4. He was undefeated in 1942, winning doubles in both the NCAA and AAU. He tied the world 100 yard record of 9.4. In 1943, he won doubles again in both meets, including a wind-aided 20.2 in the AAU. He also ran a wind-aided 220 in 20.2. World War II ended his triumphs and cancelled two Olympic Games where he would have been favored for sprint doubles. He was undefeated after his high school year in the furlong, and he lost only twice in the 100 during those four years.

Davis, Jack (USA) : 1951–1956   High Hurdles

Davis won the NCAA high hurdles all three years, adding third place in the 1951 lows, second in the 1952 200 meters flat, and first in the 1953 lows. In AAU meets, he was second in the highs in 1951 and won the lows. In 1952, he was second to Dillard in the highs. In 1953 and 1954 he won both hurdles. False starts eliminated him in the 1955 AAU and he placed only third after a world record 13.4 in his 1956 heat. He barely lost in both the 1952 and 1956 Olympic high hurdles. He ran 13.4 twice and 13.5 twice, giving him four of the six fastest times ever run. He ran 13.6 seven times, 13.7 nine times, 13.8 fifteen times, and 13.9 seventeen times. He once won thirty-seven consecutive high hurdle finals, including all of 1953 and 1954.

Davis, Walt (USA) : 1950–1953   High Jump

Buddy Davis, 6′ 8″ tall, was crippled by infantile paralysis as a boy but became an All-American in basketball. He began high jumping with 6′ 4½″ in 1950 and jumped 6′ 9″ in 1951 to rank second in the world. In 1952, he changed to the western roll, won the AAU at 6′ 10½″, and the Olympic championship at 6′ 8¼″ in cold weather. On June 27, 1953, in the AAU at Dayton, Ohio, he set a world record of 6′ 11⅝″.

Davis, Otis (USA) : 1959–1961   440

Davis ran his first good 440 in 1959 at the age of 26. That 46.2 was improved to a 45.6 400 in 1960. He won in the Olympics with a world record 44.9. He anchored the relay team for another gold medal. His only AAU victory, in 1961, ended his brief career

Doubell, Ralph (Australia) : 1966–   880

Doubell won the 1968 Olympic 800 meters while equalling the world record of 1 :44.3.

Duffey, Arthur (USA) : 1900–1902   Sprints

Duffey won several titles in the IC4A and AAU sprints but his name was removed when he was declared a professional. His 9.6 in the 1902 IC4A was also removed.

Dumas, Charles (USA) : 1955–1960   High Jump

At eighteen, Dumas cleared 6′ 10½″. At nineteen, in 1956 he was undefeated. After winning the AAU at 6′ 10″ he became history's first 7-footer in the Final Trials with 7′ ⅝″. He won the Olympic championship at 6′ 11⅜″.

In 1957 he was undefeated and won the AAU at 6′ 10¼″. In 1958 he won the AAU, tied for second in the NCAA, and ranked second in the world. In 1959, he regained his first ranking, cleared seven feet, won the AAU, and lost only once.

In 1960, he jumped 7′ ¼″, but he was hobbled by a leg injury and placed only sixth in the Olympic Games. He retired completely until 1964, when he appeared out of nowhere to clear 7′ ¼″.

Eastman, Ben (USA) : 1931–1936   440–880

Eastman tied Meredith's world 440 record of 47.4 in 1931. He lowered it to 46.4 on March 26, 1932. He ran 46.5 in May. On June 4 he broke the world 800 and 880 records with 1 :50.0 and 1 :50.9. Choosing the 400, he lost three times to Bill Carr, including the Olympic final.

In 1933 he set an official world record of 1 :09.2 for 600 yards. In 1934 he won the Princeton Invitational in 1 :49.8, a world record for 880 yards and a tie with Hampson's 800 record. He won the AAU 800 in 1 :50.8. In Europe he bettered his 600 record with 1 :08.8, ran the fastest 600 meters on record, 1 :18.4, and set an official world record of 1 :02.0 for 500 meters. After a year of rest, he ran 1 :50.1 for 800 meters in 1936, but humid, 100-degree heat sickened him and he failed to make the Olympic team.

Edwards, Phil (Canada) : 1928–1936   880–1,500

A Negro from British Guiana, Edwards attended New York University and ran in three Olympic Games for Canada. In 1928 he placed fourth in the 800 and won a bronze medal in the 1,600 meter relay. In 1932 he won three more bronze medals, in the 800, 1,500, and relay. In 1936 he took his fifth bronze medal, in the 800, plus a fifth in the 1,500 and fourth in the relay. He won the AAU 880 in 1929 and the indoor AAU 600 from 1928 through 1931.

Evans, Lee (USA) : 1966–   440

Evans burst into prominence in 1966, his first year out of high school, with an undefeated season, first in World Ranking, and the AAU championship. In 1967 he ranked first and won the AAU and Pan American titles, but he lost to Smith's world record plus three races after an injury. In 1968 he lost only two minor races and won NCAA, AAU, and Olympic championships plus a second Olympic gold medal in a world-record relay. He lowered the world 400 meter record to 44 flat at South Lake Tahoe, California, in September and to 43.8 in the Olympic final. In 1969 he won his fourth AAU title.

Ewell, Norwood (USA) : 1936–1948   Sprints–Long Jump

Barney Ewell had the longest career of any good sprinter. He started with the junior AAU 100 meters in 1936. He won six AAU sprint championships, was runner-up four times, and placed in five other races, plus once in the broad jump. In 1940 and 1941, he won NCAA sprint doubles. He won both sprints and the long jump in all three of his IC4A meets. An injury in the long jump eliminated him from the 1942 NCAA and AAU.

He won the indoor AAU long jump three times and jumped 25′ 2½ in an IC4A indoor meet. In 1948, after missing two Olympics because of the war, he won the Final Trials with a world record equalling 10.2. At London, he placed a close second in both Olympic sprints and won a gold medal in the relay.

Ewrey, Ray (USA) : 1898–1908   Standing Jumps

Ewrey was paralyzed as a boy, but exercises developed tremendous strength in his legs. In 1898, at the age of twenty-five, he began winning championships in the standing jumps, then official events. He won fifteen AAU titles even though the events were not held from 1899 to 1905.

Ewrey won ten Olympic championships in four Olympics. In 1900 he won the high jump with a world record 5′ 5″, the broad jump at 10′ 6.4″, and the triple jump at 34′ 8¼″. In 1904 he repeated his three triumphs, raising his broad jump record to 11′ 4⅞″. This mark stood unbeaten on the official world record list until it was discarded in 1938.

In the unofficial Olympics of 1906, Ewrey won both standing jumps, and he repeated in 1908 at the age of thirty-four.

Finlay, Donald (GB) : 1931–1951   High Hurdles

Unequalled for longevity, Finlay was third in the 1932 Olympic high hurdles at the age of twenty-three. He won the silver medal in 1936. He ran 14.1 and 14.2 in 1937, and won the 1938 European Championships in 14.3. He fell in the 1948 Olympics, but in 1949, at the age of forty, he won in 14.4 against France.

Flannagan, John (USA) : 1895–1909   Hammer

Flannagan set a world record of 145′ 10½″ for the hammer in Ireland in 1895. He broke it sixteen times, to 184′ 4″, at New Haven, July 24, 1909. He won AAU titles in the hammer seven times and in the 56-pound weight six times. He won three Olympics championships : 1900, 1904, and 1908, and placed third in the 1904 discus.

173

Foss, Frank (USA) : 1920   Pole Vault

Foss won the 1920 Olympic pole vault with a world record of 13' 5".

Fuchs, Jim (USA) : 1948–1952   Shot Put

Fuchs raised the world record in the shot put four times, to 58' 10¾" in 1951. He won both NCAA and AAU in 1949 and 1950, and placed third in the Olympics in 1948 and 1952. He also threw the discus 172' 7", making him fourteenth best of all time in 1949.

George, Walter (GB) : 1879–1884   Distances

One of the greatest runners of all time, George won fourteen British Championships from the 880 to 10 miles in the four years he entered. In 1884 he set his third world mile record (4:18.4) and records for 2 miles (9:17.4), 3 miles (14:39.0), 6 miles (30:21.5), and 10 miles (51:20). In 1885 he ran a well-documented practice mile in 4:10.2 on a course six yards long. The next year he ran his famous 4:12¾. He won two out of three series from Lon Myers, losing only indoors.

Gordien, Fortune (USA) : 1947–1956   Discus

Gordien set world records in the discus of 186' 11" in 1949 and 194' 6" in 1953. At that date he had sixteen of the eighteen longest throws ever made. He won three NCAA and six AAU titles. He ranked first in the world in 1947, 1949, 1953, and 1954. He was third in the 1948 Olympics, fourth in 1952, and second in 1956. He lost only four times from 1947 through 1950, when he retired temporarily. In 1947 he was third shot putter in World Ranking.

Greene, Charlie (USA) : 1964–1968   Sprints

Greene tied the world records of 9.1 for 100 yards (1967) and 9.9 for 100 meters (1968). He ranked first in the world in 1966. He placed third in the 1968 Olympic 100 and won a gold medal in the relay.

Gutowski, Bob (USA) : 1955–1957   Pole Vault

Gutowski placed second in the 1956 Olympic vault and broke Warmerdam's record in 1957 with 15' 8¼", using a steel pole.

Hägg, Gunder (Sweden) : 1940–1945   1,500–5,000

Hägg developed into a world-class runner in 1940 at the age of twenty-two after four years of training in an unstructured method now called Fartlek. He tied the Swedish record for 1,500 meters with 3 :48.8 in 1940, only 1.2 second from the world record.

In 1941, he ran 3 :48.6, then defeated Arne Andersson by seven yards in world record time of 3 :47.6. He ran a mile in 4 :09.2.

After nine months of hard Fartlek, he ran his first race of 1942 on July 1 at Göteborg. He defeated Andersson in a 4 :06.1 mile, a new world record. Two days later, he lowered the world record for 2 miles to 8 :47.8. Two weeks later, at Stockholm, he defeated Andersson and lowered his 1,500 meter record to 3 :45.8. Four days after that, at Malmö, he broke the 2,000 meter record with 5 :16.4.

August 23, 1942, at Ostersund, he lowered his 2,000 record to 5 :11.8. Five days later, in Stockholm, his 8 :01.2 was a new world 3.000 meter record. A week later, he took the mile record down to 4 :04.6 Another week later he broke the 3-mile record with 13 :55.4.

Nine days later, September 20, in Göteborg, he bettered that 3-mile time by three seconds on his way to 5,000 meters in 13 :58.2. Those two records lasted twelve years.

In a period of eighty-two days he had broken ten world records at seven distances in twenty-six victorious races.

In 1943 he made a long, hazardous, war-time voyage to the United States and won all of his races without setting a world record. In Sweden, Andersson lowered two of Hägg's records to 3 :45.0 and 4 :02.6.

On July 7, 1944, in Göteborg, Hägg recovered one record when he defeated Andersson by seven yards in 3 :43.0. Eleven days later, at Malmö, Andersson managed his lone victory over Hägg in 4 :01.6, while Hägg ran 4 :02.0.

Hägg lowered his 2-mile record to 8 :46.4 on June 5. On August 4, at Göteborg, he ran 8 :42.8, a world record for eight years.

In 1945, Hägg made a rough voyage to the United States and ran without distinction, but by July 17 he was back in shape. At Malmö he defeated Andersson by six yards in a 4 :01.3 mile, a world record for the next nine years. Both he and Andersson were barred from amateur competition in November, 1945.

175

Hägg's best distance was undoubtedly longer than a mile. When he retired he had run the six fastest 2-miles of all time, plus five of the six fastest 3,000 meters, all in separate races.

Hahn, Archie (USA) : 1903–1906   Sprints

Hahn won three Olympic sprints in 1904–60, 100, and 200. He repeated in the 100 of the unofficial 1906 Games. He won three AAU championships.

Halberg, Murray (New Zealand) : 1954–1964   Distances

Halberg, a 4:04.4 miler at the age of twenty-one, placed fifth in the 1954 British Empire mile behind Bannister and Landy. In the 1956 Olympics, he was 11th in the 1,500 meters. In 1958 he won the Empire 3-mile and ran a 3:57.5 mile behind Elliott's 3:54.5.

In March, 1960, he ran 27:52.2, the second fastest 6-mile of all time, then won the Olympic 5,000 and placed fifth in the 10,000. On July 7, 1961, he lowered the world 2-mile record to 8:30.0. On July 25, in Stockholm, he bettered the world 3-mile record with 13:10.0 and continued to 5,000 meters in 13:35.2, only a fifth off the world record.

He won the British Empire 3-mile again in 1962. In 1964, after four consecutive years as world first in the 5,000 meters, he did not qualify in the Olympic 5,000 and placed seventh in the 10,000.

Hamm, Ed (USA) : 1927–1928   Long Jump

Hamm won the NCAA long jump in 1927 and 1928. On July 7, 1928, in the AAU meet, he jumped 25′ 11⅛″ for a new world record. He won the Olympic championship with 25′ 4¼″.

Hampson, Thomas (GB) : 1930–1932   800

Hampson won the AAA title three times before he set a world record of 1:49.8 in the 1932 Olympic 800 meters.

Hansen, Fred (USA) : 1962–1964   Pole Vault

Hansen ranked eighth in the world in 1963 with a best vault of 16′ 1″. In 1964 he became the first man to clear 17 feet with

17′ 1″ in Texas on June 5. He raised his world record to 17′ 2″ at San Diego on June 13. He won the AAU at 17 feet. Against Russia, in Los Angeles, July 25, he raised the world record to 17′ 4″. He won a dramatic Olympic victory at 16′ 8¾″.

Harbig, Rudolf (Germany) : 1936–1942   400–800

Unsuccessful in the 1936 Olympics Harbig was deprived of two Olympics by World War II. He was undefeated in 1937, lost one 400 meters to Ray Mallott in 1938, and was undefeated in 1939. That year he ran 1 :46.6 at Milan on July 15, a world 800 record which lasted sixteen years. On August 12 at Frankfort, he ran 400 meters in 46 flat, a world record which lasted ten years. In 1941, he set a world record for 1,000 meters. In 1942 he lost two slow races and in 1944 he was reported missing on the Russian front. He was European 800 meter champion in 1938.

Hardin, Glenn (USA) : 1932–1936   440-Hurdles

As a freshman at Louisiana State in 1932, Hardin won the AAU 400 meter hurdles but he was disqualified. At Los Angeles, he set an Olympic record of 52.8 in the semi-final and finished a close second in the final. Tisdall, the winner in 51.8, knocked down a hurdle and so was deprived of a world record. Hardin, timed in 51.9, was credited with equalling the official world record of 52 flat.

In both 1933 and 1934, Hardin won NCAA doubles in the 440 and low hurdles, plus the AAU intermediates. His 47.1 in the 1933 NCAA was the second fastest 440 ever run on two turns. His 22.9 broke the world record for the low hurdles but it was not approved.

In 1934 he won a 440 in 46.8, second only to Eastman's world record. He improved both his NCAA marks with 47.0 and 22.7. Again his low hurdle record was not recognized, because an electric timer showed a slower time. In the 1934 AAU, his 51.6 was a new world record for the 400 meter hurdles.

He toured Europe in 1934. In Stockholm for three days, Hardin started with 47.8. On the second day he ran 300 meters in 33.7, half a second off Paddock's world record. On the third day, July 26, he ran the 400 hurdles in 50.6, which remained as the world record for nineteen years.

He was off form in 1935. He finished third in the NCAA 440 and lost to Owens in the low hurdles.

In 1936, he won his third AAU title, in 51.6, giving him the five fastest times in history. He won the Olympic championship in 52.4, completing four years without a defeat in the intermediates.

Hary, Armin (Germany) : 1958–1960   Sprints

Hary was a miraculous starter who ran the first 10-flat 100 meters, at Zurich, June 21, 1960. He also ran two unofficial 10-flats. He won the 1958 European Championships in 10.3 and the 1960 Olympic championship in 10.2.

Hayes, Bob (USA) : 1961–1964   Sprints

Hayes' career lasted through his four college years at Florida A&M. In sixty-two 100 yards or 100 meters finals he lost only two, both in one week after he had been ill. Indoors, his only loss in nine races was to an admitted rolling start when he hesitated, expecting to be recalled. Lack of conditioning probably accounted for his 220 losses although they were mostly to great runners.

Hayes was first in World Ranking his last three years in the 100. He ranked only fifth in 1961 because he was unknown and ran few races although he was undefeated and equalled the world record of 9.3.

In the 220 he ran 20.1 on a straightaway in 1961 and twice tied the world record of 20.5 around a curve. He ranked second in 1963 and fourth in 1964.

Indoors, he ran only once before 1964, lowering the record for 70 yards to 6.9. In 1964, he again ran 6.9. In his seven 60-yard races, he ran 6.1 once, tied the record of 6-flat five times, and set a new record of 5.9 in the AAU meet

His outdoor championships included the 200 in his only NCAA appearance and three AAU 100's. He lost his only AAU 220 to Paul Drayton. He won the 1964 Olympic 100 meters by seven feet and won a second gold medal with an almost inhuman burst of speed on the anchor leg.

His times at 100 yards and 100 meters were phenomenal. After 1961, the records were 9.2 and 10.1. He ran 9.2 and 10.1 in

1962. In 1963 he ran 9.1 for an official world record plus one with wind, and he ran a 9.9 100 meters with wind. In 1964 he ran three 9.1's and a 9.2. In the Olympic semi-final he ran 9.9 for 100 meters with wind. His world record 10-flat in the final was hand timed at 9.9. He ran 9.3 or faster nineteen times, plus three with wind

Hein, Karl (Germany) : 1936–1938   Hammer

Hein won the Olympic hammer in 1936. In 1938, he set a world record of 191' 1" and won the European Championships at 192' 10".

Hemery, David (GB) : 1966–   400 Hurdles

Hemery lived and trained in the United States, attending Boston University where there is no outdoor track and only a part-time coach. He ran 52.8 as a freshman in 1965. In the indoor season of 1966 he proved his strength with a 1:09.8 600. He proved his hurdling ability with two 7.2's for the 60-yard high hurdles, winning the IC4A and placing second in the NCAA.

Outdoors, he won the 1966 IC4A highs in 14.1 and ran 51.8 for second in the intermediates. He ran 13.9 in Russia and won the Commonwealth championship in 14.1. After 14.1 in a heat of the European Championships, he was injured. In 1967, after a promising start indoors, he was injured again and missed the entire outdoor season.

He ran little indoors in 1968, placing second in the IC4A 600. In early outdoor meets, he ran 14 flat, 13.9, and 13.7 with wind. His progress showed even more in the intermediates, where he clocked 2 50.7's, 50.6, and 50.5 for 440 yards before winning the IC4A at 50.4.

In the NCAA meet at Berkeley, he won in the slow curb lane with 49.8 for 400 meters. He won the AAU title of July 13 with 50.2 for 440 yards. On August 24, in London, he ran 49.6.

In the Olympic Games, Mexico City's high altitude aided quarter-milers by as much as a full second, but a hurdler had to maintain the correct step Hemery was cautious while qualifying with times of 50.3 and 49.3, but in the final he gambled on using only thirteen steps between the first six hurdles. He built up an astounding lead, then changed to fifteen steps. He won by 9

yards in 48.1, a full second faster that the official world record.
He did not run the intermediate hurdles in 1969, but he placed
second in the European Championship high hurdles in 13.7.

Hines, Jim (USA) : 1966–1968   Sprints
Hines ranked first in the world for 100 meters in 1967 and
1968 and second in the 200 in 1966 and 1967. He won three
AAU titles and the 1968 Olympic 100. His fast finish saved the
gold medal in the relay. He tied world records with 9.1 and 9.9
and he ran a 20.3 curve 220.

Höckert, Gunnar (Finland) : 1936   3,000–5,000
Höckert won the 1936 Olympic 5,000 meters in an Olympic
record 14 :22.2. On September 16, 1936, in Stockholm, he broke
the world 3,000 meter record with 8 :14.8. Eight days later, he
broke the 2-mile record with 8 :57.4.

Horine, George (USA) : 1912   High Jump
Horine invented the western roll. Only 5′ 11″ tall, he broke
the world high jump record with 6′ 6⅛″ on March 29, 1912. On
May 18, he raised it to 6′ 7″. Ill, he placed only third in the
Olympics.

Houser, Clarence (USA) : 1924–1928   Shot–Discus
Bud Houser, only 187 pounds, won the shot put and discus
throw in the 1924 Olympics. In 1928 he won the discus again.
On April 3, 1926, he set a world record of 158′ 1¾″ in the discus.
He won two AAU shot titles and three in the discus.

Hubbard, De Hart (USA) : 1922–1928   100–Long Jump
Hubbard won the broad jump in the 1923 NCAA. He won
the 1924 Olympic broad jump after falling far back on a jump
which measured 24′ 5⅛″. In the 1925 NCAA, he won the 100
and broad jumped 25′ 10⅞″ for a world record. In 1926 he tied
the world record of 9.6 for 100 yards. In 1927, he jumped 26′ 2¼″
but the landing pit was one inch too low. He won six AAU
broad jumps, 1922–1927. He was injured in 1928 and placed only
11th in the Olympics.

Iharos, Sandor (Hungary) : 1954–1958   Distances

Iharos set a European record of 3 :42.4 for 1,500 meters in 1954. In 1955, he set successive world records for 3,000 meters (7 :55.6), 2 miles (8 :33.4), 1,500 meters (3 :40.8), 5,000 meters (13 :50.8), 3 miles (13 :14.2), and, in the same race, 5,000 meters (13 :40.6). In his first attempt at 10,000 meters in four years, he set a world record of 28 :42.8 (in 1956), passing 6 miles in 27 :43.8. He missed the 1956 Olympics because of the uprising.

Iness, Sim (USA) : 1948–1953   Discus

Iness threw the discus 180′ 6½″ for a new Olympic record in 1952. In 1953 he won his second NCAA title with a world record of 190′ ⅞″.

Iso-Hollo, Volmari (Finland) : 1931–1936   Distances

Iso-Hollo won two Olympic steeplechase championships, in 1932 and 1936. His 9 :03.8 at Berlin was by far the fastest ever recorded. He placed second and third in two Olympic 10,000s. His 30 :12.6 in 1932 placed him third on the all-time list. He was a close second to Lehtinen's world record 5,000 in 1932, timed in 14 :18.3. In 1933 his 8 :19.6 was barely beaten by Lehtinen in the second fastest 3,000 ever run. On July 20, 1933, he broke the official world record for 4 miles with 19 :01.0.

Järvinen, Akilles (Finland) : 1928–1934   Decathlon

Son of a world record discus thrower, Aki placed second in two Olympic decathlons, 1928 and 1932. Under the present scoring system, he would have won them both. In 1931 he bettered the world decathlon record. In 1934 he placed second in the European Championships in the 400 meter hurdles.

Järvinen, Matti (Finland) : 1929–1938   Javelin

Brother of the world record decathlon man, Matti had the longest throw in the world at the age of twenty in 1929, his first full year with the javelin. On August 8, 1930, he broke the world record with 234′ 9½″. He raised his record nine times, to 253′ 4½″ in 1936. He won the 1932 Olympic championship, but a back injury dropped him to fifth in 1936. He won the European Championships in 1934 and 1938. In 1949, at the age of forty, he threw 220′ 10⅜″. He won the Finnish Championship eight times. At the end of the 1937 season he had to his credit the ten longest throws of all time.

Jazy, Michel (France) : 1956–1966   1,500–5,000

Jazy ran in the 1956 Olympics at the age of twenty, and placed tenth in the 1,500 meters of the European Championships of 1958. In the 1960 Olympics he ran 3 :38.4 for second in the 1,500. In 1962, he set world records of 5 :01.5 for 2,000 meters and 7 :49.2 for 3,000 meters and won the European Championships 1,500 in 3 :38.3.

In 1963 he ranked third in both 1,500 and 5,000 and lowered his 1,500 meter mark to 3 :37.8. He set a world 2-mile record of 8 :29.6. He placed fourth in the 1964 Olympic 5,000.

In 1965 he was undefeated at 1,500 meters and one mile and broke the world mile record with 3 :53.6. He lowered the 2-mile record to 8 :22.6. He was undefeated and ranked first in the 5,000, beating Keino and Clarke in 13 :27.6, only 1.8 seconds behind Clarke's new world record.

In 1966 he won the European Championships 5,000 and was undefeated. In the 1,500, he ran 3 :36.3 twice and placed second in the European Championships.

Jerome, Harry (Canada) : 1959–1968   Sprints

Jerome tied world records at 9.2 and 10.0 and ran in three Olympics. He pulled a muscle in 1960, placed third in the 100 and fourth in the 200 in 1964, and seventh in the 1968 100.

Johnson, Cornelius (USA) : 1932–1938   High Jump

'Corny' Johnson tied for the 1932 Olympic championship at eighteen. Under present rules he would have been second, but he placed fourth in a jumpoff. He was never beaten, though tied, in the AAU from 1932 through 1936. He won indoor titles in 1935, 1936, and 1938.

In 1936 he set an indoor record of 6′ 8 15/16″. At the outdoor AAU in Princeton, he arrived late and cleared 6′ 7″ on his first jump. He won at 6′ 8″. The next week, in the Final Trials, he set a world record of 6′ 9¾″. He won the Olympic championship at 6′ 8″ without a miss.

Jones, Hayes (USA) : 1957–1964   Hurdles

Jones was a Dillard-type hurdler, short (5′ 11″), fast (9.4), and consistent. He set a junior record of 13.7 at age eighteen in 1957. The next year he ran 13.6, won the AAU, and ranked first in the world. In 1959, he was second in both the NCAA and AAU and won the Pan American championship in 13.6. He won the NCAA low hurdles in 22.5 and lost narrowly to Charles Tidwell's world record 22.6 around a curve in the AAU.

In 1960, after running 13.5, he placed third in the Olympics. He ranked first again in 1961 with an undefeated season. In 1962 he ran 13.4 in the AAU but lost to Jerry Tarr. In 1963, Jones was first again, and won the AAU in 13.4.

In 1964 he ran 13.4 in the semi-final Olympic Trials and won his fifth AAU championship. He won the Olympic highs in 13.6.

Indoors, Jones was unbeatable. His last loss was in March of 1959, after which he won fifty-five consecutive major races. He lowered the 60 yard record to 6.8 in his final race in 1964. He also won sprint races indoors.

Keino, Kipchoge (Kenya) : 1964–   Distances

Keino placed fifth in the 1964 Olympic 5,000. In 1965 he ranked second in the world with a world 5,000 meter record of 13 :24.2, at Auckland, New Zealand, on November 11. He set an outstanding world record of 7 :39.6 for 3,000 meters. He ranked second in the mile with 3 :54.2, third best ever. In 1966, he ranked first in the 5,000 and second in the mile. He ran a 3 :53.4 mile and won both the mile and 3-mile in the Commonwealth Games. In 1967 he was second in World Ranking in both events and lowered his mile best to 3 :53.1.

In 1968, Keino ran 10,000 meters in 28 :06.4, a time bettered by only two men in history. In the Olympic Games he was a contender in the 10,000 meters until pain from a defective gall bladder forced him out near the end. In the 5,000, he finished a close second. In the 1,500 meter final, his sixth run in eight days, he shocked everybody with the fastest race of his career, at 7,350 feet altitude. He won by almost three seconds in 3 :34.9, an Olympic record.

King, Leamon (USA) : 1955–1957   Sprints

King was the first to run two official 10.1s for 100 meters. This came in 1956 after an injury kept him out of the Olympic sprints. He won a gold medal at Melbourne in the relay. He ran an official record equalling 9.3 and won the 1957 AAU 100.

Klim, Romuald (USSR) : 1964–   Hammer

Klim won the 1964 Olympic championship and barely lost in 1968. He won the 1966 European Championships. He threw 241' 3" in 1968 and was undefeated from 1966 to the 1968 Olympics. On June 15, 1969, at Budapest, he reached a world record distance of 244' 6".

Kolehmainen, Hannes (Finland) : 1912–1920   Distances

In the 1912 Olympics, Kolehamainen won the 10,000 meters by 46 seconds and the cross-country by 33. Jean Bouin of France led the 5,000 meters at 3 miles in 14 :07, ten seconds under the world record. Kolehamainen fought past in the homestretch to win by a yard in 14 :36.6, a world record by almost half a minute. He also set a world record for 3,000 meters (8 :36.8) in a heat of the team run.

In the United States, Kolehamainen ran an indoor 4-mile faster than Shrubb's world record and came close to Shrubb's times in two long runs. After missing a chance for more gold medals in the cancelled 1916 Olympiad, he won the 1920 marathon in the rain by 12.8 seconds in 2 :32 :35.8. On October 10, he set a world record of 1 :26 :29.6 for 25,000 meters.

Kraenzlein, Alvin (USA) : 1897–1900   Sprints–Hurdles–LJ

As a freshman at Pennsylvania in 1897, Kraenzlein won the AAU low hurdles in a meet record 25 flat. In 1898 he won both hurdles in the IC4A and AAU. His IC4A low hurdle time of 23.6 remained as the world record for twenty-five years. His 15.2 in the AAU highs was a world record.

In 1899 he again won the hurdle double in each meet. He finished second in the AAU 100 but is now credited with the championship because Duffey was suspended. Kraenzlein also won both broad jumps. His 24′ 4½″ in the IC4A was a world record.

In 1900 he won his third IC4A hurdles double and took the 100 in 10.2. At the Olympic Games in Paris, he set four Olympic records: 60 meters (7.0), high hurdles (15.4), low hurdles (25.4), broad jump (23′ 6⅞″).

Krivonosov, Mikhail (USSR): 1953–1956   Hammer
Krivonosov raised the world record in the hammer throw six times, to 220′ 10⅜″ in 1956. He won the 1954 European Championships and placed second in the 1956 Olympics.

Krzyzkowiak, Zdzislaw (Poland): 1955–1961   Distances
Krzyzkowiak placed fourth in the 1956 Olympic 10,000 and qualified for the steeplechase final, but an injury prevented him from running. He won both the 5,000 and the 10,000 in the 1958 European Championships.

On June 26, 1960, he set a world steeplechase record of 8:31.3. In the Olympics, he won the steeplechase and placed seventh in the 10,000. He lowered his steeplechase record to 8:30.4 on August 10, 1961.

Kuck, John (USA): 1926–1928   Shot Put
Kuck won the NCAA shot put in 1926 and the AAU in 1927. On April 28, 1928 at Fresno, he broke the world record with 51′ ½″. He raised it a week later in Los Angeles to 51′ 2″, but he lost it the same day to Hirschfield's 51′ 9¾″. At the 1928 Olympic Games, Kuck won with a new world record of 52′ ¾″.

Kusocinski, Janusz (Poland): 1931–1936   Distances
Kusocinski won the Olympic 10,000 in 1932 in 30:11.4, second only to Nurmi's world record. Kusocinski lowered the world record for 3,000 meters to 8:18.8 at Antwerp on June 19, 1932. In the 1934 European Championships, he finished second in the 5,000.

Kuts, Vladimir (USSR): 1953–1957   Distances
In 1953, at the age of twenty-six, Kuts ran 5,000 meters in 14:04.0 and 10,000 meters in 29:41.4. In 1954, he ran away from

Zátopek and Chataway to win the European Championships in a world record 13:56.6, plus a 3-mile record of 13:27.4. In a great race at London's White City on October 13, Kuts led Chataway at 3 miles in a record 13:27.0, but he lost by two feet to Chataway's record 13:51.6. Ten days later, at Prague, Kuts regained the 5,000 record with 13:51.0.

He lost his 5,000 record to Iharos on September 10, 1955. Eight days later he recovered it with 13:46.8 at Belgrade, only to lose it a third time to Iharos' 13:40.6 on October 23. Kuts also ran 10,000 meters in 28:59.2.

The next year, Kuts ran 5,000 meters in 13:39.6 but lost to Pirie's record 13:36.8. On September 11, at Moscow, Kuts lowered the world 10,000 record to 28:30.4. In the Olympic Games, he won the 10,000 in 28:45.6 and the 5,000 in 13:39.6.

Stomach problems assailed Kuts in 1957, but in October he returned to form. On October 6 in Prague, he barely missed the 5,000 record with 13:38.0. A week later, in Rome, he broke it for the fourth time with 13:35.0.

In his five years of international racing he was first in World Ranking three times at each distance. After 1957 he had run four of the five fastest 5,000s of all time.

Larrabee, Mike (USA): 1956–1964   440

Larrabee was an in-and-out quarter-miler to the age of thirty. His best World Ranking had been second in 1957 when he ran a 46.2 440. He ran 45.8 in 1959. In 1964, his patient determination paid off with a record tying 44.9 400 meters in the Final Trials and the Olympic championship. He won a second gold medal in the relay.

Lehtinen, Lauri (Finland): 1931–1937   Distances

Lehtinen took 11.3 seconds off Nurmi's world 5,000 record with 14:16.9 on June 19, 1932, at Helsinki. He also set a 3-mile record of 13:50.6. He won the Olympic 5,000 at Los Angeles. He placed second in 1936 after a collision in the last kilometer. His 8:19.5 for 3,000 meters was second fastest ever, in 1933. In 1937, he ran a losing 10,000 in 30:15.0, fifth fastest ever.

Lemming, Erik (Sweden) : 1899–1912   Javelin

Lemming set a world javelin record of 161′ 9¾″ at the age of nineteen in 1899. He broke it seven times, reaching 204′ 5½″ in 1912. He won the javelin at the Olympics of 1906, 1908, and 1912. He also placed third in the 1906 shot and pentathlon. He won a second gold medal in 1908 – the javelin 'held in middle'. He was fifth in the 1900 high jump.

Lippincott, Donald (USA) : 1912–1913   Sprints

Lippincott set an Olympic and world record of 10.6 for 100 meters in 1912, then finished third in the final. Second in the 200 final, he came back in 1913 to tie the world 220 record of 21.2.

Long, Dallas (USA) : 1958–1964   Shot Put

Long astounded track fans with a 61′ ½″ put of the 16-pound shot while he was still eighteen years old in 1958. With a second place in the AAU, he was second in World Ranking. As a freshman at Southern California in 1959, he bettered the world record with 63′ 7″ and was again second in the world. He raised the world record to 64′ 6½″ on March 26, 1960, but lost it to Nieder. He won the NCAA and Final Trials and placed third in the Olympics.

In 1961, Long improved to first in World Ranking. He won the NCAA and AAU and was undefeated with a best mark of 64′ 7¾″. He broke Nieder's world record with 65′ 10½″ in the 1962 Coliseum Relays. He won the NCAA with 64′ 7″, then slipped to 63′ 1¼″ in the AAU and lost to Gary Gubner. He ranked first. Now busy as a dental student, he slipped to sixth in 1963 with a best of 63′ 9″ in two meets.

Training intensively in 1964, he bettered his world record by one inch on April 4. At Fresno on May 9, he raised it to 66′ 7¼″ in a rimless ring. He put 66′ 3½″ on May 29, then declined and put only 63′ 4¾″ in the AAU, losing to Matson. Against the Soviets, on August 11 in Los Angeles, he threw 67′ 10″. His great series also included puts of 65′ 6¼″, 66′ 5¼″, 66′ 9¼″, and 67′ 1″. At Tokyo, he came from behind to win the Olympic championship at 66′ 8½″.

187

Long, Maxie (USA) : 1898–1900   440

Olympic 400 meter champion in 1900, Long set a world 440 record of 47.8 on September 29, 1900, at Travers Island, N.Y. On October 4, in New Jersey, Long ran a straightaway 440 in 47 flat. He won the AAU 440 three times (1898–1900) and the 1899 220.

Loomis, Frank (USA) : 1917–1920   400 Hurdles

Loomis won the 1920 Olympic 400 meter hurdles in world record time of 54.0. He won 2 AAU low hurdles plus one intermediate.

Lovelock, Jack (New Zealand) : 1932–1936   Mile

Lovelock attended Oxford and set a British record of 4 :12.0 in 1932. After a ninth place finish in the 1932 Olympics, he set a world mile record of 4 :07.6 at Princeton, July 15, 1933. He won the British Empire Games mile at London in 1934 and the 1935 Princeton Invitational. In the 1936 Olympics, he set a new world 1,500 meter record of 3 :47.8.

Lowe, Douglas (GB) : 1924–1928   880

In the 1924 Olympics, Lowe won the 800 and was fourth in the 1,500. In 1928, he won again in the 800 and was fifth in the relay. In 1926 he was under the world record while losing an 880 to Peltzer in 1 :51.6.

Lundkvist, Erik (Sweden) : 1928–1936   Javelin

Lundvist improved 26 feet in 1928 to win the Olympic javelin championship. Thirteen days later he broke the world record with 232′ 11½″. He retired because of mental illness but came back in 1936 with 233′ 5½″.

Lusis, Janis (USSR) : 1961–   Javelin

Lusis uses great strength and excellent technique to be the greatest of all time in the sport's most erratic event, the javelin throw.

From a best throw of 265′ 9½″ in 1961, he progressed to first in World Ranking for 1962. He had a best mark of 282′ 3½″

and was undefeated, including the European Championships at 269′ 2″.

In 1963 he scored 7,342 points in a decathlon. His best javelin throw was 274′ 5″, but he was again undefeated. In 1964 his best mark was only 270′ 11½″ and he lost three times before the Olympics. He led at Tokyo with his second throw, 264′ 4″, but he did not improve and placed third.

In 1965 he lost three times, early in the season. Then he returned to form and won all the rest to regain his first position in World Ranking. He threw over 280 feet in five meets with a best of 284. In 1966 he was an undefeated first again, with a best of 281′ 4½″. He won his second European Championships title at 277′ 2″.

In 1967, a sore shoulder caused five early defeats, but on September 7, at Odessa, he threw 298′ 4″ and 298′ 6″, the second and third best ever.

In 1968 he was over 280 feet in seventeen meets. Of all the javelin throwers in history, only Terje Pedersen's freak throw of 300′ 11″ had gone over 290 feet, but Lusis did it in eleven meets! On June 23, at Saarijarvi, Finland, he broke the world record with a throw of 301′ 9″.

And yet, in the Olympic Games, he was beaten by Jorma Kinnunen's 290′ 6″ until his last throw when he won with 295′ 7″.

1968 was his sixth year as first in World Ranking. In 1969 he won his third European Championships with a throw of 300′ 3″ and ranked No. 1 again.

Mäki, Taisto (Finland) : 1938–1939   Distances

Mäki set a world record of 30 :02.0 for 10,000 meters in 1938 and won the European Championships 5,000. He set five world records in 1939. On June 16 at Helsinki, he ran 3 miles in 13 :42.4 and 5,000 meters in 14 :08.8. On July 7 he lowered the 2-mile record to 8 :53.2. On September 17, still in Helsinki, he ran the 6-mile in 28 :55.6 and the 10,000 in 29 :52.6. The war ended his career.

Matson, Randy (USA) : 1963–   Shot–Discus

Matson was the best high school junior of all time with a shot put of 64′ 7″ and a discus throw of 186′ 6″ in 1962. As a senior, in 1963, he put the 12-pound shot 66' 10½" and the 16-pounder 60' 6". He threw the high school discus 193' 1½" and lost a national record of 199' 4" because of sloping ground. He threw the heavy discus 169' 7½", making him the second best high school thrower of all time with all four weights. He placed fourth in the AAU shot at 59' 1¼" and toured Europe.

As a freshman at Texas A&M in 1964, he gained new strength through weight training. He concentrated on the shot, but he threw the discus 182' 11". Indoors, he improved his shot record to 62' 5" five days before his 19th birthday.

Outdoors, he kept improving to 64' 10½". He beat Long for the AAU title at 64' 11". He put 65' 5½" on September 5 and made the Olympic team with 63' 10". At Tokyo, he put 66' 3¼" and nearly won the gold medal.

In 1965 he put 66' 2¼" indoors and won the NCAA. In the discus he was undefeated and set a collegiate record of 201' 1½". In the shot, he became the greatest ever. He broke the world record with 67' 11¼' on April 9. He raised it to 69' ¾" on April 30. Eight days later he put 70' 7".

In 1966 he played basketball and lost weight and strength. He ranked first in the shot and fifth in the discus in the world ratings, but his bests were 69' 2½" and 197' 11". He won both events in the NCAA. He won the AAU shot and was third in the discus.

In 1967, his first loss since the Olympics was to Steinhauer, indoors. He put the iron outdoor shot 70' 7½" indoors, but it was no kind of record.

In April, 1967, he had one of the greatest performances in track and field history. He had not trained much with the shot for a month because of a hand injury. For the first time in his life he had concentrated on the discus. On April 9, at College Station, Texas, he put the shot over 70 feet 3 times, with a best of 70' 5½". Then he threw the discus over his own collegiate record three times with a best of 213' 9", only 2½ inches from the world record.

Two weeks later, he put 71' 5½", probably the greatest single mark ever made to that date in track and field. He reached 70 feet again, then won a double at the NCAA and took the AAU shot. He won the Pan American Games title at Winnipeg.

In 1968 he started with a sprained hand and never reached

his potential. His best put was 69′ 10½″. He won his fourth AAU championship and won the Olympic gold medal at 67′ 4¾″.

At the end of 1968 he was the only man ever to put 69 feet and he had done it in nine meets. He had to his credit twenty-one of the twenty-two longest winning puts in history.

McGrath, Matt (USA) : 1906–1935   Weights

McGrath broke the world record in the hammer with 173′ 7″ in 1907 and again on October 11, 1911, with 187′ 4″. He threw 190′ in an exhibition in 1913. He set world records for 35 pound weight (53′ 11″) and 56-pound weight (40′ 6⅜″) in 1911 and later threw 61′ 8″ (1918) and 41′ 3″ (exhibition). McGrath won seven AAU hammer titles from 1908 to 1926, and seven 56-pound weight titles. He placed in four Olympic hammer throws : second in 1908, first in 1912, fifth in 1920 (with a twisted knee), and second in 1924.

McKenley, Herb (Jamaica) : 1945–1952   100–440

McKenley attended university in the United States and won NCAA 440 titles in 1946 and 1947. He won the AAU in 1945, 1947, and 1948. On June 1, 1946, he lowered the world 440 record to 46.2, then ran a 20.6 220. He tied his 46.2 in the 1947 NCAA and lowered it to 46 flat at Berkeley, June 5, 1948. He won the AAU 400 in a record 45.9. In the 1948 Olympics, at the age of twenty-six, McKenley lost the 400 meters to Wint's 46.2.

McKenley ranked first in the world for 1947 and 1948, but his career was one of fast second places in big meets. He was second in the AAU in 1946, 1949, 1950, and 1951. In the 1952 Olympics, he was a close second in the 100 and 400. He finally won a gold medal with a 44.6 relay leg, fastest ever recorded. Strangely, he never developed his 220 talent, although he ranked second in the world in 1950.

Meadows, Earle (USA) : 1935–1942   Pole Vault

Meadows tied for first in the 1935 NCAA and AAU and the 1936 NCAA. In 1936 he won the Final Trials and the Olympic gold medal, with a record 14′ 3¼″. In 1937 he tied with Bill Sefton for a world record 14′ 8½″ at Palo Alto, California, on

May 8. Three weeks later, in Los Angeles, they both cleared 14′ 11″.

Meadows won the indoor AAU in 1940 and 1941. He set an indoor world record of 14′ 7⅛″ in 1941.

Meredith, Ted (USA) : 1912–1917   440–880

Meredith was probably the greatest middle-distance runner of all time until the 1930's. In 1912, he came out of obscurity to win the Princeton Interscholastics in 49.2 and 1:55.0, far under the old high school records. The 5′ 9″, 155-pound 19-year-old made the Olympic team in both events.

In the Olympic 800 at Stockholm, Meredith fought past Sheppard in the homestretch to win in world record time of 1:51.9. He continued to 880 yards and set a new world record of 1:52.5. In the 400, he started too fast and placed only fourth. He won a second gold medal on the world record relay team.

A freshman at Pennsylvania in 1913, he set an indoor record of 1:13.8 for 600 yards. In 1914, he won the IC4A 440 in 48.4, then lost the 880 to Dave Caldwell's collegiate record 1:53.4. He won the AAU 440.

In the 1915 IC4A, he tied the collegiate 440 record with 48 flat and won the 880 in 1:54.4. In the AAU meet in San Francisco, he won the straightaway 440 in 47 flat.

In 1916, he set an indoor record of 1:21.4 for 660 yards. In a dual meet with Cornell, Vere Windnagle equalled Meredith's world 880 record, but Meredith beat him in 1:52.2. In the IC4A he set a new world record of 47.4 in the 440 and then won the 880 in a collegiate record 1:53.0.

After a mediocre 1917 season he retired, holding interscholastic, collegiate, and world records for 400 meters, 440 yards, 800 meters, and 880 yards. His 880 record lasted twenty years, his 440 record 27 years. An attempted comeback in 1920 saw him eliminated in the semi-final of the Olympic 400 meters.

Metcalfe, Ralph (USA) : 1930–1936   Sprints

In high school, Metcalfe won a sprint double in the Illinois state meet three times, and he placed fourth in the AAU 220 (1930). As a freshman at Marquette in 1931, he was fifth in the AAU 100 and second in the 220.

PETER SNELL   Appearing as calm as if sitting at home, Snell wins the 1500
metres at Tokyo. 'My run down the straight was a little easier . . .'

ROGER BANNISTER This was the scene at the Iffley Road track at Oxford when Bannister became the first man to run a mile in under 4 minutes

RON CLARKE All alone, as he often is, Clarke runs 2 miles at the Crystal Palace Stadium in London, 1968. His time – 8:19.6, another world record

In 1932, the 5' 11", 180-pounder won both metric sprints in the NCAA in 10.2 and 20.3. Neither world record was considered by the AAU. He won both sprints in the AAU, but in the Los Angeles Olympics he had bad luck. His chest touched the tape first in the 100 meters, but under existing rules Tolan was the winner because his back crossed the line first. In the 200, Metcalfe's lane was measured wrong and he ran five feet too far, finishing third. In Canada, he ran a 220 in 19.8 with wind.

In 1933, he won doubles again in both the NCAA and AAU, and added the indoor AAU title. His 9.4 and 20.4 in the NCAA were not recognized. In Budapest, August 12, he entered the record books twice, with a 10.3 100 meters and a 20.6 200 meters. The latter was amazing because it was around a turn.

In 1934 he became the only man ever to win three NCAA doubles. He again doubled in the AAU and won his second indoor title, even though he was a notoriously slow starter. In Japan, he ran 200 meters in 20.2 with wind.

In 1935 he lost his AAU 100 championship to Peacock, but he won the 200. In 1936 he won his third indoor AAU and his fifth AAU 200 meters. No other sprinter has ever won five times in one event. He made the Olympic team behind Owens in the 100, but for the only time in his life he failed in the 200, placing fourth after leading into the homestretch. He was second to Owens in the 100 meters at Berlin, gaining two yards after a poor start. He finally won his gold medal in the relay.

Metcalfe tied the world 100 meter record of 10.3 ten times and broke it once. He received credit for only three of the 10.3's. He broke the 220 record twice without recognition In five years of competition he lost only five times in the 100 and three times in the 200.

Jesse Owens' coach, Larry Snyder, said of Metcalfe : 'He had no adequate coaching in how to start properly . . . but how he could fly at the finish ! . . . I am convinced that Metcalfe was potentially the best of them all.'

Mills, Billy (USA) : 1960–1968   Distances

Mills won the 1964 Olympic 10,000 and placed 14th in the marathon. In 1965, he set a world record of 27 :11.6 in the AAU 6-mile, plus an American record of 28 :17.6 for 10,000 meters.

Mimoun O'Kacha, Alain (France) : 1950–1956   Distances

Mimoun, an Algerian, ran second to Zátopek in five major races : 1948 Olympic 10,000, 1952 Olympic 5,000 and 10,000, and the 1950 European Championships 5,000 and 10,000. In 1956 at the age of thirty-four, he won the Olympic marathon in 2 :25 :00 He won the International Cross-country four times.

Moore, Charley (USA) : 1949–1952   440–LH–IH

Moore won the NCAA 440 in 1949 and the low hurdles in 1951. He won four AAU titles in the intermediate hurdles. He was first in World Ranking in 1949, 1951, and 1952. He won the 1952 Olympic 400 meter hurdles in 50.8.

Morris, Glenn (USA) : 1934–1936   Decathlon

Morris, in his single year as a decathlon man, won the 1932 AAU with a world record and raised it 20 points with his victory in the Olympic Games.

Morrow, Bobby (USA) : 1955–1960   Sprints

Morrow was the best all-around sprinter of all time before his injury in 1959. He was undefeated as a high school senior in 1954, and he continued undefeated in his freshman year at Abilene Christian until he had won the AAU 100. His only loss was his fourth place in the AAU 220.

He had won thirty consecutive 100s when Sime caught a flyer and defeated him in the 1956 Drake Relays. Morrow was undefeated that year in the 200–220. He won both sprints in the NAIA, NCAA, and Final Olympic Trials, plus the AAU 100.

In the Olympic Games at Melbourne, he won both sprints and anchored the winning relay team. He ran 9.4 three times and 10.2 four times, each within one tenth of a second of the world record. Also in 1956, he ran 20.6 around a curve three times, tying the best ever record.

In 1957 he tied the world record of 9.3 three times and ran another 20.6. He lost only one race all year, winning the NAIA and NCAA doubles again In 1958, he ranked first in the world for the third straight year, but he slipped to second in the 220. He won both sprints in the AAU.

In 1959 he ran 10.2 and three 9.4's before his injury. In 1960, hobbled by injuries, he barely missed making the Olympic team in the 200.

Myers, Lawrence (USA) : 1879–1887   100-Mile

Lon Myers was one of the most versatile and remarkable runners in history. A thin 5' 8", 112-pounder, he beat the best in both the United States and Britain in races from 50 to 1,000 yards, setting American records at all those distances. He was the first man to run 440 yards under 50 seconds.

Myers won fifteen AAU championships – two in the 100, four in the 200, six in the 440 (1879 to 1884), and three in the 880. In 1880 he won all four distances in one afternoon and repeated in the Canadian Championships. In 1881, after winning three AAU titles, he went to England to run in the biggest international meet available. He won the AAA championship in 48.6, fastest time on record. His 6.4 for 60 yards, his 35-flat 330, and his 2 : 13 for 1,000 yards lasted more than twenty-five years.

Myers equalled the world record of 10-flat in the 100, ran 22.5 in the 220, and a 4 : 27.6 mile. In 1884 he lowered his world 880 record to 1 : 55.4. In 1885 he tied it and won a 440–880 double in the AAA.

He turned professional in 1885. As an amateur, he had raced the great W. G. George in a series consisting of 880, mile, and ¾ mile, witnessed by crowds totaling 130,000 at the New York Polo Grounds. Myers won only the 880 (1 : 56.4). As professionals, they raced in two more series. Indoors, in New York in 1886, Myers won all three. In 1887, in Australia, Myers won only the 880. His best pro mile was 4 : 22.6.

His most amazing professional race came at Rochdale, England, on August 19, 1885. After a 1 : 57 880, he came back two hours later and spotted England's best professional quarter-miler, Mason, a 24-yard handicap. The race ended in a tie in 46.4.

Myyrä, Jonni (Finland) : 1912–1925   Javelin

Myyrä placed eighth in the 1912 Olympic javelin, then broke the world record with 205' 3½" in 1914. He bettered it four times, ending with 216' 10½" in 1919. He won the javelin in the Olympic Games of 1920 and 1924. He had an unofficial throw of 224' 11" in 1925.

Nambu, Chuhei (Japan) : 1928–1932   LJ–TJ

Nambu placed fourth in the 1928 Olympic triple jump and ninth in the long jump. On October 27, 1931, in Tokyo, Nambu, a 10.5 100 meter man, broke the world long jump record with 26′ 2¼″. In the 1932 Olympics, he placed third in the long jump, and he won the triple jump with a world record 51′ 7″.

Nemeth, Imre (Hungary) : 1939–1952   Hammer

Nemeth set a world hammer record of 193′ 7½″ on July 14, 1948. Ten days later he won the Olympic championship. He raised the world record to 195′ 5″ in 1949 and to 196′ 5½″ in 1950. He placed third in the 1952 Olympics.

Nieder, Bill (USA) : 1955–1960   Shot Put

The first high school 60-footer, Nieder was set back by a severely damaged knee. He won the 1955 NCAA at 57′ 3″, then became history's second 60-footer with 60′ 3¾″ in 1956. He placed second to O'Brien in the 1956 Olympics.

In 1957 he beat O'Brien with 62 ′2″ and ranked No. 1 in the world. In the army in 1958, he slipped to fourth in World Ranking. In 1959 he improved to third with a best of 62′ 9″.

He started 1960 with a world record 65′ 7″ in the Texas Relays. An injured leg dropped him to fourth in the Final Trials. His leg healed, and after four meets around 64 feet, he improved the world record to 65′ 10″ at Walnut, August 12. He won the Olympics with 64′ 6¾″. At his retirement he owned twelve of the thirteen longest puts ever made.

Nikkanen, Yrjo (Finland) : 1935–1946   Javelin

Nikkanen set a world javelin record of 258′ 2⅜″ in 1938, which lasted fifteen years. He was second in the 1936 Olympics and in the European Championships of 1938 and 1946.

O'Callaghan, Patrick (Ireland) : 1927–1937   Hammer

In 1928, O'Callaghan came from behind on his fourth throw to win the Olympic championship. In the 1932 Olympics, he came from behind on his last throw to win another gold medal. He raised the European record to 183′ 11″ in 1931 and to 186′ 10″

in 1933. He was ineligible for the 1936 Olympics because of a federation 'war'. In 1937, throwing from a circle five inches too small and with a hammer six ounces too heavy, he bettered the world record with 195' 4"⅞, a mark not beaten officially for twelve years.

Oda, Mikio (Japan) : 1924–1932   LJ–TJ

Oda placed sixth in the 1924 Olympic triple jump and won the Olympics in 1928. Injured, he placed 12th in 1932. He raised the Asian record to 50' 6¾" in 1928. On October 27, 1931, in Tokyo, he set a world record of 51' 1½". His best long jump was 24' 8".

Osborne, Harold (USA) : 1922–1936   HJ–Decathlon

Dr Osborne was one of the most remarkable of all athletes, with national recognition in 1922 and again in 1936.

In 1922, he tied for first in the NCAA and AAU high jumps. He lost the AAU title in a jumpoff. He also placed second in the hop-step-jump and decathlon. In 1923 he won the AAU indoor high jump and the decathlon.

In 1924, after winning the indoor AAU high jump, he set a world outdoor record of 6' 8¼" at Urbana, Illinois, on May 27. In the Olympic Games, he won the high jump with an Olympic record of 6' 6". Then he won the decathlon with a world record score. No other man ever won an Olympic decathlon with a world record score. No other man ever won an Olympic decathlon plus an individual event, let alone world records in both.

In 1925, in the indoor AAU, he won four championships and placed fourth in the shot put. He won the 70 yard high hurdles in a good 8.6, the high jump, and the standing high and broad jumps. In that same indoor season, he set a world indoor record of 6' 6¼" and a standing high jump record of 5' 5¾", equal to the outdoor world record.

Outdoors in 1925, he jumped 6' 8 5/16" but it was not accepted as a world record. He won the AAU high jump (6' 7") and the decathlon. In 1926 he won the indoor AAU high jump and standing broad jump, plus the outdoor high jump and decathlon. In 1927, his only title came in the indoor standing broad jump.

In the AAU high jump, he placed third in 1927 and 1928, and tied for fourth in 1935. In the indoor AAU, he was fourth in 1927, won in 1928, and placed in 1929 and from 1931 through 1935.

He competed in his second Olympic Games in 1928, but placed only fifth in the high jump.

Indoors, he won the AAU standing high jump three more years until it was abandoned after 1931. He was second in the indoor standing broad jump in 1930. In 1934 he tried the pentathlon and placed second in the AAU. He was fifth in 1935.

In 1936, at the age of thirty-seven, Osborne climaxed his career indoors at St Louis on April 4 when he cleared 5' 6" in the standing high jump. This is still the best on record, indoors or out.

Thus, he won eighteen AAU championships in six different events, and won thirty-five AAU medals in a total of nine different events.

Paddock, Charley (USA): 1919–1928   Sprints

Paddock dominated the sprints in the 1920s although he lost many races. He won AAU 100's in 1921 (9.6) and 1924. He won the 220 in 1920 (21.4), 1921, and 1924 (20.8). He won the Olympic 100 in 1920 and placed fifth in 1924. He was second in the 200 in both Olympics. He won a gold medal in the 1920 relay and ran unplaced in 1928.

In 1921 he tied the world record of 9.6 for 100 yards and broke the 220 record with 20.8. A few weeks later he ran a world record 100 meters in 10.4, then ran 300 yards in 30.2 and 300 meters in 33.2. The 30.2 was not official because only the time for the full distance could be accepted as a world record. Two months later he ran 110 yards in 10.2 but it was not accepted as a world 100 meter record because it was a longer distance! He entered the record books with six official 9.6's, but one, on May 15, 1926, in Los Angeles, was the first official 9.5.

Patton, Mel (USA): 1947–1949   Sprints

Patton was regarded as the fastest sprinter of all time but he was reluctant to compete. He won all five NCAA sprints he entered, but he ran no AAU races after he came into prominence in 1947. He placed fifth in the 1948 Olympic 100 meters and won the 200. He won a second gold medal in the relay.

He tied the world 100 record of 9.4 in 1947 and ran the first 9.3 in 1948. On May 7, 1949, in Los Angeles, he ran 9.1 with a wind of 6.5 m.ph, then broke Owens' 220 record with a legal 20.2. His 20.7 around a curve in the 1948 Final Trials equalled Owens' American record. He ran 20.4 four times, giving him half of the ten fastest 220 times ever run. He lost only three races in three years.

Peacock, Eulace (USA) : 1933–1948   100–LJ–Pentathlon

Peacock had unlimited potential but leg injuries defeated him. Second best in history only to Owens in the high school and indoor AAU broad jumps, he won the national AAU pentathlon in 1933 and 1934. On tour in Europe, he tied the world record with 10.3 at Oslo.

After losing the NCAA 100 and broad jump to Owens in the 1935 meet, he beat Metcalfe and Owens in the AAU 100 meters. His 10.2 was aided by a wind of 7.7 m.p.h. His 26′ 3″ broad jump victory over Owens was second longest in history He defeated Owens in two 100s in the next week.

When he won a 1936 indoor 50 at Cleveland for his fourth consecutive victory over Owens, he seemed to be a certain Olympian, and his 6.0 world record 60 yards at Toronto confirmed it. But he pulled a muscle and he was never again a contender.

He won four more AAU pentathlons, in 1937, 1943, 1944, and 1945. He placed in indoor AAU 60's in 1939, 1940, and 1941, in the outdoor 100 in 1940, and in the outdoor broad jump in 1944. He won the Metropolitan AAU broad jump in 1948.

Peltzer, Otto (Germany) : 1924–1932   500–1,500

Dr Peltzer outkicked Douglas Lowe to set a world record of 1 :51.6 in the AAA 880 in 1925. In 1926, his stretch sprint defeated Wide and Nurmi in a world record 3 :51.0 1,500 meters. His speed is indicated by his official world record of 1 :03.6 for 500 meters in 1926.

In 1927 his famed kick beat Sera Martin at 1,000 meters in a world record 2 :25.8. Illness caused him to miss the 1924 Olympics. Injured, he failed to qualify in 1928. In 1932, at age thirty-two, he finished last in the Olympic 800 meter final.

Pirie, Gordon (GB) : 1952–1960   Distances

Pirie placed seventh in the 1952 Olympic 10,000 and fourth in the 5,000 at the age of twenty-one. He set a world record 13 :36.8 for 5,000 meters, June 19, 1956, in Bergen, Norway. Three days later, he tied the world 3,000 meter record with 7 :55.6. On September 4, at Malmö, he beat the great Hungarians in 7 :52.8. In the 1956 Olympics he tried to beat Kuts in the 10,000 and finished eighth. In the 5,000 he placed second.

He was third in the 1958 European Championships 5,000. He ranked second in the world behind Kuts in both 1956 and 1957. He did not qualify for the final of the 5,000 and placed tenth in the 1960 Olympic 10,000.

Pörhölä, Ville (Finland) : 1920–1936   Shot–Hammer

Pörhölä won the shot put in the 1920 Olympics and placed seventh in 1924. He turned to the hammer and was a close second in the 1932 Olympics, won the 1934 European Championships, and placed 11th in the 1936 Olympics.

Porter, Bill (USA) : 1947–1948   Hurdles

Porter won the 1948 Olympic high hurdles in 13.9. He ran two other 13.9s in 1948. He beat Dillard three times, including the 1948 AAU and Final Trials and a 22.7 low hurdles race in 1947. He ran 22.5, equal to the second fastest of all time, behind Dillard's 22.3.

Potgieter, Gerhardus (South Africa) : 1955–1962   440 Hurdles

Potgieter, at nineteen, fell over the last hurdle in the 1956 Olympic intermediates when he was in third place. He won the Commonwealth title in 1958 with a world record 49.7 for 440 yards. On April 16, 1960 – his 23rd birthday – he broke the world record for the 440 intermediates with 49.3. Undefeated for four years and first in 1959 in the world rankings, he was eliminated from the 1960 Olympics by an automobile accident.

Prinstein, Myer (USA) : 1898–1906   LJ–TJ

Prinstein, of Syracuse, set a world broad jump record of 23' 8⅜" in the 1898 IC4A meet, and won the AAU at 23' 7". In the 1900 Penn Relays, he raised the world record to 24' 7¼". He led the qualifiers in the Olympic broad jump with 23' 6½", but he would not jump in the final because it was on Sunday, and he lost the championship by ¼ inch. He won the hop-step-jump on Monday.

He won the AAU broad jump in 1902 and 1904. In the 1904 Olympics, he won both the broad jump (24′ 1″) and the hop-step-jump on the same day, three days after placing fifth in the 400 meters.

In 1906, he won the AAU broad jump. In the 1906 Olympics he sprained his ankle on his first jump, but it was 23′ 7½″ and it held up for the championship. In the hop-step-jump three days later he could place only 11th.

Reiff, Gaston (Belgium) : 1947–1952   Distances
Reiff won the 1948 Olympic 5,000 meters. He set a world record of 5:06.9 for 2,000 meters at Brussels in 1948. He set a 3,000 meter record of 7:58.7 at Gävle, Sweden, in 1949. In 1952, after dropping out of the Olympic 5,000, he went to Paris on August 26 and set a world 2-mile record of 8:40.4. He ran 1,500 meters in 3:45.8 in 1949 and 5,000 in 14:10.8 in 1951.

Rhoden, George (Jamaica) : 1949–1952   220–440
Rhoden set a world 400 meter record of 45.8 in 1950. He won the 1952 Olympic 400 and won another gold medal in the relay. He won three AAU 400s, three NCAA 440s, and an NCAA 220.

Richards, Bob (USA) : 1946–1957   PV–Decathlon
Richards was the second man in history to vault 15 feet and he cleared it a total of one hundred and twenty-six times. Only 5′ 9¾″, he was not tall enough to vault higher with a steel pole, and his best vault was 15′ 5″ outdoors and 15′ 6″ indoors.

In college he managed to tie for first in the NCAA only once. He improved enough to win the AAU nine times, including two ties. He won the indoor AAU eight times, including one tie.

He vaulted in three Olympics. Third at London in 1948, he won in 1952 and 1956 to become the only man to win two gold medals in the Olympic pole vault.

He also competed in the decathlon. He won the AAU all-round in 1953 and the decathlon in 1951, 1954, and 1955. He made the Olympic team in 1956, but an injured tendon caused him to finish 12th.

201

He was first in World Ranking for eight consecutive years between his third of 1948 and his second of 1957. He was undefeated for three years in a row – 1953–55. He ranked first in the decathlon in 1951 and 1954.

Ritola, Ville (Finland) : 1921–1928   Distances

Willie Ritola won three Olympic championships, plus two gold medals for team championships. He won four silver medals, all behind Nurmi. In the 1924 Olympics, he won the steeplechase and 10,000 meters, both in world record time. He was second to Nurmi in a close 5,000, the cross-country, and the 3,000 meter team race. In 1928, he lost a close 10,000 to Nurmi, but he beat Nurmi in the 5,000.

Ritola won fourteen AAU championships as a resident of the United States, from the time he was seventeen. He placed second in the (short) 1921 Boston Marathon in 2 :21. Indoors on February 24, 1925, he bettered all records for 3 miles and 5,000 meters. His 13 :56.2 was 15 seconds faster than Nurmi's outdoor record and his 14 :23.2 was five seconds faster than Nurmi's 5,000 record. Five weeks before, he had bettered Shrubb's world 5-mile record by 11 seconds with 24 :21.8 indoors.

Roelants, Gaston (Belgium) : 1960–1968   Distances

Roelants placed fourth in the 1960 Olympic steeplechase. He won the 1962 European Championships. On September 7, 1963, he broke the world record with 8 :29.6. He won the 1964 Olympic championship in 8 :30.8. In the 1965 Belgian Championships on August 7, he lowered his world record to 8 :26.4. He also ranked second in the World Ranking in the 10,000 with the second fastest ever run – 28 :10.6.

In 1966 he ran under 8 :30 twice but placed only third in the European Championships, plus eighth in the 10,000. At Louvain, Belgium, on October 28, he amazed the track world by running 20,000 meters in 58 :06.2. His second world record of the day came when he ran 12 miles 1,474 yards (20,644 meters) in one hour. In 1967 he lost his second steeplechase in six years but regained his first in World Ranking. In 1968, an injury and Mexico City's altitude knocked him back to seventh in the Olympic steeplechase.

Rose, Ralph (USA) : 1904–1912   Shot Put

A 6' 6", 235-pound giant, Rose broke the world record and won the Olympic championship in the shot put at the age of twenty with 48' 6" in 1904. He regained the record in 1907 (49' 7¼"), raised it to 49' 10" in 1908, to 50' 6" in 1909, and 51' ¾" one week later. This was the official world record for nineteen years.

On June 26, 1909, in an unsanctioned meet at Healdsburg, California, he put the shot 54' 4", a mark not bettered until 1934, and he threw the hammer 178' 5", better than the world record. His best official hammer throw was 164' 4".

Rose set a record for the shot put with both hands, totaling 91' 10½" in 1912. This was the official record for 19 years. He won the AAU shot put four times. The third time, in 1909, he also won the discus and javelin. His first AAU championship came in the 1905 discus.

Rose won six Olympic medals. In 1904 he won the shot, took the silver medal in the discus, and the bronze in the hammer. In 1908, he repeated his shot put triumph. In 1912, he lost the shot by 3½ inches, but he won the shot for both hands.

Ryan, Pat (USA) : 1913–1921   Hammer

Ryan broke the world record with a hammer throw of 189' 6½" on August 17, 1913, in Celtic Park, Long Island. It lasted twenty-four years. He won eight AAU hammer titles and two with the 56-pound weight. In 1920, he won the Olympic hammer throw.

Ryun, Jim (USA) : 1964–   880–Mile

Ryun set an age-16 mile record of 4 :07.8 in 1963. In 1964, he ran 3 :59.0 and 1,500 meters in 3 :39.0. Youngest ever to make the U.S. Olympic team, he was ill at Tokyo. In 1965, he won the AAU from Snell in 3 :55.3 and ranked fourth in the world.

In 1966, at the age of nineteen, he won the 2-mile at the Coliseum Relays from Jim Grelle and Keino in 8 :25.2, an American record. At the Compton Invitational, he missed the world mile record by one tenth with 3 :53.7. A week later, at Terre Haute, Indiana, he broke Snell's 880 record with a surprise 1 :44.9. He won the AAU in 3 :58.6.

On July 17, at Berkeley, he set a world record of 3 :51.3. A week later he ran the third fastest 880 ever run – 1 :46.2.

In 1967, he ran 3 :53.2 at Compton, and he won the NCAA championship. In the AAU meet at Bakersfield, he paced himself to 3 :51.1, another world record.

On July 8, in the Los Angeles Coliseum, Ryun smashed Keino by 20 yards in the 1,500 meters. His last 880 in 1 :51.3 brought him under Elliott's world record with 3 :33.1. He beat Keino again in London in 3 :56.0. On August 17 he sprinted away from Tummler and Norpoth to win a 3 :38.2 1,500 by 30 yards. His last 400 was 50.6, his last 300 was 36.4, and his last 200 was 24.8.

Injuries to his back and ankle slowed him but he won the 1968 NCAA indoor 2-mile from Lindgren and doubled in the mile. Mononucleosis kept him out of the 1968 spring season, and high altitudes prevented fast times. He ran 3 :55.9 in August.

In the Olympics, he lost to an incredible altitude run by Keino, finishing second in 3 :37.8, faster than he thought possible.

Saling, George (USA) : 1930–1932 High Hurdles
Saling won the 1932 NCAA high hurdles in unrecognized world record time of 14.1. He won the 1932 Olympics in 14.6.

Salminen, Ilmari (Finland) : 1934–1939 Distances
Salminen won the 1936 Olympic 10,000 meters, then fell in the 5,000 and finished sixth. On July 18, 1937, in Kouvola, Finland, he broke Nurmi's world 10,000 record with 30 :05.5. Salminen won the 10,000 at the European Championships in both 1934 and 1938, and placed third in the 1934 5,000. His fastest 5,000 was 14 :22.0 in 1939.

Saneyev, Viktor (USSR) : 1965– Triple Jump
Saneyev came into prominence as late as 1967 when he ranked second in the world with a best triple jump of 54′ 8¼″. In 1968 he was undefeated, winning the Olympic championship with a world record 57′ ¾″. He won the 1969 European Championships with a wind-aided 56′ 10¾″.

Schmidt, Józef (Poland) : 1957–1968 Triple Jump
Schmidt improved from a triple jump of 51′ 2½″ in 1957 to win the 1958 European Championships with 53′ 11″. On August 5, 1960, in the Polish Championships, he leaped 55′ 10½″ for a

world record. Then, even though injured, he won the Olympic championship at 55′ 1¾″.

In 1961, a weak ankle reduced him to second in the world with a best of only 53′ 9¾″. He won the 1962 European Championships with his best jump of the year, 54′ 3½″.

In 1963, undefeated, he reached 55′ 9″ twice in the Polish Championships, 55′ ¼″ with wind against the USA, and 55′ 4½″ in September. He long jumped 26′ 1½″. In 1964 he was injured and jumped in only two meets, including the Olympic Games, where he won again with 55′ 3½″.

In 1965, his best was 54′ 11″ and he ranked first for the sixth year. In 1966, injuries continued to hobble him and he ranked fifth. His best was 54′ 7¼″ and he placed only fifth in the European Championships at 53′ 11¾″.

In 1967 he slipped to sixth even though he won the Polish Championships at 55′ 3″. In 1968, a bad leg held him to a best of 54′ 3½″ in his World Games victory. Injured again, he managed 55′ 5″ at Mexico City's altitude for seventh in the Olympics.

Scholz, Jackson (USA) : 1920–1928   Sprints
Scholz placed in three Olympics Games : fourth in the 1920 100, second in the 1924 100, first in the 1924 200, and fourth in the 1928 200. He won a gold medal in the 1920 relay. He claimed an advantage over Paddock in their career competition, but he won only one AAU title. He ran an unofficial 9.5 in 1925.

Seagren, Bob (USA) : 1965–1969   Pole Vault
From a best of 16′ 4″ in 1965, Seagren developed to a world record 17′ 5¼″ at Fresno, May 14, 1966. He lost it two months later, and regained it with 17′ 7″ at San Diego, June 10, 1967. He lost that one thirteen days later, and regained it with 17′ 9″ in the Final Trials at South Lake Tahoe, September 12, 1968. He won both titles in 1969.

He won the 1968 Olympic championship with 17′ 8½″. He set indoor records six times, beginning with 17′ ¾″ in 1966. He cleared 17′ 6″ in 1969. He won the AAU in 1966 and 1969 and the NCAA in 1967 and 1969.

Sexton, Leo (USA) : 1931–1932   Shot Put
Sexton won the 1932 Olympic shot put, then broke the world record with 53′ ½″.

Sheppard, Mel (USA) : 1908–1912   800–1,500

Sheppard won the 1908 Olympic 1,500 and doubled with a world record 1 :52.8 in the 800. In the 1912 Olympics he barely lost in a world record 800 and won a third gold medal in the 1,600 meter relay. He won five AAU titles.

Sheridan, Martin (USA) : 1902–1912   All-Round

Called 'the world's greatest athlete,' Sheridan won the AAU all-round championship in 1905, 1907, and 1909. He also won the shot put in 1904, 1906, 1907, and 1911.

His greatest feat was winning three Olympic discus championships, in 1904, 1906, and 1908. He placed fourth in the shot put in 1904 and won in 1906. In 1906 he also placed second in throwing the 14-pound stone and in the standing broad jump. He tied for second in the standing high jump, was disqualified in the Greek style discus, and was expected to win the pentathlon until his knee went bad.

In the 1908 Olympics, he also won the Greek style discus and was third in the standing broad jump, bringing his Olympic total to five gold medals, three silver, and one bronze.

He held the world record in the discus from 1902 to 1912, with a best of 143′ 3″ in 1905. He threw the hammer 162′ 8½″ in 1906 when the world record was 175′ 1¾″. He placed ninth in the 1908 triple jump.

Shrubb, Alfred (GB) : 1903–1905   Distances

Shrubb became the world's best distance runner in 1903 at the age of twenty-four, winning the British AAA mile and cross country, the International Cross Country, and a world record 9 :11.0 for 2 miles and 14 :17.6 for 3 miles. In the spring of 1904 he ran four world record races : 5 miles (24 :33.4), 3 miles (14 :17.2), 2 miles (9 :09.6), 4 miles (19 :23.4).

On November 5, 1904, he ran 11¾ miles in 1 :00 :2.2 and put his name into the official record book six more times : 6-mile (29 :59.4), 7-mile 35 :04.6), 8-mile (40 :16), 9-mile (45 :27.6), 10-mile (50 :40.6), and one hour (11 miles, 1,137 yards). His unofficial 31 :02.4 was better than the world 10,000 meters record. His 6-mile record fell to Nurmi after 26 years, while his 7, 8, and 9-mile records lasted thirty-three years until they were removed from the official list. Shrubb was declared a professional in 1905 and he ran successfully in the United States and Canada until he was forty-two.

Sidlo, Janusz (Poland) : 1952–1968 Javelin
The most durable of competitors, Sidlo threw in the 1952 Olympics and in four more. He set a world record of 262' 11½" at the age of twenty in 1953. He won the European Championships in 1954 and 1958. He placed second in the 1956 Olympics, eighth in 1960, fourth in 1964, and seventh in 1968. He ranked first in the world five times and second five times.

Silvester, Jay (USA) : 1961– Discus
Silvester first set a world record in the discus with 199' 2½" in 1961. He won AAU championships in 1961, 1963, and 1968. He was fourth in the 1964 Olympics and fifth in 1968. He raised the world record to 218' 3½" in May of 1968. After many long throws, he reached 224' 5" in a high wind at Reno, Nevada, September 18, 1968.

Sime, Dave (USA) : 1956–1960 Sprints–LH
Sime won no major championships, but he ran three 9.3 100's when that was the world record. He ran 10.1 for 100 meters. He set a world record of 20-flat for a straight 220 on June 9, 1956. That same year he ran 20.1, 20.2, 20.3 twice, and 20.4. He tied the world record of 22.2 in the low hurdles, on May 5. He was a close second in the 100 meters of the 1960 Olympics.

Simpson, George (USA) : 1929–1932 Sprints
Simpson ran the first 9.4 100, while winning an NCAA double in 1929, but the use of starting blocks nullified his record. He won the 220 in both NCAA and AAU in 1930. In the 1932 Olympics, he was fourth in the 100 and second in the 200. His unofficial 20.6 in 1929 equalled the world record.

Smith, Tommie (USA) : 1966–1968 Sprints
Smith tied the world record for 200 meters on a straightaway in 1965. In 1966 he lowered the 200–220 record to 19.5 and gained a 200–220 record of 20-flat around a curve. He also ran 9.3, 10.1, 45.3 for 400 meters, and long jumped 25' 11". In

207

1967 he set world records of 44.5 for 400 meters and 44.8 for 440 yards on May 20. He won AAU furlong titles in 1967 and 1968, and the 1968 Olympic championship in 19.8. He ranked first in the world for 200 meters in 1966, 1967, and 1968.

Stanfield, Andy (USA) : 1949–1956   Sprints
Stanfield won a sprint double in the 1949 AAU (10.3 and 20.4) and took the 200 title in 1952 and the 220 in 1953. At Philadelphia, in 1951, he ran a turn 220 in 20.6, equal fastest ever and broad jumped 25' 9". Injuries kept him out of fast-start 100s, but he won the Olympic 200 in 1952 and placed second in 1956. He also won some low hurdle races and ranked fourth in the lows in the World Ranking for 1951. He was second in the 100 for 1949 and 1950 and in the 200 for 1949 and 1951. He was first in the 200 in 1952 and 1953.

Steers, Les (USA) : 1938–1941   High Jump
Steers broke the world record with a high jump of 6' 10¾" on April 14, 1941, at Seattle, Washington. That year he had the five highest jumps of all time, raising the record to 6' 10⅞" and 6' 11", but he lost the AAU after clearing 6' 9¾". He won the AAU in 1939 and 1940 and the NCAA in 1941.

Sternberg, Brian (USA) : 1962–1963   Pole Vault
After setting a junior record of 15' 8" at 18 in 1962, Sternberg set world records of 16' 5", 16' 7", and 16' 8" at age nineteen in 1963. He won the NCAA and AAU and was undefeated. His last competition was the AAU victory on his twentieth birthday. Shortly after, he was paralyzed in a trampoline accident.

Taipale, Armas (Finland) : 1912–1924   Discus
Taipale won the 1912 Olympic discus throw, placed second in 1920, and 12th in 1924. He was 10th in the 1920 shot put. In 1914 he bettered the world discus record with an unrecognized 160' 5".

Tajima, Naoto (Japan) : 1936–   LJ–TJ
Tajima had the best jumps of his life in two events in the 1936 Olympics. His 25' 4¾" placed third in the long jump, and he won the triple jump with a world record 52' 6".

Taylor, F. Morgan (USA) : 1924–1932   400 Hurdles

Taylor won the 1924 Olympic 400 meter hurdles in world record time of 52.6, but a fallen hurdle nullified the record. His earlier 52.6 was only an American record. On July 4, 1928, in Philadelphia, he set a record of 52-flat. He finished third in both the 1928 and 1932 Olympics. He won a 48.2 440, won the 1925 NCAA low hurdles, and once broad jumped 25' 2" with wind. He won four AAU championships in the intermediate hurdles.

Thomson, Earl (Canada) : 1916–1922   High Hurdles

Thomson, a 6' 3", 185-pounder, attended Dartmouth after running the first high hurdles in 14.8, in 1916. He set another world record in the IC4A with 14.4 at Philadelphia on May 29, 1920. He won the Olympic championship in 14.8. In 1921, he tied his record of 14.4 and it lasted until 1931. He won three AAU titles in the highs and one in the lows.

Thorpe, Jim (USA) : 1908–1912   Decathlon

If Thorpe had concentrated on track and field he might well have been the greatest of all. A legendary hero in football and a professional baseball player, he fitted track into his schedule only during the short season.

Five-eights Indian, Thorpe spent his boyhood hunting, working, playing, and breaking wild horses. He is reputed to have run 18 miles at age ten. At nineteen, he came under the influence of the famous coach, Pop Warner, at Carlisle Indian School. The next year he tied for first in the high jump at the Penn Relays, clearing 6' 1", and placed third in the broad jump. In collegiate meets that year, he won both hurdles, both jumps, and the hammer throw.

In 1909, he won seven events against Lafayette. In 1910 and 1911 he was out of school and took no part in track and field. In 1912, he competed in five to seven events per meet, getting in condition for the Olympic Games.

'I may have had an aversion for work,' Thorpe admitted, 'but I also had an aversion for getting beat. I was always in condition, and I never left my best performance on the practice field.'

With this limited background, Thorpe was thrust upon the unsuspecting track world at the 1912 Olympic Games in Stockholm. He won the pentathlon by winning four of the five events.

He placed fourth in the Olympic high jump and seventh in the broad jump. In the decathlon, he beat his nearest opponent by 700 points. The King of Sweden was so impressed that he told Thorpe :

'Sir, you are the greatest athlete in the world. I consider it an honor to shake your hand.'

Thorpe smiled in appreciation and said, 'Thanks, King.'

Some idea of Thorpe's tremendous ability can be gained by an examination of each separate event.

Sprints – He once ran 100 yards in 10-flat. His Olympic decathlon mark was 11.2, compared with 10.8 for the Olympic winner. He said, 'I ran a 220 in a little over 21 seconds.'

440 – His Olympic 400 was 52.2, but he has an official 51-flat 440 on record. He said, 'Some of my real good marks were made down at Carlisle. You won't find 'em in the books. One day, I got out 24 feet in the broad jump and ran a quarter mile in close to 48 seconds.'

1,500 – His pentathlon 1,500 was 4 :44.8 and he ran 4 :40.1 in the decathlon, He is supposed to have run a mile in 4 :35.

High hurdles – He ran 15.6 in the decathlon. In a post Olymppic meet at Rheims, he defeated Olympic champion Fred Kelly in 15-flat, equal to the world record.

Low hurdles – He ran 23.8, one-fifth off the world record.

High jump – He won the Final Trials in the New York Polo Grounds at 6' 5", only $\frac{5}{8}$ of an inch from the world record.

Broad jump – His best official jump was 23' 6".

Shot put – In a post Olympic meet he put 47' 9", two feet better than the bronze medalist at Stockholm.

Decathlon – His 1912 score was not bettered for 15 years.

Tisdall, Robert (Ireland) : 1932   IH–Decathlon

Tisdall won the 1932 Olympic 400 meter hurdles in 51.7 but did not receive an official world record because he knocked over a hurdle. He also placed eighth in the decathlon.

Tolan, Eddie (USA) : 1929–1932   Sprints

In 1929, Tolan tied the world record of 9.5 while winning the NCAA 100. He won the AAU sprint double. He tied the world 100 meter record of 10.4 in Europe. In 1930 he did not reach his peak until the college season ended. In Canada, he ran an unofficial 10.2 and barely lost to Simpson in 20.6, both world record times. He won the AAU 100 but lost to Simpson in the 220.

In 1931, Tolan lost the NCAA 100 to Wykoff, but he won the 220 by four yards. In the AAU he was third in the 100, but he won the 220. In the 1932 AAU, he made the Olympic team by placing second to Metcalfe in both sprints. In the Olympics, he barely beat Metcalfe in a world record equalling 10.3. Then he came from behind Simpson in the homestretch of the 200 to win.

Toomey, Bill (USA) : 1959–   Decathlon

Lacking the natural talent of Mathias, Campbell, Johnson, and Yang, Toomey outscored all of them by developing himself over many years. At Colorado University, he broad jumped 24′ 8½″ and ran the 400 meter hurdles in 51.7, but he never placed in the NCAA.

He tried the pentathlon in 1959 and placed sixth in the AAU. In 1960 he won it, and in 1962, on his home track at Boulder, Colorado, he won again with an American record of 3,482. He also won in 1963 and 1964.

In 1963 he placed fifth in the AAU decathlon. In 1964, he placed fifth in the AAU and fourth in the Final Trials. After winning the 1965 AAU (7,764) for third in World Ranking, he spent six months in Germany coached by Friedel Schirmer. He became ill, returned to the United States, and spent six weeks in a hospital. On April 2, 1966, he began training again.

On July 2 and 3, in Salina, Kansas, his AAU marks included personal records in the first four events : 10.3, 25′ 6″, 45′ 8¾″, and 6′ 4⅞″. His 47.3 400 gave him a first-day record of 4,430. On the second day he ran his fastest ever 110 meter hurdles (14.8) and set a personal record of 147′ 5½″ in the discus. He finished with 13′, 198′ 11″, and 4 :30.0 for a world record 8,234.

Three weeks later, he scored 8,219 and lost by 11 points to Russ Hodge, but he was first in World Ranking.

In 1967, Toomey was injured, but he won the AAU (7,880), lost in Los Angeles (7,779), won the Pan American Games (8,044), and won against West Germany (7,938), but he lost his world record to Kurt Bendlin's 8,319 and was second in World Ranking.

In 1968 he won at Mt. San Antonio (7,800) and the AAU (8,037). He was ill in Germany (7,628) and lost to Bendlin and Wolde. He won in London (7,985) and the Final Trials (8,222).

At Mexico City, in the Olympic Games, his first day marks were 10.4, 25′ 9¾″, 45′ 1½″, 6′ 4¾″, and an amazing 45.6 for the highest ever score of 4,499. An injured leg slowed him the second day but he won the championship with 8,193 points. It was his sixth decathlon score over 8,000 points. (For comparison, Rafer Johnson's best was 8,063.)

He won his fifth AAU title in 1969, and scored 4,123 points in a pentathlon in London, best in history. In December, at Los Angeles, he scored 8,417 points to regain the world record. He had eight of the twelve best scores of all time.

Towns, Forrest (USA) : 1935–1937   High Hurdles

'Spec' Towns, a 9.7 sprinter, had one great year. With the world high hurdle record standing at 14.2, he ran 14.1 nine times in 1936. He won the Olympic title in 14.2. On August 27, in Oslo, he shocked the track world with a 13.7, which lasted until 1948.

Tuulos, Vilho (Finland) : 1920–1928   Triple Jump

Tuulos was first in the 1920 Olympic hop-step-jump and third in both 1924 and 1928. In 1923 he jumped 50′ 9½″, only half an inch from the world record.

Wefers, Bernie (USA) : 1895–1897   Sprints

Wefers won three AAU sprint doubles, 1895–97. He equalled the 100 record at 9.8, held the 220 record at 21.2 for twenty-five years and the 300 yard record at 30.6 for thirty-nine years.

Whitfield, Mal (USA) : 1946–1956   440–880

Whitfield was one of the greatest competitors of all time and probably the fastest doubler among middle-distance runners.

After early second places in the 1946 NCAA and AAU half-miles and the 1947 NCAA 880 and AAU 400, he became invincible in the half-mile.

He lost no championship races from 1948 through 1954, including two NCAA's, five AAU's, two Final Trials, and two Olympic Games. At a quarter mile, he won the 1952 AAU, both Final Trials, placed third in the 1948 Olympics, and made the Olympic final in 1952. He won a gold medal on the Olympic relay team in 1948 and a silver medal in 1952.

He was first in World Ranking in the half-mile from 1948 through 1953, except for 1951. That year he was sixth while losing only one race after five months as a tail gunner in Korea. In the 440, he ranked first in 1949 and 1953 and third in 1948, 1950, and 1952 in the World Rankings.

Indoors, he was first four times at 600 yards and twice at 1,000 yards. He won an AAU title at each distance.

He seldom ran for time, but he set world records in the 880 (1:48.6) and 1,000 meters (2:20.8). His 45.9 at 400 meters was only one tenth off the world record. His world indoor records were for 500 yards (56.6), 500 meters (1:029), and 600 yards (1:09.5). He set additional American records for 400 meters (45.9), 440 (46.2), 500 meters (1:01.0), 600 meters (1:17.3), and 800 meters (1:47.9). Before 1954, he ran nine of the sixteen fastest 800–880 times ever recorded. He had faster times from the 100 through the mile than any runner in history (10.7 100 meters, 4:12.6 mile).

Perhaps his greatest accomplishments came as a doubler. In one day of the 1948 Final Trials, he won the 800 in 1:50.6, ran a heat of the 400 in 47.3, and won the final in 46.6. Indoors in 1953, he set a Madison Square Garden 880 record of 1:50.9 and came back little over an hour later with a world record 600 in 1:09.5. On July 29, in Cologne, he ran a 1:48.4 800 and came back in 45 minutes with a 46.2 400. In Finland on August 16, he broke the world 1,000 meter record with 2:20.8. One hour later he ran his American record 440 in 46.2.

Williams, Archie (USA): 1936–   440

Williams won the 1936 NCAA in 46.5 and was timed in a world record 46.1 at 400 meters. He won the Olympic 400 in 46.5.

Williams, Percy (Canada) : 1928–1930   Sprints

Williams won a double sprint victory in the 1928 Olympics. On August 9, 1930, at Toronto, he ran the first official 10.3.

Wint, Arthur (Jamaica) : 1948–1952   400–800

Wint won the 400 meters in the 1948 Olympics and was second in the 800. In 1952, he was fifth in the 400 and second in the 800, and he won a gold medal in the relay.

Winter, Archibald (Australia) : 1924–1928   Triple Jump

Winter won the 1924 Olympic hop-step-jump with a world record 50' 11¼". He was 12th in 1928.

Wolcott, Fred (USA) : 1938–1942   Hurdles

Wolcott was the greatest hurdler of all time before Dillard. In his three collegiate seasons he lost only three races, one a 100 yard dash in which he ran 9.5. He also lost the high hurdles in the 1939 AAU and the 1940 NCAA.

Wolcott equalled the American record with 14-flat in 1938 and 13.9 in 1940. At Stockholm, in 1938, he became the second man ever to run under 14 seconds. His 13.7 in the 1940 Texas Relays was a collegiate record but it was not recognized by the AAU. His 13.7 in the 1941 AAU officially equalled the world record.

In the low hurdles, Wolcott won everything (three of his five NCAA titles and four of his seven AAU titles). His 22.9 in the 1930 AAU was the fastest ever around a curve but it was wind aided. At the 1940 Princeton Invitational, he broke Owens' 220 record with 22.5 and set a 200 meter record of 22.3 which lasted sixteen years.

Indoors, Wolcott set high hurdle records at four distances plus a 60-yard low hurdle record of 6.9. He won the 1942 AAU indoor highs in 7.2. The war kept him out of Olympic competition.

Wooderson, Sydney (GB) : 1936–1946   800–5,000

Wooderson was a successful internationalist from 800 meters to 5,000. On August 28, 1937, at Motspur Park, London, he set a world mile record of 4 :06.4. Then he won the 1,500 meters in the 1938 European Championships. On August 20, 1938, at Motspur Park, he set world records for 800 meters (1 :48.4) and 880 (1 :49.2).

After the war had eliminated him from two Olympics (an ankle injury stopped him in 1936), Wooderson made an amazing comeback. He went to Sweden in 1945 and lost a close mile to Andersson with a time of 4 :04.2. In 1946, he won the European Championships 5,000 in 14 :08.6, second only to Hägg's world record.

Woodruff, John (USA) : 1936–1940   440–880

As a freshman at Pittsburgh in 1936, Woodruff lost the AAU title by one foot through inexperience. In the Final Trials he ran 1 :49.9, third fastest of all time, in his heat. He won the final and his superior talent blundered through to a tactical Olympic victory at Berlin.

He won the difficult 440–880 double in three consecutive IC4A meets, running 47-flat in all three 440's. He won the NCAA 880 each year. His only AAU victory came in 1937.

In 1937 he defeated new world record holder Elroy Robinson in 1 :47.8 at a distance five feet short of 800 meters. In 1940 he ran 1 :47.0 for 800 meters and 1 :47.7 for 880 yards on Dartmouth's five-lap indoor track. In the Compton Invitational, he won the 800 meters in 1 :48.6, an American record.

Wykoff, Frank (USA) : 1928–1936   Sprints

Wykoff was credited with the first 9.4 100. He won three IC4A 100's, two NCAA 100's, and two AAU 100's. He ran 200 meters in 20.8 as an 18-year-old in 1928. He ran in three Olympic Games, winning a gold medal in the relay each time. He placed fourth in the 100 in 1928 and 1936. He was the only man before Owens to run two 9.4s, both in 1930.

Yang Chuan-Kuang (Formosa) : 1958–1964   Decathlon

C. K. Yang competed in the 1956 Olympics as a 6' 7½" high jumper and placed eighth in the decathlon. In May, 1958, he set an Asian record of 7,319 in the decathlon. In late May, he won the decathlon in the Asian Games. He also placed second in the high hurdles (14.8) and broad jump 24' 6⅞"), and third in the 400 meter hurdles (53.0). In June, at the age of twenty-six, he moved to the United States for training. He placed second to Rafer Johnson in the AAU decathlon. His 7,625 placed him seventh on the all-time list.

In 1959, he ran in the big California meets as a high hurdler, with a best of 14.2. In August, he scored 7,835 and ranked third for the year in the World Ranking. He enrolled as a freshman at UCLA to train with Johnson and recorded marks of 13.9, 25' 5", 14' 1¼", and 233' 2½". He raised his decathlon record to 7,892 in April, then broke the world record with 8,426 while placing second to Johnson in the AAU. In the Olympic Games he pushed Johnson all the way, finishing a close second with 8,334.

In 1962, Yang won the AAU decathlon with 8,249 and was first in World Ranking. In 1963 he developed suddenly with the fiberglass pole into a near-record vaulter. He cleared 16' 3½" for a world indoor record and he cleared 16' 5" outdoors. He was sixth vaulter in World Ranking.

He used his vaulting ability to such an extent that he caused the adoption of new tables in 1964 when he shattered Johnson's world record with 9,121 points. In his record decathlon, he vaulted 15' 10½", ran 10.7 and 47.7, and hurdled in 14-flat.

He won the 1964 AAU decathlon with 8,641. Then the new scoring tables were issued, lowering his world record from 9,121 to 8,089. Discouraged and injured, he placed only fifth in the Olympics.

Yrjölä, Paavo (Finland) : 1924–1932   Decathlon

Yrjölä set a world record in the 1928 Olympic decathlon. He placed ninth in 1924 and sixth in 1932.

Zsivótzky, Gyula (Hungary) : 1960–   Hammer

Zsivótzky was second in the 1960 and 1964 Olympic hammer throws and he won in 1968. He won the 1962 European Championships and was second in 1966. He set a world record of 241' 11½" in 1965 and raised it to 242 feet in 1968.

INDEX

Albans, Bill, 75-7
Albuquerque, 163
Algeria, 63
Amsterdam Olympic Games (1928), 21-2, 160, 164-5, 172, 176, 180-1, 185, 188, 196, 198-9, 202, 205, 209, 212, 214-16
Anderson, Billy, 51
Anderson, George, 29
Andersson, Arne, 175, 215
Ann Arbor, 27-9
Antwerp, 185
Antwerp Olympic Games (1920), 13-14, 174, 184, 188, 191-2, 195, 198, 200, 203, 205, 208-9, 212
Anufriev, Aleksandr, 62-3, 67
Argentina, 72
Ashenfelter, Horace, 160
Athens, 113
'Athens Olympic Games' (1906), 173, 176, 187, 201, 206
Atlantic City, 95
Attlesey, Dick, 52, 160
Auckland, 149-50, 154, 156, 158, 166, 183
Australia, 88, 195

Babka, Rink, 118-21
Bacon, Charlie, 160
Baillie, Bill, 154
Bakersfield, 97, 99, 111, 113, 131, 204
Baldwin-Wallace (U.S.A.), 46
Bannister, Roger, 160, 176
Bantum, Ken, 87-8
Barnes, Lee, 160
Bausch, Jim, 161

Beamon, Bob, 161
Beatty, Jim, 153, 155-6
Beccali, Luigi, 161
Belgium, 56, 60
Belgrade, 186
Bell, Greg, 97
Bendigo, 135-6
Bendlin, Kurt, 212
Berea, 51
Bergen, 200
Berkeley, 29, 39, 43, 82-3, 96-7, 108-9, 111, 179, 191, 203
Berlin, 21-2, 38, 162
Berlin Olympic Games (1936), 31-4, 46, 172-3, 177-81, 183, 186, 188, 191, 193, 196-7, 200, 204, 208, 212-13, 215
Bern, 68, 102, 113, 165
Bernard, Michel, 137
Berruti, Livio, 162
Bikila, Abebe, 162
Bislet Idrettsplass, 134
Bloomfield, 70
Blue, Tony, 136, 138, 150
Bochum, 34
Bolotnikov, Pyotr, 162
Bolshov (U.S.S.R.), 140-4
Borg, Eino, 21
Boston, 39, 42, 142, 162
Boston, Ralph, 163-4
Bouin, Jean, 22, 164, 184
Boulder, 86, 95, 113, 211
Bowerman, Bill, 102
Bragg, Don, 164
Brazil, 67
Brisbane, 130, 135
Britain, 64, 90, 142, 148, 195

217

British Guiana, 172
Brumel, Marina, 144
Brumel, Valeriy, 139–47
Brussels, 60, 67, 201
Bucarest, 67
Budapest, 58, 68, 112, 184, 193
Budd, Frank, 164
Buffalo, 20
Burghley, David (Marquis of Exeter), 114, 164
Burleson, Dyrol, 154–6

Caldwell, Dave, 192
Calhoun, Lee, 54, 97, 102, 105, 165
Campbell, Milt, 77–8, 97–8, 211
Canada, 92, 193, 207, 211
Cardiff, 131
Carlsen, Gary, 125
Carlton, James, 165
Carr, Bill, 165, 172
Carr, Henry, 165
Carr, Sabin, 165
Cartmell, Nat, 45
Cawley, Warren, 166
Celakovice, 68
Celtic Park, 203
Central Lenin Stadium, 142
Cerutty, Percy, 128–32, 134, 136–7
Chandler, Otis, 84
Chataway, Chris, 64, 68, 186
Chicago, 26, 30, 44–5, 48, 51, 119–20
China, 141
Christchurch, 152
Clarke, Ron, 128–9, 162, 166–7, 182
Cleveland, 25, 30, 199
Clowser, Jack, 50, 52
Cochran, Roy, 167
College Station, 190
Collymore, Ed, 112
Cologne, 34, 213
Compton, 41, 51, 83, 85, 89, 95, 97, 101, 105, 111, 121, 131, 136, 156, 159, 170, 204, 215
Conger, Ray, 22
Connolly, Harold, 168

Consolini, Adolfo, 117, 168
Copenhagen, 16
Courtney, Tom, 168
Craig, Ralph, 168
Crawfordsville, 97
Crothers, Bill, 157, 159, 169
Csermák, József, 169
Culbreath, Josh, 108–10
Cunningham, Glenn, 169
Cushman, Clif, 113–14
Czechoslovakia, 55–7, 59, 67, 122

Dallas, 38
Danek, Ludwig, 122–3, 126
Danielson, Egil, 169
Dartmouth, 215
Da Silva, Adhemer Ferreira, 169
Davenport, Willie, 170
Davies, John, 155–8
Davies, Lynn, 163
Davis, Dave, 91
Davis, Glenn, 107–15, 148
Davis, Hal, 170
Davis, Jack, 51–4, 76, 79, 97, 165, 170
Davis, Otis, 113, 171
Davis, Walt, 170
Dayton, 110, 118, 171
Deacon, Bud, 40
Delany, Ron, 131–3, 138, 150
Des Moines, 86, 167
Dillard, Harrison, 46–54, 97, 170, 183, 200, 214
Dills, Ken, 40
Dixon, Craig, 51–2
Dodson, Murl, 94
Doubell, Ralph, 171
Drake, Ducky, 101, 105
Draper, Foy, 34
Drayton, Paul, 178
Dublin, 131–2, 150–1
Duffey, Arthur, 171, 185
Dumas, Charles, 139, 171
Dyachkov, Vladimir, 139, 141, 143

Eastman, Ben, 165, 172
Easton, Bill, 126
Edstrom, Dave, 102–3

Edwards, Phil, 172
Elliott, Herb, 128–38, 150–1, 176, 204
England, 15, 71
Estadio Olimpico, 125
Eugene, 76, 82, 87, 101, 104
Evans, Lee, 172
Evans, Louis, 105
Evanston, 49
Ewell, Barney, 49–50
Ewell, Norwood, 172–3
Ewrey, Ron, 173

Finland, 14–17, 19–20, 23–4, 58, 60, 213
Finlay, Donald, 173
Finnigan, Eddie, 46, 49–50
Flagstaff, 164
Flannagan, John, 173
Foss, Frank, 174
France, 14, 63, 73, 137, 146, 173, 184
Frankfort, 47, 89, 177
Fresno, 40, 43, 81, 83, 85–6, 160, 185, 187, 205
Fuchs, Jim, 82–4, 174

Gävle, 101
Geelong, 167
George, Walter, 174, 195
Georgetown, 51
Gerhdes, Jim, 51
Germany, 20, 22, 31–2, 63, 114, 212
Gieve, Bob, 28
Gilbert, Elias, 111, 113
Glasgow, 38, 51
Gordien, Fortune, 86, 117–18, 174
Gorno, Reinaldo, 66
Göteborg, 134, 175
Greene, Charlie, 174
Grelle, Jim, 155–6, 159
Guardia, Fiorello La, 44
Gubner, Gary, 91, 187
Guillemot, Joseph, 14
Gutowski, Bob, 174

Hägg, Gunder, 58, 67, 175–6, 215

Hahn, Archie, 176
Halberg, Murray, 132–4, 149–51, 154, 176
Hamilton, Brutus, 33, 72, 77–9
Hamm, Ed, 176
Hampson, Thomas, 172, 176
Hanner, Flint, 37
Hansen, Fred, 176–7
Harbig, Rudolf, 177
Hardin, Glenn, 29, 167, 177–8
Hary, Armin, 178
Hawaii, 154
Hayes, Bob, 178–9
Healdsburg, 203
Hein, Karl, 179
Heino, Viljo, 55–61
Heinrich, Ignace, 73–4
Heitanen, Mikko, 66
Hellfrich, Allan, 20
Helsinki, 16, 23, 58, 60, 62, 144, 151, 160, 186, 189, 191
Helsinki Olympic Games (1952), 24, 52–3, 62–7, 70, 76–9, 84, 117, 151, 160, 168–71, 174, 181, 194, 196, 200–1, 207–8, 212, 214
Hemery, David, 179–80
Hewson, Brian, 131–2, 134
Hines, Jim, 180
Hirschfield (U.S.A.), 185
Höckert, Gunnar, 180
Hodge, Russ, 211
Holland, 56
Honolulu, 92
Hooper, Darrow, 81–5
Horine, George, 180
Houser, Clarence, 180
Houstka Spa, 61, 66–7
Houston, 110, 124
Howard, Dickie, 113–14
Hubbard, De Hart, 180
Hungary, 68, 112, 117

IAAF, 16, 23
Ibbotson, Derek, 131, 133
Iharos, Sandor, 181, 186
Iness, Sim, 83, 85, 181
Iso-Hollo, Volmari, 23, 181
Italy, 117

Index

Ivanov, Albert, 68

Jackson, Virgil, 70, 74
Jansson, Gustav, 65–6
Japan, 122
Järvinen, Akilles, 181
Järvinen, Matti, 181–2
Jazy, Michel, 137, 166, 182
Jerome, Harry, 182
Johnson, Ben, 26
Johnson, Cornelius, 182–3
Johnson, Jimmy, 26
Johnson, Rafer, 94–106, 211–12, 216
Jones, Hayes, 110–11, 113, 183
Jordan, Payton, 123, 126
Jungwirth, Stanislav, 134

Keino, Kipchoge, 167, 182–4, 204
Kelly, Fred, 210
Kenya, 157
Kerr, George, 111, 149, 151, 154, 157
Kiev, 62, 141, 145, 162
King, Leamon, 184
Kingsburg, 99
Kinnunen, Jorma, 189
Kiprugut, Wilson, 157
Kistenmacher, Carlos, 72–3
Klics, Ferenc, 117
Klim, Romuald, 184
Knoxville, 170
Kolehmainen, Hannes, 13–14, 19, 184
Korobkov, Gabriel, 106, 146
Košice, 162
Kouvolo, 204
Kovacs, Josef, 67–8
Kraenzlein, Alvin, 184–5
Krivonosov, Mikhail, 185
Krzyzkowiak, Zdzislaw, 185
Kuck, John, 185
Kuopio, 19
Kusocinski, Janusz, 185
Kuts, Vladimir, 67–8, 129, 137, 185–6, 200
Kutyenko, Yuriy, 102–3
Kuznetsov (U.S.S.R.), 98, 100–3

LaBeach, Lloyd, 50
Lafayette, 111, 209
Lampert, Stan, 86
Landy, John, 129, 160, 176
Larrabee, Mike, 186
Lawrence, Al, 71
Lehtinen, Lauri, 23–4, 181, 186
Leichum, Wilhelm, 34
Lemming, Erik, 187
Leningrad, 141, 144
Lewis, Aubrey, 98, 108
Lincoln, 29, 39, 48
Lincoln, Merv, 129–33, 135
Lindgren, Gerry, 204
Lippincott, Donald, 187
Lituyev, Yuriy, 109
London, 23, 34, 68, 120, 132, 134, 150–1, 167, 186, 188, 204, 212
London Olympic Games (1908), 160, 173, 186, 191, 203, 206
London Olympic Games (1948), 49–50, 55–8, 71–4, 76, 117, 167–9, 174, 191, 194, 196, 199–201, 213–14
Long Beach, 52, 83,
Long, Dallas, 89–91, 187, 190
Long, Luz, 32–3
Long, Maxie, 188
Loomis, Frank, 188
Losch, –, 126
Los Angeles, 41, 51–2, 88, 97, 107, 120, 122, 124, 130, 144–5, 153, 155, 163, 166–8, 177, 185, 187, 192, 198–9, 204, 212
Los Angeles Olympic Games (1932), 23–4, 161, 164–5, 169, 172–3, 176–7, 181–2, 185–6, 188, 193–4, 196–7, 199–200, 204–5, 207, 209–11, 215–16
Loukolo, Toivo, 22
Louvain, 202
Lovelock, Jack, 188
Lowe, Douglas, 188, 199
Lugansk, 141
Lundkvist, Erik, 188
Lusis, Janis, 188
Lydiard, Arthur, 150, 152–3, 156–7

220

Madison Square Garden, 19, 47, 74, 86–7, 142, 213
Madrid, 163
Mäki, Taisto, 189
Mallott, Ray, 177
Malmö, 134, 175, 200
Manila, 89
Marquette, 192
Martin, Sera, 199
Mason (G.B.), 195
Mathias, Bob, 70–80, 94, 96, 106, 211
Matson, Randy, 91, 187, 189–91
Mauger, Jack, 38
Mayer, Bernie, 84
McGrath, John, 91
McGrath, Matt, 191
McKenley, Herb, 191
Meadows, Earle, 37–40, 42, 191–2
Melbourne, 130, 150, 166
Melbourne Olympic Games (1956), 69, 88, 96, 98–9, 104, 106–7, 109–10, 114, 116–18, 128–9, 136, 162, 165–6, 168–71, 174, 176, 181–2, 184–6, 194, 196, 200–1, 207–8, 215
Memphis, 43
Meredith, Ted, 172, 192
Metcalfe, Ralph, 26–7, 29–32, 34, 192–3, 199, 211
Mexico City, 86, 95, 163, 169
Mexico City Olympic Games (1968), 116, 124–6, 161, 164, 167–8, 170–2, 174, 179–80, 182–4, 189, 191, 202, 204–5, 207–8, 212, 216
Milan, 168, 177
Milde, –, 126
Mills, Billy, 193
Milwaukee, 38, 49, 108
Mimoun, O'Kacha Alain, 56, 63–4, 194
Minneapolis, 47
Modesto, 43, 124, 131, 155, 163
Moens, Roger, 148–9, 151
Mondschein, Irving, 71–2, 75
Moore, Charley, 194
Moore, Tom, 136

Morris, Glenn, 74, 76, 194
Morrow, Bobby, 97, 112, 194–5
Mortensen, Jesse, 83
Moscow, 100, 112, 118, 139, 142, 144, 163, 186
Motspur Park, 214–15
Mt San Antonio, 120–1, 212
Myers, Lawrence, 174, 195
Myyrä, Jonni, 195

Nambu, Chuhei, 196
Nemeth, Imre, 196
Népstadion, 68
Neufeld Stadium, 68
New Brunswick, 122
New Haven, 173
New Jersey, 188
New Zealand, 148–9, 151, 153–5, 158, 165
New Orleans, 42
New York, 26, 31, 37, 44–6, 122, 142, 144, 195, 210
Nieder, Bill 88–90, 187, 196
Nikkanen, Yrjo, 196
Norpoth, Harald, 204
Norris, Ken, 68
Norton, Ray, 112
Norway, 112
Nurmi, Paavo, 13–24, 185–6, 199, 202, 204, 206
Nyberg, Evert, 58

Oakland, 167
O'Brien, Parry, 81–93, 196
O'Callaghan, Patrick, 196–7
Oda, Mikio, 197
Odessa, 141, 189
Oeter, Al, 88, 116–27
O'Hara, –, 156–7
Olympic Games *see*
    Amsterdam (1928)
    Antwerp (1920)
    Athens ('1906')
    Berlin (1936)
    Helsinki (1952)
    London (1908 and 1948)
    Los Angeles (1932)

Index

Melbourne (1956)
Mexico City (1968)
Paris (1900 and 1924)
Rome (1960)
St Louis (1904)
Stockholm (1912)
Tokyo (1964)
Ontario, 109
Osborne, Harold, 197–8
Osgood, Bob, 30
Oslo, 57, 75, 112, 134, 167–8, 199, 212
Ostersund, 175
Ostreva, 59
Owens, J., 163, 178
Owens, Jesse, 25–35, 46–7, 50–1, 53–4, 115, 193, 199, 214
Oxford, 160

Packard, Bobby, 31
Paddock, Charley, 25, 177, 197, 205
Padway, Milt, 42
Palmyra, 100
Palo Alto, 119, 143, 191
Paris, 50, 67, 82, 201
Paris Olympic Games (1900), 173, 185, 187–8, 200–1
Paris Olympic Games (1924), 16–19, 22, 160, 180, 188, 191, 195, 197–200, 202, 205, 208–9, 212, 214, 216
Pasadena, 70–1, 87, 94
Patton, Mel, 49–50, 198–9
Peacock, Eulace, 27, 29–30, 193, 199
Pedersen, Terje, 189
Peltzer, Otto, 21, 188, 199
Perth, 136, 154
Peters, Jim, 64–5
Pettersson (Sweden), 139, 145
Philadelphia, 51, 107, 119, 146, 208–9
Philpott, –, 154
Piatkowski, Edmund, 120
Pikkala, Lauri, 17
Pirie, Gordon, 63, 68, 133, 186, 200

Pocatello, 44
Poland, 120
Pörhöla, Ville, 200
Porter, Bill, 47–9, 200
Potgieter, Gerhardus, 109, 200
Prague, 58, 61, 67–8, 186
Princeton, 30, 38, 172, 182, 188, 192, 214
Prinstein, Myer, 200–1

Rambo, John, 145–6
Rawson, –, 132
Ray, Joie, 20
Reiff, Gaston, 56–8, 60–1, 63, 201–2
Reno, 125, 207
Rheims, 210
Rhoden, George, 201
Richards, Bob, 45, 95, 201
Riley, Charley, 25
Ritola, Ville, 16–22, 202
Robinson, Barry, 152
Robinson, Elroy, 215
Robinson, Mack, 31, 33–4
Rochdale, 195
Roelants, Gaston, 202
Rome, 186
Rome Olympic Games (1960), 89, 99, 102–3, 113–14, 116, 118–19, 135–42, 148–51, 162–5, 168–9, 171, 176, 178, 182–3, 185, 187, 195–6, 200, 202, 205–7, 216
Rose, Ralph, 203
Rowe, Arthur, 90
Rozsavogyi, I., 137
Russia, 100–1, 103, 106, 112, 121, 139, 163, 177, 179
Ryan, Pat, 203
Ryun, Jim, 159, 203–4

Saarijarvi, 189
Sacramento, 124
St Louis, 86, 198
St Louis Olympic Games (1904), 173, 176, 201, 203, 206
Salina, 211
Saling, George, 204

Salminen, Ilmari, 204
Salt Lake City, 47, 87
San Antonio, 47
San Diego, 159, 177, 205
San Francisco, 44, 146, 192
Saneyev, Viktor, 204
Santa Ana, 88
Santry, 132
Sao Paulo, 169
Schade, Herbert, 63–4
Schirmer, Friedel, 211
Schmeitz, Fred, 42
Schmidt, Józef, 204–5
Schmidt, Paul, 149, 151
Scholz, Jackson, 205
Scott, Clyde, 48
Seagren, Bob, 205
Seaman, Bobby, 156
Seattle, 81, 92, 208
Sefton, Bill, 37–8, 191
Sexton, Leo, 205
Shavlakadze (U.S.S.R.), 140–2, 145
Sheppard, Mel, 192, 206
Sheridan, Martin, 206
Shinnick, Phil, 163
Shrubb, Alfred, 22, 184, 202, 206–7
Sidlo, Janusz, 207
Silvester, Jay, 120–6, 207
Sime, Dave, 194, 207
Simmons, –, 73
Simpson, George, 165, 207, 211
Slykhuis, Willi, 56–8
Smith, Tommie, 172, 207
Snell, Peter, 138, 148–59, 169, 203
Snell, Sally, 151, 157
Snyder, Larry, 26–7, 29–31, 54, 112, 115, 193
Sofia, 142
South Africa, 156
South Lake Tahoe, 172, 205
Southern, Eddie, 108–13
Stade de Colombes, 17, 67
Stadio Olimpico, 89, 114, 119, 137, 139
Stanfield, Andy, 208
Stanford, 39–40, 113, 143
Steers, Les, 208
Steinhauer, Neil, 92, 190

Sternberg, Brian, 208
Stockholm, 15, 20, 23, 38, 48, 68, 133, 167, 175–7, 180, 214
Stockholm Olympic Games (1912), 13, 164, 168, 180, 184, 187, 191–2, 195, 203, 208–10
Stockton, 87
Stoller, Sam, 30
Stone, Curt, 63
Stora Mossan, 133
Strandberg, Lennart, 31
Sweden, 15, 34–5, 65, 133, 139, 151, 215

Taipale, Armas, 208
Tajima, Naoto, 208
Tarr, Jerry, 183
Taylor, F. Morgan, 209
Templeton, Dink, 72
Temu, N., 167
Tennessee, 43
Texas, 177, 196, 214
Thomas, Alby, 132–4
Thomas, John, 140–6
Thompson, Wilbur, 81
Thomson, Earl, 209
Thorpe, Jim, 209–10
Tidwell, Charles, 183
Tisdall, Robert, 177, 210
Toivonen, Armas, 23
Tokyo, 142, 154, 196–7
Tokyo Olympic Games (1964), 90–2, 116, 122–3, 145–6, 154, 156–7, 162–6, 168–70, 176–9, 182–4, 186–7, 189–90, 193, 202–3, 205, 207, 216
Tolan, Eddie, 193, 211
Toomey, Bill, 211–12
Toronto, 199, 214
Towns, Forrest, 212
Travers Island, 188
Trinidad, 51
Trusenyov, Vladimir, 120–1
Tulare, 74–6, 79, 94, 96
Tulloh, Bruce, 152
Tummler, –, 204
Turku, 24, 60, 166
Tuulos, Vilho, 212

Index

Urbana, 197
USA, 16, 19–20, 22, 50–3, 63, 70–1, 77, 88, 91, 102, 106–7, 114, 126, 131, 145, 150, 154–5 165, 175, 184, 195, 207, 216
Uzhgorod, 141

Vancouver, 92, 159
Varoff, George, 39–9
Vastoras, 167
Viborg, 20
Vienna, 53
Viipuri, 19, 23
Virtanen, Lasse, 23
Visalia, 41

Waern, Dan, 134, 138, 151
Wales, 131
Walker, George, 47
Walnut, 120–1, 124, 163, 196
Wanganui, 151–2, 156
Ward, Willis, 27
Warmerdam, Cornelius, 36–45, 174
Warner, Pop, 209
Warren, Earl, 74
Warsaw, 112
Washington, Booker T., 35
Wefers, Bernie, 212
Weiershauser, Jack, 76, 78

Weill, Dave, 123
Weisiger, Cary, 155–6
Wembley, 49, 55, 72
Whetton, John, 157
White City, 34, 53, 132, 134, 151, 215
Whitfield, Mal, 212
Wide, Edvin, 15–18, 21–3, 199
Williams, Archie, 213
Williams, Percy, 213
Windnagle, Vere, 192
Winnipeg, 190
Wint, Arthur, 191, 213
Winter, Archibald, 213
Winter Stadium, 141
Wolcott, Fred, 48, 97, 213
Wolde, M., 162, 212
Wooderson, Sydney, 57, 213–14
Woodruff, John, 215
Wykoff, Frank, 31, 34–5, 211, 215

Yang, Chuan-Kuang, 100–5, 211, 215–16
Yrjölä, Paavo, 216

Zátopek, Dana, 58–60, 62, 64
Zátopek, Emil 55–69, 91, 186, 194
Zsivótzky, Gyula, 216
Zurich, 79, 178

DATE DUE			
OCT 2 3 73			
OCT 2 3 73			
OCT 4 77			